Lion of Light

Robert Anton Wilson
on Aleister Crowley

HILARITAS
⊚PRESS

Lion of Light

Robert Anton Wilson
on Aleister Crowley

Introduction by Lon Milo DuQuette
Foreword by Richard Kaczynski
Five Footprints of a Camel by Oz Fritz
Enduring Magical Biography by Gregory Arnott
23 Riffs by R. Michael Johnson

Print: ISBN: 978-1-952746-26-0

eBook: ISBN: 978-1-952746-25-3

Print Edition: 2023 Hilaritas Press
eBook Version 1.0 : 2023, Hilaritas Press

Cover Design by Richard Rasa
with AI design from Templedweller
eBook Design by Pelorian Digital

Hilaritas Press, LLC.
P.O. Box 1153
Grand Junction, Colorado 81502
www.hilaritaspress.com

TABLE OF CONTENTS

EDITOR'S NOTE

In a September, 2022 email exchange between Martin Wagner, archivist at RAWilsonFans.de, Jesse Walker, books editor of Reason.com, and Tom Jackson, blogger at RAWIllumination.com, Martin casually mentioned that a typescript of Robert Anton Wilson on Aleister Crowley titled "Do What Thou Wilt" had arrived at Harvard University, citing a listing in worldcat.org, a global library super-catalog. Tom notified Rasa of Hilaritas Press, and blogged about the discovery. Speculations arose and inquiries were made. RAW Biographer Gabriel Kennedy suggested that the document originated from the estate of Herbert Roseman. Eventually, the fine folks at Harvard's Houghton Library emailed a PDF of a photocopy of the typescript.

In fact, the typescript comes with a letter from Bob Wilson in Berkeley to "Herb" dated November 11th, 1974. Herb Roseman would have been in Brooklyn at that time working on his upstart Revisionist Press. Herb and RAW had worked together at the School for Living in Yellow Springs, Ohio where Herb edited the School publication, *Way Out,* which Bob contributed to from 1962-63. Herb credited RAW with having written some of the best modern essays on anarchism.

Why did Bob send this typescript to Herb? Within Bob's

letter to Herb, he discusses the typos from the student of his who retyped the typescript from the master copy. Bob chose to work on other projects instead of correcting the errors "because I need to sell something for hard cash." So, one could presume that he sent it to Herb for unpaid publication, or payment at later date, or maybe he sent it to Herb for 48 years safekeeping so that it could be published posthumously along with several other important pieces he wrote on that multidimensional rascal, Edward Alexander Crowley.

Curiously, Bob discusses other projects he's currently working on as follows:

> Llewellyn will be publishing a book of essays by me next Summer under the title *Prometheus Rising: a Magick Manual for the Space Age*. Playboy Press will be bringing out the paperback of *Sex n' Drugs* in January. And Dell will be bringing forth *Illuminatus* finally (!) in 3 volumes, Sept-Oct-Nov. after sitting on it since August 1971!!!! (Arrrrgh.)

> Meanwhile, I've been writing *The Starseed Signals*, a book on Tim Leary's interstellar telepathic experiments; *Death Shall Have No Dominion*, on molecular biologists in quest of anti-aging drugs; *Lion of Light*, the long book on Crowley; and *The Homing Pigeon*, a new novel.

Those familiar with the work of Robert Anton Wilson will note that *Illuminatus!* did in fact go into print less than a year later. The third book of the *Schrödinger's Cat trilogy* was published under the title of *The Homing Pigeons* in *1981,* and Bob did have a rather popular book titled *Prometheus Rising*, but certainly not as a collection of essays published by Llewellyn in the mid-70s. *The Starseed Signals* went unpublished until very recently, discovered after Bob left us, by Discordian archivist Adam Gorightly who found a copy in the archives of Discordian co-founder Greg Hill. And "Do What Thou Wilt" turned up at Harvard University.

INFORMED SOURCES

Veteran Press Agency ● Worldwide Contacts ● Founded 1888

2035 Channing Way
Berkeley, Cal 94704
November 7, 1974

Dear Herb,

Do what thou wilt shall be the whole of the law.

Here's the copy of the Crowley essay as typed by one of my
students -- with an error on nearly every page, alas...

I have another copy (my original) in case this gets lost in
the mail.

I only made one or two corrections in here, where it was
necessary to clarify the meaning. The other errors are left
intact, with the thought that a professional typist can perhaps
white them out and re-type thereby saving many a page without
total retyping of the whole page.

Llewelly will be publishing a book of essays by me next
Summer under the title Prometheus Rising: A Magick Manual
for the Space Age. Playboy Press will be bringing out the
paperback of Sex'N'Drugs in January. And Dell will be bringing
forth Illuminatus finally (!) in 3 volumes, Sept-Oct-Nov. --
after sitting on it since August 1971!!!! (Arrrrgh.)

Meanwhile, I've been writing The Starseed Signals, a book on
Tim Leary's interstellar telepathic experiments; Death Shall
Have No Dominion, on molecular biologists in quest of anti-aging
drugs; Lion of Light, the long book on Crowley; and The Homing
Pigeon, a new novel. I have put my energies into these projects
instead of retyping the enclosed slowly and painfully because
I need to sell something for hard cash. "Necessity knows no
law."

Regards and warm vibes...

Bob W

Meanwhile, *Lion of Light* may or may not have ever been
written as Wilson intended, but the title was too good to pass
up. Wilson was somewhat notorious for juggling multiple
projects that often went unpublished, and for an ephemeral
approach to record keeping and archives. One can only
wonder what else of the unpublished Wilson canon lies out
there hidden in the files and archives of old friends, defunct
publishers, and the FBI. But I digress.

Our wheels were turning. What else could we package

with this to make a full book, á la the recently released *Natural Law* essay and its companions (Hilaritas Press, 2021)? Within short order, Michael Johnson emailed a long list of Crowley and Crowley related essays by Wilson. Adam Gorightly offered up some unpublished material from his Discordian Archives. A team of Chad Nelson, Oz Fritz, Michael Johnson and myself gelled together. We chewed on our list of options for a while, and clear choices soon rose to the top.

We start with an invocation – "Starbride" from a December 1974 issue of *Gnostica*, discovered and posted on Twitter by RAW archivist Martin Wagner in July of 2022.

Next, we move onto a piece near and dear to my heart, "The Great Beast" essay from *The Realist*, 1971-72, for an in-depth introduction to this character, Crowley. This was the first work of RAW besides his books, that I purchased online in the start of what would become RAWilsonFans. org. Michael Johnson alerted me of its existence in 2003, and I found it, or most of it, for sale online at an underground bookstore carrying back issues of *The Realist*, MonkeysRetreat.com. Every day starting January 1st, 2004, I typed up a chapter and posted it to alt.fan.rawilson. That particular issue only contained the first 16 of 22 chapters and it circulated about the internet for a couple years or more in that shortened form before I found the next three issues of *The Realist* which contained the remaining 6 chapters.

Then we have our centerpiece, the previously unpublished typescript "Do What Thou Wilt" as sent to Herbert Roseman in November of 1974. Martin Wagner's detective work led us to an undated letter from Wilson to Timothy Leary in prison that indicated that Herb was to publish the essay in the Fall of 1975. One presumes that never happened. Jumping ahead to a 2007 forum post that Martin discovered on the Crowley website Lashtal.com, we find "Chiswick Demon," purveyor of now-defunct 666Books. com, who commented that he had possession of the document in question from the press archives he received directly from Herb. Fast forward to 2018 and we find that the typescript went up for sale on Weiser Antiquarian Book's website. It then showed up later that year in Houghton Library at Harvard University who revealed that the document had been purchased from Carl Williams Rare Books in London. Carl tells us he purchased the document from Weiser and immediately sold it to Harvard because he felt it fit in well with their LSD library and some other Crowley material he had also provided them.

Oz Fritz first recommended the following RAW trio: The 1982 Introduction to Israel Regardie's *The Eye in the Triangle*, Falcon Press; the foreword to the mysteriously published and out-of-print *Portable Darkness*, Harmony, 1989; and "Hidden Heritage," the foreword to Charles Kipp's out-of-print *Astrology, Aleister, & Aeon*, New Falcon, 2001. After some trouble tracking down the publisher for *Portable Darkness* in order to obtain permission to reprint, we turned to the author who gave us some clues and some cautions. Eventually Rasa received a reply from "Sun God X" explaining that the publishing rights to the Foreword belonged to the author and that, "Any new use of the Wilson essay would need permission from Wilson or his estate." Check.

We close out our selection of RAW on Crowley with "The Lord of Force and Fire," first published in 1976 in *Gnostica*, Vol. 5, No. 4 (#40). I must have found that issue of *Gnostica* on eBay in the late aughts, and sent it to Tom Jackson for conversion from analog to digital, where he posted it to his RAWIllumination blog in May of 2011.

To provide a rich tapestry in which to surround such an important collection, I asked Lon Milo Duquette, Richard

Kaczynski, Oz Fritz, Michael Johnson, and Gregory Arnott to say a few words to which they all agreed and delivered fantastic additions to the book you are reading right now. Beyond writing his introduction, Richard Kaczynski provided us with his notes on the typescript with corrections ranging from typos and formatting to historical inaccuracies and misinterpretations which led us to a more thorough editing and proofing reading process.

This book would not have happened without the efforts of Oz Fritz and Chad Nelson, and particularly, an ongoing dialog between Oz, Chad, Rasa, Michael Johnson, and myself. Their continuous feedback informed the direction of this project from start to finish.

When brain storming topics to cover for the Hilaritas Podcast, I once scanned the index of Cosmic Trigger 1 for the most cited topics, and found that Timothy Leary and Aleister Crowley stood an order of magnitude above all the rest. Bob loved Tim, and Bob loved Uncle Al. I hope that the six essays (and much more!) contained herein form a multi-layered, multi-dimensional introduction to a multi-layered, multi-dimensional one of us.

Mike Gathers
Golden, Colorado
Fools' Day, 2023

ROBERT ANTON WILSON
VIS-Á-VIS
ALEISTER CROWLEY

A FEW WORDS OF INTRODUCTION

By Lon Milo DuQuette

Do what thou wilt shall be the whole of the Law

1975 was a very magical year for me. I turned 27 in July, and on November 15th I became a new initiate member of Aleister Crowley's magical order, *Ordo Templi Orientis* (O.T.O.). I say 'new initiate' because, even though the order had existed since the turn of the century, it had lain dormant as a functioning magical society since Crowley's death in 1947.

Upon Crowley's death, leadership of the order passed to the organization's Grand Treasure General, Karl Germer, who made the unpopular decision to discontinue initiations and group events and focus the order's attention and resources exclusively toward publishing Crowley's writings. As the years passed, the remaining members (approximately two dozen) died off one-by-one until in 1961 when Germer himself passed to *that undiscovered country from whose bourn no traveler returns.* News of Germer's death was not immediately revealed to the remaining members. Indeed, it was nearly six years before it was made known, and it was 1969 before the ageing surviving members took steps to resume initiations and return the O.T.O. to a functioning initiatory order. A series of unlikely accidents would conspire to allow me to be among the first of these new initiates.

My initiator was the new head of the organization himself, Major Grady L. McMurtry (known by his O.T.O. magical name, Hymenaeus Alpha, 777)*. McMurtry was an alumnus of Agape Lodge O.T.O. in Los Angeles in the late 1930s and early 1940s, and a personal student of Aleister Crowley. As a young US Army Lieutenant he had been the only order member able to visit Crowley in England during World War II.

~•~

* Assisting him in my initiation was his (then) wife, Phyllis Seckler who was also an Agape Lodge O.T.O. alumnus Ninth Degree O.T.O. initiate.

~•~

McMurtry was a colorful character whose illustrious pre-war colleagues in the Hollywood science fiction subculture included his O.T.O. lodge brother John Whiteside (Jack) Parsons, Ray Harryhausen, Forrest Ackerman, and Ray Bradbury.

At the ceremonial dinner that followed my O.T.O. initiation McMurtry regaled me with tales of Crowley and magick. It was obvious to me that this man was a wealth of magical and qabalistic wisdom, but he was also one of the coolest and *hippest* individuals I had ever met. After allowing me to divine my magical future using Crowley's own hand-made *I Ching* oracle sticks, he announced, "I've got something I think you'll enjoy." He then disappeared into the living room library and returned with a small paperback book with a colorful but rather corny-looking cover. He pushed it across the dining room table and said, "These guys are brilliant! They have fun with Crowley. If you don't have fun with Crowley you'll go mad! Sex, drugs, magick, aliens, conspiracies . . . You'll love it. Bob Wilson was an editor at Playboy."

The book, of course, was *Illuminatus! – The Eye in the Pyramid* by Robert Shea and Robert Anton Wilson, and I did indeed enjoy it immensely. That November evening became for me the alchemical marriage of two of the aeon's outrageous and brilliant minds engaged in the very act of mutating the consciousness of the planet.

Worldwide interest *in* and respect *for* the work of Aleister Crowley has exploded since that night in 1975. Ordo Templi Orientis is now arguably the largest and most influential magical order in the world. In the first 15 years our local lodge in Newport Beach officiated scores of Degree initiations. Of the new initiates I interviewed in those years at least 75% told me they had been initially drawn to magick and Aleister Crowley because they had read *The Illuminatus! Trilogy* and the works of Robert Anton Wilson.

In 1981 Grady McMurtry and I would again find ourselves sitting at a dining room table; this time at a home in Sacramento, California. Joining us that afternoon was film-maker Kenneth Anger and Robert Anton Wilson. The four of us were guests of one of the organizers of a weekend event held that weekend at California State College Sacramento. It was billed as the *Neuro-Romantic Infraision*. As you might imagine, the table-talk was delicious. When Bob learned I was the O.T.O. Lodge Master in Newport

Beach he laughed and asked if I was the one who presented Dr. Timothy Leary some kind of "Adam Weishaupt Illuminati Award" the previous year. I proudly told him, "Yes." Then, without thinking I added, "We'll be giving *you* the next one."

I'm sure he thought I was joking, and he seemed more anxious to speak with Grady about knowing Crowley personally. Grady was only too delighted to oblige. Later that evening both of them would lecture at the college. Bob opened his talk with the words, "Aleister Crowley is an Eye! Whose Eye no one knows."

After that night, Bob and I stayed in touch and would eventually share a publisher. For several years running, we were both booked as presenters at PantheaCon.* The organizers (knowing that neither Bob nor myself would be spending much time in our comped rooms) booked us together as roommates on the Presenter's Floor of the hotel. Each year we would hang out a little in our room to dress and freshen up and chat about our work. Bob was in a wheelchair at the final Pantheon we both attended, and it was my distinct privilege to chauffer to the stage the man (and the mind) of what I consider to be an *honest-to-god(dess)* "Illuminati."

~•~

* From 1994 to 2020 PantheaCon was a conference for Pagans, Heathens, Indigenous Non-European and many of diverse beliefs that occurs annually over President's Day weekend. Well over 2000 people attended more than 200 presentations that range from Rituals to Workshops and from Classes to Concerts.

~•~

I am particularly honored to be asked to introduce this particular collection of Bob's thoughts about another *honest-to-god(dess)* "Illuminati", Aleister Crowley. I can think of no better way to conclude than with the words engraved upon the plaque our O.T.O. lodge presented to him in 1989 as he took the stage to speak at a Masonic Lodge in Santa Monica, California . . .

Robert Anton Wilson & Grady L. McMurtry
(Hymenaeus Alpha, 777)
Caliph of Aleister Crowley's Ordo Templi Orientis
October 24, 1981

ADAM WEISHAUPT
ILLUMINATI AWARD

Guild of Advanced Thought (G\O\A\T\) of
Heru-ra-ha Lodge Ordo Templi Orientis

O.T.O. Peace Tolerance Truth Salutation
on all points of the Triangle

Do what thou wilt shall be the whole of the Law.

The Guild Of Advanced Thought (G.O.A.T.) of
Heru-Ra-Ha Lodge O.T.O. is honored to present to

ROBERT ANTON WILSON

The Third Annual Adam Weishaupt Illuminati Award in
recognition of incalculable service to humanity and others.
Because of his inspiring novels and astonishing research, Mr.
Wilson is directly responsible for raising the consciousness of
our planet (and of other worlds beyond our realm).

"No man can aspire than this: That he be remembered as one
who selflessly obeyed the harsh dictates of logic and reason;
that he was truly disinterested and objective."
– Hanfkopf, Worke, VI, "Was ist Wahrheit?"

Love is the law, love under will.

Given this 21st day of January, 1989.

Victor Koman of Heru-ra-ha Lodge,
Ordo Templi Orientis Newport Beach
Presenting Robert Anton Wilson with the Third Annual Adam
Weishaupt Illuminati Award, January 21, 1989

FOREWORD

By Richard Kaczynski

You are holding a time machine.

The centerpiece of this book – Robert Anton Wilson's never-before-seen essay "Do What Thou Wilt: An Introduction to Aleister Crowley" – takes readers through a portal back to 1974. Not through modern tech (darn) or entheogens (double darn), but through the magick of one of mankind's earliest inventions: the written word.

While 1974 isn't exactly the dawn of time, it *was* the dawn of RAW's career as mystic, futurist and psychonaut. It was a time when his books *Sex n' Drugs* and *The Illuminatus! Trilogy* were about to appear. It was a time when, if you wanted to know about Aleister Crowley's life, your choices were largely limited to John Symonds' lurid *The Great Beast*, Crowley's own sprawling autobiographical *Confessions*, his former secretary Israel Regardie's apologetic *The Eye in the Triangle*, and his former publisher P. R. Stephensen's defensive *The Legend of Aleister Crowley*. But 1974 was also a golden age when books by Crowley were plentiful and inexpensive (unlike the sky-high prices they fetch on today's secondhand market).

RAW and AC seem like they've always gone together. Like peanut butter and shrooms. It started with Wilson's essay "The Great Beast" in the September/October 1971 issue of *The Realist*. In 1974, the occult "establishment" of Israel Regardie, Francis King, John Symonds and Kenneth Grant may not have known of RAW, but he was certainly aware of them. "Do What Thou Wilt" references them all. But he also pushes his outsider view of both Crowley and the occult philosophy of Thelema.

Although that essay would not see the light of day for nearly fifty years (right here!), RAW soon became a giant of the counterculture. The runaway success of his collaboration with Robert Shea, the *Illuminatus! Trilogy*, minted RAW as a newly-risen star. He followed up with so many books that we can only mention a few highlights: His semi-autobiographical *Cosmic Trigger: Final Secret of the Illuminati* (1977). His novel *Masks of the Illuminati* (1981). His reworked psychology dissertation, *Prometheus Rising* (1983). And his exploration of psychological programming and how to break out of it, *Quantum Psychology* (1990). Rather than RAW writing about Timothy Leary – who at times considered himself Crowley's successor – Leary contributed a foreword to *Cosmic Trigger*, and he and RAW became collaborators on *Neuropolitics* (1978) and *The Game of Life* (1979).

In the late 1980s, when I dove into the sci-fi con and pagan festival circuits, one or both of Wilson and Leary were frequent guests of honor. To me it seemed like more of the attendees had come to Crowley's magick through *The Illuminatus! Trilogy* than all the aforementioned "establishment" authors combined.

RAW's Thelemic street cred extended beyond his celebrated books and collaborations. That's because, after penning "Do What Thou Wilt," he kept writing about Crowley. This included *Gnostica* magazine contributions like the poem "Starbride" (1974) and his review of *The Law is For All*, "The Lord of Force and Fire" (1976). After he became a recognizable celebrity and Discordian pope, he began writing introductions and forewords for other people's books: a new edition of Regardie's *Eye on the Triangle* (1982), Scott Michaelson's Crowley anthology *Portable Darkness* (1989), and Charles Kripp's *Astrology, Aleister, and Aeon* (2001). All of it is collected between these covers.

But let's return to RAW's long-lost and long, lost essay, "Do What Thou Wilt." It draws us in with thought-provoking excerpts from Crowley's published works. It entertains with newspaper and tabloid coverage of the Beast, treating us to quotes – pro, con and ridiculous – about Crowley's larger-than-life character. We also find passages from his early biographers and, more importantly, people who actually knew him: students, secretaries, friends, and colleagues.

The essay goes on to paint a broad-strokes portrait of Crowley's life. Despite the paucity of biographical material at the time, RAW presents a spellbinding overview of the Beast. This is 28 years before the twenty-first century's critical re-evaluation of Crowley, heralded by the trio of 2002 biographies: Laurence Sutin's *Do What Thou Wilt*, Martin Booth's *A Magick Life*, and my own *Perdurabo*. In light of this, we can forgive the occasional inaccuracies and appreciate RAW's larger accomplishment.

"Do What Thou Wilt" truly takes off when RAW expounds his unique spin on Crowley's teachings. He covers *The Book of the Law*, the concept of True Will, the A∴ A∴ grade system, sex magick, entheogens, and much more. RAW appreciates Crowley's humor and trickster nature . . . a facet of the Beast that gets lost, even today, in caricatures of him as wicked, or as some kind of dark edgelord. RAW's description of the Aeon of Horus in terms of the Three Grades (Hermit, Lover and man of Earth) in *The Book of the Law* (I:40) is as provocative today as it was when he first wrote it: a decidedly different counter to Crowley's Ordo Templi Orientis-centric implementation. Likewise, "The Soldier and the Hunchback: ! and ?" – one of my favorite essays by Crowley, and one of his more under-appreciated – finds lots of love and extrapolations from RAW's pen.

He connects Crowley's ideas to a who's who of 1970s thought leaders and influencers: a testament to the breadth of RAW's knowledge. He draws parallels with an array of religious and mystical traditions including Tibetan, Theravada and Mahayana Buddhism, Voodoo, Alchemy, Sufism, Confucianism and Kabbalah. He also invokes then-current authorities on topics as diverse as entheogens (R. Gordon Wasson, John Allegro and Andrei Pujarich), psychology (Thomas Szasz, R. D. Laing and Eric Berne) and occultism (David Conway, Carlos Castaneda, Isaac Bonewits, and Osho . . . before he started calling himself Osho). He draws heavily from rebels and disrupters like Timothy Leary, Alfred Korzybski, and Malaclypse the Younger. He's equally comfortable citing Joseph Campbell's *The Masks of God* as he is Thomas Pynchon's brand-new novel, *Gravity's Rainbow* (which, despite being chosen for the Pulitzer Prize in fiction, was refused the award by the Pulitzer Prize advisory board). The originality and scope of all the dots that RAW connects is breathtaking.

Aleister Crowley's recommended reading lists encouraged students of magick to examine traditional occult practices through the lens of the latest science, anthropology, history and philosophy. So does RAW, nearly half a century later, interpret Crowley, magick and Thelema through the lens of cutting-edge thinkers and teachers of *his* time. Which begs the question, dear reader, what current ideas shape *your* worldview? This, perhaps, is the challenge posed by the present anthology: to take RAW's kaleidoscope of ideas, nearly fifty years on, and understand them through the lens of *our* latest understanding of science, anthropology, history and philosophy. As RAW amply demonstrates, the real magick is what of ourselves we bring to the table of understanding.

Richard Kaczynski
Raleigh, March 2023

Five Footprints
of a Camel

A Foreword by Oz Fritz

A cry came in the digital wilderness of the World
Wide Web some eighteen years ago announcing an online
course, *Crowley 101*, to be led by one of the most articulate
voices on the subject, Robert Anton Wilson. I signed up
immediately. This opened the door to the collective space and
timeship known as the Maybe Logic Academy. I collected my
wits and hopped on board.

Naturally the news generated much buzz and excitement.
Wilson explains, explicates, and writes about the ideas,
practices and life of Aleister Crowley like none other: direct,
engaging and often humorous. (Actually, this also describes
another contributor to this work, but in a different way). He
also shared some of his practical experiments in Magick with
the public. The first volume of the *Cosmic Trigger* series,
Final Secret of the Illuminati, at times reads like a magical
diary supplemented with extensive background material on
his influences of whom Crowley appears one among many.

Wilson has a reputation for skepticism. After 45 years

of research and experience, how skeptical would he be of Crowley and Thelema itself, I wondered? How true would he stay in the course to the teachings as given by the Great Beast?

The rationale behind "The Soldier and the Hunchback: ! and ?," Aleister Crowley's investigation of skepticism and revelation published in *The Equinox* Volume I, Number I (the journal that announced the advent of Scientific Illuminism) began the real dive into *Crowley 101* following an introductory discussion regarding the most useful way to signify 'magical critters'. RAW chose to not reference the *Equinox* article directly. Instead, he asked the students to "ponder DEEPLY " the Hunchback and the Soldier found in the first two chapters of *The Book of Lies*. Those two chapters consist solely of "?" in the first, and "!" in the second. The commentary to the second chapter suggests reading "The Soldier and the Hunchback: ! and ?" in the *Equinox*. Students who took it upon themselves to follow that link had more than two punctuation marks to deeply ponder upon.

One of the first things I noticed was that he began all his comments and some of his assignments, with 'Do what thou wilt shall be the whole of the Law,' and ended them with 'Love is the law, love under will' exactly as Crowley practiced and instructed Thelemites to do in their communications. That opening phrase, probably Uncle Al's most famous, had a featured role in the course. When will 'Do what thou wilt become the whole of the law?' was a discussion question he raised. Later, he compared the "shall be" of 'Do what thou wilt shall be the whole of the law' with "is" the whole of the law and used that to segue into the practice of writing in e-prime. As the course proceeded through April of 2005, I noted the synchronicity that *Crowley 101* coincided with the 101st anniversary of the reception of *The Book of the Law*.

In the third week we were assigned to examine different correspondences with the number 23. In *Cosmic Trigger Volume I* RAW writes: "I accepted the 23 enigma as a signal that I should attempt to decipher." Later, he compares his confrontation with 23 numerology to the intuitive leap Dr. James Watson made when he came down a spiral staircase that led to cracking the DNA code. Observing and noting all the synchronicities he experienced around 23 lifted a veil inspiring Wilson's entry into applying Cabala in his life and literature. Tradition holds that one doesn't speak directly of Cabala. RAW followed that tradition in the course despite Cabala being foundational to the structure of Crowley's teaching. However, he provided a key, the 23 enigma and its network of correspondences, for opening-up to occult reception and multiple vision. You can take the horse to water and let them make the decision.

At times I had the impression that Wilson was workshopping ideas with everyone in the group discussions. For instance, asking for our take on the violent rhetoric in the third chapter of *The Book of the Law*. He cautiously agreed with the view that posited it best be read as metaphorically representing intense inner work. Another time, he asked for opinions regarding Jack Parson's assertion that his received text, *Liber 49 The Book of Babalon*, constituted the fourth chapter of *The Book of the Law*. I recall the consensus saying, not so much. I don't remember RAW expressing a strong opinion on the question, one way or another. Interesting, though, that he brought it up.

Interesting, for one reason, because it indicates the attitude that Thelema isn't static and fixed. It progresses and changes as the world and people who practice it progress and change. In one discussion, I paraphrased from *Liber 77*: "There is no God but WoMan." Wilson replied that he and Arlen had written up *Liber 77* changing every "Man" to "WoMan." WoMan, of course, is the neologism Timothy Leary coined as an updated way to generically represent humans. It's also the title of one of his books, *What Does WoMan Want?*

Wilson directed the class to read *The Widow's Son*, perhaps his most advanced transmission of Magick. Advanced particularly in terms of symbolism, Cabala and allusion; multiple visions on multiple levels. He didn't explain any of that, but with another question he did give a demonstration of the way his Cabalistic analysis works.

This is RAW answering a question he posed earlier. He is making allusions to the 1960's TV comedy show *Gilligan's Island*. My avatar's name at this point in the course was "Skipper," the Captain of their ship that got stranded on a desert island. Earlier, the show's primary characters had been compared to the 8 Circuit model of consciousness that Leary and Wilson promoted. Skipper corresponds to the second circuit.

Wilson:

Doesn't anybody have any bright ideas about skidoo and skedaddle?

Gilligan appears to have been pondering this all day in his primitive sage-like way but no coconuts have fallen.

I'll give it a go.

skidoo by gematria = 234

key 2 = Chokmah

key 3 = Binah

key 4 = the value of Daleth, the path that connects Binah and Chokmah with love – the Empress tarot trump and a door.

234 could therefore represent Adam Kadmon, the cojoining of the male and female in one unit. This connectedness creates a door that leads to Kether via the paths represented by the Fool and Magus cards.

It could be said that 234 symbolizes the supernal triad. When this occurs, then all the impurities of the lower nature automatically skeedaddle on OUT.

Another interpretation:

ski-doo and skee-daddle

Both ski and skee add to 90, one by i – the Hermit, the other by 2 ee's, e symbolized by The Star (could this refer to the double star Sirius?)

90 = The Emperor, "This is the swift creative energy, the initiative of all Being" (from *The Book of Thoth*)

doo = 144 = 12x12 = active Magick = Do what thou wilt

daddle = 48 = 4x12 = magick multiplied by love = Love under will.

Also Chapter 48 from *The Book of Lies* corresponds with hard work.

Skidoo therefore = The Emperor doing active magick in Hermit mode.

Do what thou wilt shall be the whole of the Law.

Skeedaddle therefore = The Emperor doing magick with love and working hard at it.

Love is the law, love under will

Both Skidoo and Skeedaddle initiate being swiftly thru the formula of GET OUT. One thru will, one thru love. Both mean GET OUT fast. GET OUT the impurities and GET OUT of town.

Note: The Emperor connotates an archetypal patterning of energy (got all these fancy words from The Professor, by the way) and does not refer to gender. There may be as many female Emperors as male Empresses.

Skidoo is the title of the 23rd Chapter in *The Book of Lies* and "get OUT" represents the formula analyzed there. The Skeedaddle addition apparently comes from Wilson.

The atmosphere and mood around the online group had periods of high intensity, in a good, traveling into the unknown kind of way; skimming through the outer layers of Chapel Perilous. You could pick up the sense of that from the posts, a sort of psychic ambience alongside the literal message. One lost soul appeared discombobulated, teetering over the edge, jagged and schizo. They only lasted a few weeks. Other players of the magick game turned up with interesting insights, stories, fears and strong energy. Once I felt contact with a presence recalling Mary Desti Sturges, Crowley's Scarlet Woman at one point and co-author of *Magick.*

A strong synchronicity in a student's workplace: getting a call from someone with the same name as another student's avatar in the class, immediately after hearing "Wilson," shocked the receiver of this overlay by triggering past tragedies following other intense synchs. A discussion about what may or may not be behind synchronicities ensued, their effects and possible prognostications, alongside suggestions for handling these occult encounters. Another time, objections were raised to Nietzsche's old chestnut, "what doesn't kill you makes you stronger." Some people REALLY don't appreciate hearing that phrase. Bob Wilson jumped in on this one defending the right to these objections and calling for respect for belief systems you don't agree with.

Aleister Crowley's first published novel, *Diary of a Drug Fiend* was not covered in the course. The book espouses an ideology that dangerous, addictive drugs, in this case cocaine and heroin, may be used safely if they are put at the service of one's True Will. Crowley's own journals detail painful failures at conquering heroin addiction. Other diaries describe cocaine overindulgence. The use of psychedelic drugs did come up in a discussion thread. RAW surprised me with the comment that he didn't recommend anyone under the age of 40 take psychedelics saying something to the effect that by then they would have a strong enough foundation to risk this kind of experimentation. "I don't want to make the same mistake Leary did."

Along with hashish, Crowley did use what we now call a psychedelic drug, a compound derived from peyote called anhalonium lewinni, a precursor to mescaline. In his collection of Crowley's writings on hashish, *Roll Away the Stone*, Israel Regardie succinctly describes the Great Beast's attitude toward drugs: "His fundamental premise was stated over and over again in a hundred different ways. It was *never* that the drug experience *per se* could possibly replace the mental and spiritual discipline that he stood for, and which all previous occult teachers insisted upon." (Emphasis in the original).

Concurrent with the class, in the universe next door on the net, the Maybe Logic Academy's main forum ran a parallel thread called *Magick 101* with some interesting odds and ends not directly related to the course curriculum but related to a Magick curriculum. For instance, someone posted excellent step-by-step instructions for how to invoke/evoke a deity; a DIY method for contacting Higher Intelligence.

The eighth week of the course was reserved for asking any question you want. Wilson responded to them all quite immediately with short, aphoristic-type answers. I asked why Crowley chose to identify with The Great Beast. RAW replied because animals act on instinct, they do their will without thinking about it. In the final essay in this book, *The Lord of Force and Fire*, he delves into that further. Someone asked a question to do with Crowley's character. RAW replied:

> Forgiveness seems implied in
> Crowley's refusal to hold fixed emotions
> or fixed mental states

My own position derives from hedonic
engineering – 'They live happiest
who have forgiven most'

• • •

In 1970, Alan Watts turned Robert Anton Wilson on
to Aleister Crowley by suggesting he read *The Eye in the
Triangle* by Israel Regardie. Somewhere around a year later,
give or take, Wilson began a life-long career as a magick
educator beginning in print with the article, "The Great Beast
– Aleister Crowley," included here. *Illuminatus!,* Wilson's
first novel, co-written with Robert Shea, completed in the
fall of 1971, infused a significant amount of instruction in
Crowley's philosophy within its science fiction, psychedelic,
satirical swirl of conspiracy, romance and enlightenment.

For many like myself, RAW served as an entry point
into understanding both the man, Crowley, his jokes, and his
often arcane and confusing writings. RAW has an uncanny
knack of extracting the gist of Crowley's philosophy and
experiments making them more easily comprehensible.
In a very short time of being exposed to Crowley, Wilson
displayed a profound understanding of Magick. This may
in part be explained by the fact that he contacted and
corresponded with people who personally knew and spent
time with the Mage, namely Israel Regardie and Grady
McMurtry. These contacts seemingly passed the baraka on.

Wilson immediately set to work putting the magical
exercises into practice. I recall a recorded talk with Wilson
on the subject of Crowley where he recounts people telling
him they didn't understand or didn't know how to access key
concepts in Thelema like True Will. He would always ask
them if they had tried any of the practices, they inevitably
replied they had not.

Perhaps another contributing factor for RAW taking to
Magick so quickly involves his longtime study and frequent

reading of James Joyce. Joyce includes a great deal of magic and esoteric subjects in all his writings, appearing to increase with successive works. RAW frequently compared Crowley and Joyce in the articles he wrote and talks he gave. This dynamic duo became the main nexus point where Magick and Literature meet in all of RAW's fiction beginning with *Illuminatus!*. In a talk on Joyce, RAW says that he was responsible for introducing a lot of Eastern thought and philosophy into Western literature. Crowley introduced various Eastern philosophies and practices into Western Hermeticism.

Language plays a key role in Magick. James Joyce experiments with language to create magickal effects particularly in *Ulysses* and *Finnegans Wake* such that readings from these books have been known to alter consciousness. Crowley seems to have acknowledged this in a review of Joyce where he called him a genius, a word that Crowley rarely, if ever, used to describe a contemporary. RAW experiments with writing in Joyce's various styles (stream of consciousness, jump cuts, portmanteau words, different narrative styles etc.) throughout his fiction. It's an essential part of his magick.

Wilson made a succinct comparison of two of their books in *Crowley 101*:

> To me, dialectics involves the ability
> to transcend opposites.
> *Finnnegans Wake* and *The Book of
> Lies* seem [to me] to accomplish
> this better than any other works
> I've read.
>
> One example from FW [remember
> kosmos in Greek means order] –
> JJ's word 'chaosmos.'

Apart from Joyce, RAW's presentation modifies and

expands Crowley's teaching incorporating various elements from other systems of thought such as General Semantics, John Lilly, Zen Buddhism, and Gurdjieff among multiple others. At the last workshop I attended by RAW, he suggested that Gurdjieff and Crowley gave completely different presentations of the same system. I agree with him. Studying Gurdjieff can help with understanding Crowley and vice versa. Practicing Lilly's *Beliefs Unlimited* metaprogramming tape, frequently advocated by RAW, can help remove internal barriers and limiting beliefs to effectively practicing ritual magick. The method of eclectic, comparative Hermeticism RAW explored and included under the umbrella of model agnosticism, became very useful for me.

• • •

Following the Crowley course, the various, ever-changing constellation of stars at the Maybe Logic Academy's main forum continued to create a significant online presence. Some became good friends. RAW would turn up and post from time to time over the next year or so. It always felt special to see his presence there. About six months before he permanently transitioned out of body, a caregiver posted on the Forum that if we had something to say to RAW, now was the time. I sent him a joke about a ventriloquist dog, and a quote from *The Book of Lies*:

> Now and again Travelers cross the desert; they come from the Great Sea, and to the Great Sea they go.
>
> As they go they spill water, one day they will irrigate the desert, till it flower,
>
> See! Five footprints of a Camel! V.V.V.V.V.

> Ewige blumenkraft!

Oz Fritz
February 14, 2023
Nevada City, CA

LION OF LIGHT

WRITINGS BY
ROBERT ANTON WILSON
ON ALEISTER CROWLEY

STARBRIDE

O Nuit, continuous one of heaven,
let it be ever thus: that men speak not
of Thee as One but as None . . .
since thou art continuous!

Your time has come, O nightmare life-in-death,
Corpse-god, slime-god, compost ghoul,
Now we dare the right of stifled breath,
Become *der reine Thor*, the Tarot Fool

"That is not dead which can eternal lie"
(Who needs to fear the merge and blend?)
"And with strange eons even death shall die"
When even incarnation has its end.

Your time has come, O skull-beneath-the-skin,
Osiris, mummy-Christ of eyeless sockets,
Now if ever we will dare Promethean sin,
Bring fire back to heaven on our rockets.

The last of the terrestrial mortals dies;
The cosmic immortals are already born;
Farewell to planet Earth: O open skies,
Gods not Men arise on Judgement Morn

Your time has come, O God of cages' bars,
Do What Thou Wilt shall be the only law:
Our mother-bride awaits us in the stars
A smiling sphinx with velvet paw.

Robert Anton Wilson

~~~~~~~

Starbride
Gnostica, Volume 4, Number 4, December 1974

THE GREAT BEAST — ALEISTER CROWLEY

0 – The Fool

"All ways are lawful to innocence. Pure folly is the key to initiation."

–The Book of Thoth

Crowley: Pronounced with a *crow* so it rhymes with *holy*: Edward Alexander Crowley, b. 1875 d.1947, known as Aleister Crowley, known also as Sir Aleister Crowley, Saint Aleister Crowley (of the Gnostic Catholic Church), Frater Perdurabo, Frater Ou Mh, To Mega Therion, Count McGregor, Count Vladimir Svareff, Chao Khan, Mahatma Guru Sri Paramahansa Shivaji, Baphomet, and Ipsissimus; obviously, a case of the ontological fidgets – couldn't make up his mind who he really was; chiefly known as The Beast 666 or The Great Beast; friends and disciples celebrated his funeral with a Black Mass, or so the newspapers said.

Actually it was a Gnostic Catholic Mass (even John Symonds, Crowley's most hostile biographer, admits that

at most it could be called a Grey Mass, not a Black Mass –
observe the racist and Christian-chauvinist implications in
this terminology, but it was certainly not an orthodox R.C.
or Anglican mass, I mean, cripes, the priestess took off her
clothes in one part of it, buck naked, and they call *that* a
Mass, gloriosky!

So the town council had a meeting – this was the Ridge,
in Hastings, England, 1947, not 1347 – and they passed an
ordinance that no such heathen rites would ever be tolerated
in any funeral services in their town, not *never*; I sort of
picture them in the kitsch, Alpine-Balkan garb of Universal
Studios' classic monster epics, and I see Aleister himself, in
his coffin, wearing nothing less spectacular than the old black
cape of Bela Lugosi: fangs showing beneath his sensual lips,
but his eyes closed in deep and divine Samadhi.

Because that's the sort of images that come to mind
when Aleister Crowley is mentioned: this damnable man
who identified himself with the Great Beast in St. John's
Revelation in an age when the supernatural is umbilically
connected with Universal Studios, Hearst Sunday
Supplement I-walked-with-a-zombie-in-my-maidenform-
bra gushing and, God's socks, *Today's Astrology* ("Listen,
Scorpio: This month you must look before you leap and
remember that prudence is wiser than rashness: Don't trust
that Taurus female in your office" – I repeat: God's socks and
spats); this divine man who became the Logos when Logos
was just a word to pencil into Double-Crostics on rainy
Sundays; this damnable and divine paradox of a Crowley!

Listen, some critic (I forgot who) wrote of Lugosi
"acting with total sincerity and a kind of demented cornball
poetry" and the words, like the old, crimson-lined black
cape, seem tailored equally well for the shoulders of
Master Therion, To Mega Therion, the Great Beast, Aleister
Crowley. This is the final degradation: this avatar of anarchy,

this epitome of rebellion, this incarnation of inconsistency, this man Crowley whom his contemporaries called "The King of Depravity," "The Wickedest Man in the World," "A Cannibal at Large," "A Man We'd Like to Hang," "A Human Beast"; and, with some anti-climax, "A Pro-German and Revolutionary."

Now, to us, he is quaint. Worse: he is Camp. Worse yet: he is corny.

We don't even believe his boast that he performed human sacrifice 150 times a year, starting in 1912.

None of these cordial titles was invented by myself. All were used, in Crowley's lifetime, by the newspaper *John Bull*, in its heroic and nigh-interminable campaign to save England from the Beast's pernicious influence. See P.R. Stephensen, *The Legend of Aleister Crowley*.

I − The Magician

"The True Self is the meaning of the True Will: know Thyself through Thy Way."

−The Book of Thoth

For there is no clear way, even on the most superficial level of the gross external data, to say what Edward Alexander Crowley (who called himself Aleister, and other names) really was trying to do with his life and communicate to his fellows.

Witness: here is an Englishman (never forget that: an Englishman, and bloody English at times he could be) who in the stodgiest year, of the dreariest decade of the age we call Victoria, commits technical High Treason, joins the Carlists, accepts a knighthood from Don Carlos himself, denounces as illegitimate all the knighthoods granted by "the

Hanoverian usurper" (he also called her a "dumpy German hausfrau" – poor Vicky), yes, and then for years and decades afterward continues, with owl-like obstinacy, with superlative stubbornness, with ham heroism, with promethean pigheadedness, to sign himself "Sir Aleister" – a red flag in the face of John Bull.

But more: the same romantic reactionary, the same very parfait bogus knight, hears that the French authorities, scandalized by the heroic size of the genital on Epstein's statue of Oscar Wilde, have covered it with a butterfly – and, *bien bueno*, you guessed it, there he is, at twilight with hammer and chisel, sworn enemy of the Philistines, removing the butterfly and restoring the statue to its pristine purity – but why by all the pot-bellied gods in China, why did he turn that gesture into a joke by walking, the same night, into London's stuffiest restaurant, wearing the same butterfly over the crotch of his own trousers?

A Harlequin, then, we might pronounce him, ultimately: the archetypal Batty Bard superimposed upon the classic Eccentric Englishman? And with a touch of the Sardonic Sodomist – for didn't he smuggle homosexual jokes (hidden in puns, codes, acrostics and notarikons) into his various volumes of mystical poetry?

Didn't it even turn out that his great literary "discovery" the *Bagh-i-Muattar* [*The Scented Garden*] was not a discovery at all but an invention – all of it, all, all! from the pious but pederastic Persian original, through the ingenious but innocent English major who translated it (and died heroically in the Boer War), up to the high Anglican clergyman who wrote the Introduction saluting its sanctity but shivering at its salacity – all, all from his own cunning and creative cranium?

Yes: and he even published one volume, *White Stains* (Krafft-Ebing in verse) with a poker-faced prologue pronouncing that "The Editor hopes the Mental Pathologists, for whose eyes alone this treatise is destined, will spare no precaution to prevent it falling into other hands" – and, hot damn, arranged that the author's name on the title-page would be given as "George Archibald," a pious uncle whom he detested.

Sophomore pranks? Yes, but in 1912, at the age of 37, he was still at the same game; that was the year he managed to sell *Hail Mary*, a volume of versatile verses celebrating the Virgin, to London's leading Catholic publishers, Burns and Oates; and he even waited until it was favorably reviewed in the Catholic press ("a plenteous and varied feast for the lovers of tuneful verse," enthused the *Catholic Times*) before revealing that the real author was not a cloistered nun or an uncommonly talented Bishop, but himself, Satan's Servant, the Great Beast, the Demon Crowley.

But grok in its fullness this fact: he really did it. You or I might conceive such a jest, but he carried it out: writing the pious verses with just the proper tone of sugary sanctimoniousness to actually sell to a Papist publisher and get cordial reviews in the Romish press – as if Baudelaire had forced himself to write a whole volume of Edgar Guest: And just for the sake of a horse-laugh?

To understand this conundrum of Crowley we will have to Dig.

II — The High Priestess

"Purity is to live only to the Highest: and the Highest is All; be thou as Artemis to Pan."

–The Book of Thoth

These jokes sometimes seem to have an obscure point, and one is uneasily suspicious that there might be

Hamlet-like method in this madness. Even the alternate identities can be considered more than games. They might be Zen counter-games. Here's the Beast's own explanation of the time he became Count Vladimir Svareff, from *The Confessions of Aleister Crowley: An Autohagiography*:

> I wanted to increase my knowledge of mankind. I knew how people treated a young man from Cambridge. I had thoroughly appreciated the servility of tradesmen, although I was too generous and too ignorant to realize the extent of their dishonesty and rapacity. Now I wanted to see how people would behave to a Russian nobleman. I must say here that I repeatedly used this method of disguise – it has been amazingly useful in multiplying my points of view about humanity. Even the most broad-minded people are necessarily narrow in this one respect. They may know how all sorts of people treat them, but they cannot know, except at second hand, how those same people treat others.

And the Hail Mary caper has its own sane-insane *raison d'etre*:

> I must not be thought exactly insincere, though I had certainly no shadow of belief in any of the Christian dogmas . . . I simply wanted to see the world through the eyes of a devout Catholic, very much as I had done with the decadent poet of *White Stains*, the Persian mystic of *Bagh-i-Muattar*, and so on . . . I did not see why I should be confined to one life. How can one hope to understand the world if one persists in regarding it from the conning tower of one's own "personality?"

Just so: the procedure is even scientific these days (Role-Playing, you know) and is a central part of Psychodrama and Group Dynamics. "You have to go out of your mind before you can come to your senses," as Tim Leary (or Fritz Perls) once said. Sure, you can even become Jesus and Satan at the same time: Ask Charles the Son of Man.

For Artemis, the goddess of nature, is eternally virgin: she only surrendered once, and then to Pan: and this is a clue to the Beast's purpose in his bloody sacrifices.

III — The Empress

"This is the Harmony of the Universe, that Love unites the Will to create with the Understanding of that Creation."

– The Book of Thoth

The infant Gargantua was sent to a school run by the Plymouth Brethren, the narrowly Fundamentalist sect to which his parents belonged. He commends the school in these cordial words from his essay "A Boyhood in Hell":

May the maiden that passes it be barren and the pregnant woman that beholdeth it abort! May the birds of the air refuse to fly over it! May it stand as a curse, as a fear, as a hate, among men. May the wicked dwell therein! May the light of the sun be withheld therefrom and the light of the moon not lighten it! May it become the home of the shells of the dead and may the demons of the pit inhabit it! May it be accursed, accursed – accursed for ever and ever.

One gathers that the boy Alick was not happy there. In fact, the climax of his miseries came when somebody told the Headmasters that he had seen young Crowley drunk on hard liquor. Our anti-hero was put on a diet of bread and water and placed in coventry (i.e., nobody, student or teacher, was allowed to talk to him), without being told what offense he committed; this Christian punishment (for his own good, of course) lasted one full year – at which point his health collapsed and a relative not totally committed to Plymouth Brethren theology insisted that he be removed from that environment before it killed him.

This incident is a favorite with the Beast's unsympathetic critics; they harp on it gleefully, to convey that *they* are not the sort of religious bigots who would torture a child in this fashion; and they also use it to explain his subsequent antipathy to anything bearing the names or coming under the auspices, of "Jesus" or "Christ."

It was this school, they say, which warped his mind and turned him to the service of the devil; a nice theory for parlor analysts or term papers, but it has the defect of not being quite true. The King of Depravity never did embrace Satan, as we shall see, and he kept a very nice mind full of delicate distinctions and discriminations; of this experience he himself says, "I did not hate Jesus and God; I hated the Jesus and God of the people I hated."

But now we jump ahead, past adolescence (skipping the time he seduced a housemaid on his mother's bed; sorry, Freudians), past Cambridge (missing a nice 1890-style student riot) and past mountain-climbing (by 1901, he and his favorite fellow-climber, Oscar Eckenstein, held most of the climbing records in the world between them – all but one to be exact); we come now to the Hermetic Order of the Golden Dawn; caveat lector; we enter the realm of Mystery, Vision – and Hallucination; the reader is the only judge of what can be believed from here on.

IV — The Emperor

"Find thyself in every Star. Achieve thou every possibility."

–The Book of Thoth

It seems that the Golden Dawn was founded by Robert Wentworth Little, a high Freemason, based on papers he rescued from a hidden drawer in London's Freemason Hall during a fire. No: it wasn't Little at all, but Wynn Wescott, a Rosicrucian, acting on behalf of a mysterious Fraulein Sprenger in Germany, who herself probably represented the original Illuminati of Adam Weishaupt.

No: not so either. Behind the Golden Dawn was actually a second Order, the Rose of Ruby and Cross of Gold – i.e. the original medieval Rosicrucians still in business at the old stand; and behind *them* was the Third Order, the Great White Brotherhood – i.e., the Nine Unknown Men of Hindu lore – the true rulers of earth. One can only say, if the last theory be true, that the Great White Brotherhood are Great White Fuckups.

The true *true* story of the Illuminati, Rosicrucians etc. – or another damned lie – is given in *Illuminatus: or Laughing Buddha Jesus Phallus Inc.*, by Robert J. Shea and this writer, to be published by Dell this year, unless the Nine Unknown Men suppress it.

Well anyway, wherever the Hermetic Order of the Golden Dawn came from, there it was almost practicing in the open in London in the 1890's, with such illustrious members as Florence Farr (the actress), Arthur Machen (the horror-story writer: you must have read his *Great God Pan*?), George Cecil Jones (a respectable chemist by day and a clandestine alchemist by night) and William Butler Yeats (a poet who thought his verse was superior to Crowley's, he is described in *Autohagiography* as "a disheveled demonologist who could have given much more care to his appearance without being accused of dandyism.").

In 1898, the King of Depravity was admitted to the Order. Crowley took the new name Frater Perdurabo which means Brother I-Will-Endure-To-The-End; he later changed it to Frater Ou Mh or Brother Not Yet – and began acquiring great proficiency in such arts as the invocation of angels and demons, making himself invisible, journeying in the astral body and such-like Wonders of the Occult.

In one critical operation of magick the Wickedest Man in the World failed abjectly in those early days; and this was the most important work of all. It consisted in achieving the Knowledge and Conversation of one's Holy Guardian Angel – what, precisely, that may mean will be discussed later.

The usual operation, as found in *The Book of Sacred Magick of Abra-Melin the Mage*, requires six months' hard work and is somewhat more grueling than holding the Ibis position of Hatha Yoga for that interlude, or working out pi to the thousandth place in your head without using paper or pencil. The Beast's critics like to proclaim that he couldn't manage this because he was incapable of obeying Abra-Melin's commandment of chastity for the necessary 180 days. We will later learn how true that claim actually is.

Invisibility, by the way, isn't as hard as Lamont Cranston's Tibetan teachers implied. After only a few months practice, guided by the Beast's training manuals, I have achieved limited success twice already; and my cats, Simon and Garfunkel, do it constantly. There is no need to look for mysteries when the truth is often right out in the light of day.

V – The Hierophant

"Be thou athlete with the eight limbs of Yoga; for without these thou art not disciplined for any fight."

– The Book of Thoth

Early in February, 1901, in Guadalajara, Mexico, the Beast began seriously working on *dharana*, the yoga of concentration. The method was that long used in India: holding one single image in the mind – a red triangle – and banishing all other words or pictures. This is in no wise any easy task, and I, for one, would have much more respect for Aleister's critics and slanderers if there were any shred of evidence that they ever attempted such self-discipline, and, attempting it, managed to stay with it until they achieved results.

For instance, after three weeks of daily practice, the Beast recorded in his diary that he had concentrated that day for 59 minutes with exactly 25 "breaks" or wanderings from the triangle: 25 breaks may not sound so great to those who haven't tried this; a single hour, however, will convince them that 3600 breaks, or one per second is close to average for a beginner.

Toward the end of April, the Beast logged 23 minutes with 9 breaks; on May 6th, 32 minutes and 10 breaks. I repeat, anyone who thinks Acid or Jesus or Scientology has remade his or her life ought to attempt a few weeks of this; it is the clearest and most humiliating revelation of the compulsive neurosis of the "normal" ego.

On August 6 the Beast arrived in Ceylon, still working on daily *dharana* – oh yes, in Honolulu he'd had an affair with a married woman, later celebrated in his sonnet sequence *Alice: An Adultery*, published under the auspices of his fictitious "Society for the Propagation of Religious Truth." His critics always mention that, to prove that he wasn't *sincere*; one sometimes gets the cynical notion that these critics are either eunuchs or hypocrites.

Under the guidance of Sri Parananda and an old friend, Allan Bennett, now the Buddhist monk Maitreya Ananda, he plunged into the other "seven limbs" of yoga. I say that his mountain-climbing involved *less* self-discipline. I will not argue; I will give a hint only. Here are the first two steps in beginning to do *pranayama*:

1. Learn to breathe through your two nostrils alternately. When this becomes easy, practice exhaling through the right

nozzle for no less than 15 seconds and then inhaling through the left orifice for a like time. Practice until you can do this without strain for 20 or 30 minutes.

2. Now begin retention of breath between inhalation and exhalation. Increase the period of retention until you can inhale for 10 seconds, retain for 30 second and exhale for 20 seconds. This proportion is important: if you inhale for as long as, or longer than, the exhalation, you are screwing up. Practice until you can do this – comfortably – for an hour.

Got it? Good; now you are ready to start doing the real exercises of *pranayama*. For instance, you can add the "third limb," *asana*, which consists of sitting like a rock, no muscle moving anywhere; the Hindus recommend starting with a contortion that seems to have been devised by Sacher-Masoch himself, but choose a position that seems comfortable at first, if you want – it will turn into Hell soon enough.

All this has a point, of course; when *pranayama* and *asana* are mastered, you can begin to do *dharana* without constant humiliating failures. Congratulations, now you can add the other "five limbs." Of course, the temptation (especially after your foot is no longer merely asleep but has progressed to a state gruesomely reminiscent of rigor mortis) is to decide that "There isn't anything in yoga after all" or "I just can't do it" and maybe there's something in Christian Science or the Process or probably another acid trip would really get you over the hump.*

~•~

* Oh yes, brethren and sistern, we have known people capable of much rationalization. Back in 1901, even, the Beast discovered that some of the "lesser yogis," as he called them, used hashish to fuel the last gallop from *dharana* to *dhyana*; and he later recommended this to his own disciples – but always with the provision that the results so obtained should be regarded as an indication and foreshadowing of what was sought, not as a

Lion of Light

substitute for true attainment. The Beast achieved *dhyana*, the non-ego trance, on October 2, 1901, less than 8 months after beginning serious *dharana* in Guadalajara.

~•~

VI — The Lovers

" . . . rest in Simplicity, and listen in the Silence."

–The Book of Thoth

This may be getting heavy, but it has to be endured for a while before the band starts playing again. Specifically, we should have some understanding of what we mean by *dhyana* and what the Beast has accomplished in those 8 months. The best analysis is probably that given by the Wickedest Man in the World himself in his *Confessions*:

> The problem is how to stop thinking; for the theory is that the mind is a mechanism for dealing symbolically with impressions; its construction is such that one is tempted to take these symbols for reality. "That is, we manufacture units such as the inch, the chair, the self, etc., in order to organize our sense-impressions into coherent wholes, but the mind which performs this kind service is so built that it cannot then escape its own constructs. Having imagined inches and chairs and selves, the mind then perceives them *out there* in the physical world and finds it hard to credit that they exist only in the mind's own sorting machinery.

> Conscious thought, therefore, is fundamentally false and prevents one from perceiving reality. The numerous practices of yoga are simply dodges to help one acquire the knack of slowing down the current of thought and ultimately stopping it altogether.

The mind's self-hypnosis, of course, arises anew as soon as one comes out of *dhyana*. One never retains the ego-less and world-less essence of *dhyana*; one retains an impression thereof polluted by the mind's pet theories and most resonant images. The Beast calls this adulterated after-effect of *dhyana* "mixing the planes" and regards it as the chief cause of the horrors perpetrated by religious nuts on the rest of us throughout history:

> Mohammed's conviction that his visions were of imperative importance to 'salvation' made him a fanatic . . . The spiritual energy derived from the high trances makes the seer a formidable force; and unless he be aware that interpretation is due only to the exaggeration of his own tendencies of thought, he will seek to impose it on others, and so delude his disciples, pervert their minds and prevent their development . . .

> In my system the pupil is taught to analyze all ideas and abolish them by philosophical skepticism before he is allowed to undertake the exercises that lead to *dhyana*.

By 1904, the Beast had come to the conclusion that all he had seen and performed, among the Magicians and among the yogis, could be explained by combining the known psychology with the emerging beginnings of psycho-chemistry. He had pushed mysticism as far as one can, and retained his Victorian Rationalism.

Then came the cataclysm of Cairo.

VII — The Chariot

> "The Issue of the Vulture, Two-in-One, conveyed; this is the Chariot of Power."

– The Book of Thoth

Ever since his initiation into the Hermetic Order of the Golden Dawn in 1898, the Beast has been practicing astral voyaging almost daily. This is considerably easier than *pranayama, asana, dharana*, and it's good clean fun even from the beginning.

If you are an aspirant, or a dupe, merely sit in a comfortable chair, in a room where you won't be interrupted, close your eyes, and slowly envision your "astral body," whatever the blazes that is, standing before you. Make every detail clear and precise; any fuzziness can get you into trouble later.

Now transfer your consciousness to this second body – I don't know why, but some people stick at this point – and rise upward, through the ceiling, through the other rooms in the building, through the stratosphere, until you have left the physical universe entirely – to hell with it, Nixon and his astronauts are taking it over anyway – and find yourself in the astral realm, where NASA isn't likely to follow with their flags and other tribal totems.

Approach any astral figures you see and question them closely, especially about any matters of which you wish knowledge not ordinarily available to you.

Return to the earth-body, awake, and record carefully that which has transpired. The diary of such astral journeys, carefully transcribed, is the key to all progress in High Magick, once the student learns to decipher his own visions.

The skeptical reader, if there are any skeptics left in this gullible generation, might point out that this process begins as an exercise of imagination and that there is no reason to think it ever crosses the line to reality. Quite so: but that objection does not diminish the value of the visions obtained.

The Beast has been at some pains to write a little book called "777" which is a copious catalog, in convenient table form, of the 32 major "astral planes" and their typical scenery, events and inhabitants. Using one's own Magical Diary and the tables in "777" together with a few standard reference works on comparative religion, one can quickly discover where one has been, who has been there before and what major religions were founded on the basis of some earlier visitor's account of what he had seen there.

One need not hold any occult hypothesis about these visions; you can even say that you have been exploring Carl Jung's "Collective Unconscious" – or, more fashionably, that you have been deciphering the ethological record of the DNA code (Tim Leary's favorite theory about LSD voyages, which fits these astral trips just as neatly). The important discipline is to avoid "mixing the planes" and confusing your explanation with the actual vision itself; or, as the Beast says in *Liber O*:

> In this book it is spoken of the Sephiroth, and the Paths, of Spirits and Conjurations; of Gods, Spheres, Planes and many other things which may or may not exist.
> It is immaterial whether they exist or not. By doing certain things certain results follow; students are most earnestly warned against attributing objective reality or philosophical validity to any of them . . .
> The Student, if he attains any success in the following practices, will find himself confronted by things (ideas or beings) too glorious or too dreadful to be described. It is essential that he remain the master of all that he beholds, hears, or conceives; otherwise, he will be the slave of the illusion and the prey of madness . . .
> The Magician may go a long time being fooled and flattered by the Astrals that he has himself modified or manufactured . . . He will become increasingly interested in himself, imagine himself to be attaining one initiation after another. His Ego will expand unchecked, till he seems to himself to have heaven at his feet . . .

The teachers of Zen have the proper tactics against this danger of grandiosity: Crowley's independent discovery of this strategy led to those behaviors – the jokes, the "blasphemies," the shifts in name and identity – which led to his reputation as a kook, a Satanist, and the Wickedest Man in the World.

Having watched the decline into dogmatism and self-aggrandizement of various heroes of the New Wave of dope and occultism, some of us are maybe ready to see that the Beast's incessant profane mockery against himself and his Gods was a necessary defense against this occupational hazard of the visionary life.

But then came the Mystification of Cairo – and beyond it, the Mindfuck in China . . . and the discovery of the value of human sacrifice.

VIII – Adjustment

"Balance against each thought its exact opposite. For the Marriage of these is the Annihilation of Illusion."

–The Book of Thoth

In March, 1904, the Beast and his first wife, Rose, were in Cairo, and he was trying to teach her some Magick, a subject which bored her profoundly. And now this is the part we warned you about, take it or leave it, this is what seems to have happened – Rose went into a kind of trance and began murmuring various disjointed phrases, including "It's about the Child" and "They are waiting for you."

It soon developed that some god or other was trying to communicate; Crowley asked 12 questions to determine which god and, gulp, her answers were correct, consistent, and revealed a knowledge of Egyptology which in her conscious mind she did not possess.

Like: "What are his moral qualities?" "Force and fire." "What opposes him?" "Deep blue" – until one god emerged that fit the box just as sure as Clark Kent fits the phone booth at *The Daily Planet*; Ra-Hoor-Khuit, or Horus in his War God aspect.

The Beast then took Rose to the Boulak Museum and

asked her to pick out the god in question. She walked past several statues of Horus – which The King of Depravity observed stolidly, although, he says, "with silent glee" – and then (shiver!) she stopped before Stele 666, Ra-Hoor-Khuit. "This is him," she said.

Sorry about that, fellow rationalists.

And, of course, alas and goddam it, 666 – the Number of the Beast in *St. John's Revelation* – was Crowley's own magick number and had been for years.

Those who want to invoke the word "coincidence" to cover the rags of their ignorance are welcome to do so. Some of us have a new word lately, *synchronicity*, coined by no less than psychologist Carl Jung and physicist Wolfgang Pauli – and I've read their books and must admit I came out as confused as I went in; as far as this brain can comprehend, *coincidence* is meaning-*less* correspondence, and synchronicity is meaning-*ful* correspondence, and if that makes you feel superior to the custard-headed clods who still say *coincidence*, you're welcome to it.

And there's more: when the Beast acknowledged Ra-Hoor-Khuit on the other side of the astral phone hook-up, he was turned over to an underling, one Aiwass, an angel, who told him among other things that the true Word of Power isn't abra-*ca*-dabra but abra-*ha*-dabra and the letters add up to 418, which was the number of Crowley's home on Loch Ness in Scotland; and Aiwass's own name adds up to 93, which is also the number of *love* and *will*, the two chief words in his total communication, which is known as *The Book of the Law* – But enough; the proofs, mathematical and cabalistic and *coincidental* (if you must) run on for pages.

In summary, the Beast had been playing a Game against himself for six years, since 1898, invoking the miraculous and the proving after the fact that it was "only" his mind.

Now he had to begin considering that he had made

himself the center of an "astral" field effect, having the qualities of an intelligence greater than his, and signifying same by multi-lingual and numerological correspondences coming not from "inside" but from "outside": Rose's mind, the "independent" decisions of the curators of the Boulak Museum and, then, a certain Samuel bar Aiwass.

For, in 1918, Crowley had adopted the name To Mega Therion, which means The Great Beast in Greek, and adds to 666, and, in an article in *The International*, he asked if any of his readers could find a word or phrase of similar meaning, in Hebrew, which would also add to 666.

He was himself no mean cabalist and had tried all sorts of Hebrew synonyms for "beast" but none of them added to anything like 666; yet the answer came in the mail – Tau, Resh, Yod, Vau, Nun, equal 666 – and it was signed Samuel bar Aiwas.

Aiwas is the Hebrew equivalent of Aiwass, and also adds to 93, the number of his Holy Guardian Angel.

But meanwhile came the Chinese Mindfuck.

IX — The Hermit

"Wander alone; bearing the Light and thy Staff."

–The Book of Thoth

One day in Rangoon, in 1905, Crowley happened to mention to a man named Thornton that there is no necessary connection between the separate quanta of sense-impression. Philosophy-buffs are aware that this has been observed by David Hume, among others, and Thornton replied with another truism, pointing out that there is no necessary connection between the successive states of the ego, either.

The Beast, *naturlich*, was aware that the Buddha had spotted that disturbing fact a long time ago, but suddenly the full import of it hit home to him on an emotional level.

Chew on it: he could not absolutely prove that there was an external world to Aleister Crowley, but merely that there appeared to be a tendency for sense-impressions to organize themselves to suggest such a world, Lord help us; and he could not absolutely demonstrate that there was an "Aleister Crowley" doing this organizing but only that there seems to be a tendency to aggregate internal impressions in such a way as to suggest such an entity. (Get the Librium, mother). All intelligent people have noticed that at one time or another – and quickly brushed it aside, to carry on in the only way that seems pragmatically justified, assuming the reality of the World and the Self.

The Beast, after the workings of his Magick, the experience of his *dhyana* (in which Self, indeed, had vanished for a time) and his encounter with the ever-lovin' Aiwass, was not satisfied to rest in assuming anything.

There was no absolute proof that he had ever achieved *dhyana*, for instance, but only a tendency to organize some impressions into a category called "memory and to assume that they corresponded to "real" events in a time called the "past." Nor could reason alone prove that he had seen a "miracle" in "Cairo," or performed "Magick" in "London," or suffered in a "school" run by "Plymouth Brethren," or had a "biological" "relationship" "with" "beings" known as "Father" and "Mother."

"About now," he scribbled in his diary on November 19, "I may count my Speculative Criticism of the Reason as not only proved and understood, but realized. The misery of this is simply sickening – I can write no more."

He started on a walking journey across China with his wife and daughter, or his earth-body did; his mind was on a far weirder trip. "He had become insane," writes unsympathetic biographer John Symonds in *The Great Beast*; "If this happened to any of us," adds sympathetic biographer Israel Regardie in *The Eye in the Triangle*, "we too might feel we had become insane." Of course, lately it has happened to a lot of us, thanks to the free enterprise pharmacopia of the streets, and we know with bitter memory what the suffering Beast was going through.

And it wasn't six or ten hours in his case; it lasted four solid months, while China drifted by like the eye in the triangle. We've been there, and some of us did the Steve Brodie out the window (the triangle?) and never came back and some of us found weird clues in songs like *Helter Skelter* – what triangle? – Rocky Raccoon went up to his room and Sharon Tate must die – doesn't it? – Because John Lennon wouldn't lie to us when a man is crashing out like American life bomb went authoritarian (what eye?) – So we'll write PIG on the wall and they'll blame it on the spades, see? Oh, yes, Charlie, I see – Sixty-four thousand, nine hundred twenty-eight, because 7-Up Commercials and we start from Void and anything we manufacture is necessarily composed of the elements of Void even when you call it your Self or your World – And then there was the strawberries . . .

Manson, hell; you could turn into *Nixon* that way.

X — Fortune

"The axle moveth not; attain thou that."

–The Book of Thoth

The Beast described this 120-Days-of-Bedlam in a poem called *Aha!*:

The sense of all I hear is drowned;
Tap, tap, tap and nothing matters!
Senseless hallucinations roll
Across the curtain of the soul.
Each ripple on the river seems
The madness of a maniac's dreams!
So in the self no memory-chain
Or casual wisp to bind the straws!
The Self disrupted! Blind, insane,
Both of existence and of laws,
The Ego and the Universe
Fall to one black chaotic curse . . .
As I trod the trackless way
Through sunless gorges of Cathay,
I became a little child!

"They are waiting for you," Rose, in a trance, had said, a year earlier. "It's about the Child."

When Crowley returned to England, after becoming "a little child," he received a letter from chemist George Cecil Jones, a friend in the Golden Dawn. Jones, who recognized what happened, wrote: "How long have you been in the Great Order, and why did I not know? Is the invisibility of the A.A. to lower grades so complete?"

Israel Regardie, a biographer sympathetic to Crowley, but dubious about the existence of the A.A. (the Third Order, or Great White Brotherhood, behind the Rose of Ruby and Cross of Gold) comments thoughtfully, "I do not wholly understand this."

Herman Hesse, who described the Third Order very clearly in *Journey to the East*, gives the formula for initiation in *Steppenwolf*:

PRICE OF ADMISSION:
YOUR MIND

XI — Lust

"Mitigate Energy with Love; but let Love devour all
things."

–The Book of Thoth

One act remained in the drama of initiation: the
achievement of the Knowledge and Conversation of the Holy
Guardian Angel. This most difficult of all magical operations
had been started anew even before Crowley left China,
and, for all of his previous failures, he was determined to
complete it successfully this time. As mentioned earlier, this
invocation takes six months and requires a rather full battery
of magical and mystical techniques.

Sometime after his return to England, the Beast
arranged to have George Cecil Jones "crucify" him (I am
not totally sure what this means, but suspension on a cross,
even via ropes, gets quite painful in a very short while) and,
while hanging on the cross, he swore an oath as follows:
I, Perdurabo, a member of the Body of Christ, do hereby
solemnly obligate myself . . . and will entirely devote my
life so as to raise myself to the knowledge of my higher and
Divine Genius that I shall be He.

In Chapter 9, "The Redemption of Frank Bennett," in
The Magick of Aleister Crowley, John Symonds tells how
with a few words Crowley brought a species of Samadhi or
Satori to Frank Bennett, a magician who had been striving
unsuccessfully for that achievement over many decades.

The words were, in effect, that the Real Self or Holy
Guardian Angel is nothing else but the integration that
occurs when the conscious and subconscious are no longer
segregated by repression and inhibition. It is only fair to warn
seekers after either-or answers that in *Magick Without Tears*
Crowley flatly denies this and asserts that the Angel is a

separate "Being . . . of angelic order . . . more than a man . . ."

After the Crucifixion, the King of Depravity went on plowing his way through the required 180 days (the essence of the Abra-Melin operation is "Invoke Often") while adding other various techniques.

On October 9, 1906 The Beast recorded in his Magical Diary:

> Tested new ritual and behold it was very good . . . I *did* get rid of everything but the Holy Exalted One, and must have held Him for a minute or two. I did. I am sure I did.

On October 10, he added: "I am still drunk with Samadhi all day." And a few days later, "Once again I nearly got there – all went brilliance – but not quite." By the end of the month, there was no longer any doubt. Eight years after commencing the practice of Magick, Aleister Crowley had achieved the Knowledge and Conversation of the Holy Guardian Angel.

XII — The Hanged Man

> "And, being come to the shore, plant thou the Vine and rejoice without shame."

–The Book of Thoth

The Beast lived on for 41 more years, and did work many wonders and quite a few blunders in the world of men and women. In 1912, he became the English head of the Ordo Templi Orientis, a secret Masonic group tracing direct descent from Knights Templar. In 1915, he achieved a vision of the total explanation of the universe, but afterwards was only able to record, "Nothing, with twinkles – but WHAT twinkles."

In 1919, he founded the Abbey of Thelema in Sicily,

but was quickly expelled by a moralist named Benito Mussolini after English newspapers exposed the scandalous *sex-and-dope orgies* that allegedly went on there.

Somewhere along the line, he became the Master of the A.A. or Great White Brotherhood (assuming it ever existed outside his own head, which some biographers doubt) and began teaching other Magicians all over the world.

He married, and divorced, and married, and divorced.

He wrote *The Book of Thoth*, in which, within the framework of a guide to divination by Tarot cards, he synthesized virtually all the important mystical teachings of East and West; we have used it for our chapter-heads.

He landed on Bedloe's Island one day, representing the IRA, and proclaimed the Irish Republic, repudiating his English citizenship.

He wrote *The Book of Lies*, a collection of mind-benders that would flabbergast a Zen Master, including the pregnant question, "Which is Frater Perdurabo and which is the Imp Crowley?" He got hooked on heroin; kicked it; got hooked again; kicked again; got hooked again . . .

He died, and his friends buried him with a Gnostic Catholic Mass which the newspapers called Black.

But he is best remembered for writing in 1928 in *Magick in Theory and Practice* that the most potent invocation involves human sacrifice, that the ideal victim is "a male child of perfect innocence and high intelligence," and that he had performed this rite an average of 150 times per year since 1912.

XIII — Death

" . . . all Acts of Love contain Pure Joy. Die daily."

—The Book of Thoth

Crowley's admirers, of course, claim that he was

engaged in one of his manic jokes when he boasted of performing human sacrifice 150 times a year; he was not joking at all, as we shall see.

Even his bitterest critics (except Rev. Montague Summers, who was capable of believing anything) admit that it's unlikely that a man whose every move was watched by newspapers and police could polish off 150 victims a year without getting caught; but they are, most of them, not above adding that this ghastly jest indicates the perversity of his mind, and, after all (summoning those great and reliable witnesses, Rumor and Slander) there was some talk about Sicilian infants disappearing mysteriously when he was running his Abbey of Thelema there . . .

We have got to come to a definitive conclusion about this matter or we will never grasp the meaning of his life, the value of his Magick, the cause of his vilification, or the true meaning of the Knowledge and Conversation of the Holy Guardian Angel.

XIV — Art

" . . . make manifest the Virtue of that Pearl."

—The Book of Thoth

In 1912, we said, the Beast became English head of the Ordo Templi Orientis. This occurred in a quite interesting manner: Theodore Reuss, Head of that Order in Germany, had come to him and implored him to stop publishing their occult secrets in his magazine, *Equinox*.

The Beast (who had been publishing some of the secrets of the English Rosicrucians – but this wasn't one of them) protested that he didn't know anything about the O.T.O. and its mysteries. Reuss then proclaimed that the Beast did know, even if he had discovered it independently, and that he must accept membership in the 9th degree with the accompanying pledges and responsibilities.

The Beast, who was already a 33-degree Freemason, thanks to a friend in Mexico City, accepted – and found that his "new ritual" to invoke the Holy Guardian Angel in 1906 was the most closely-guarded secret of the Ordo Templi Orientis.

"Now the O.T.O. is in possession of one supreme secret," the Beast writes in his *Confessions*. "The whole of its system . . . was directed towards communicating to its members, by progressively plain hints, this all-important instruction. I personally believe that if this secret, which is a scientific secret, were perfectly understood, as it is not even by me after more than twelve years' almost constant study and experiment, there would be nothing which the human imagination can conceive that could not be realized in practice."

Israel Regardie, the Beast's most perceptive biographer, comes close to revealing the secret in a book called *The Tree of Life*. However, he remarks that the method in question is "so liable to indiscriminate abuse and use in Black Magic" that it is not safe to reveal it directly; he therefore employs a symbolism which, like a Zen riddle, can be decoded only after one had achieved certain spiritual insights.

Charlie Manson understands at least part of this Arcanum of Arcanums; his misuse of it is a classic example of the danger warned of by Crowley in *Liber O*: "he will be the slave of illusion and the prey of madness . . . His Ego will expand unchecked, till he seem to himself to have heaven at his feet . . . "

The secret, of course, is the formula of the Rose and Cross which, as Frazier demonstrated in *The Golden Bough*, is the magic foundation under all forms of religion.

XV — The Devil

"With thy right Eye create all for thyself . . ."

—The Book of Thoth

A word about Evil; the Beast's frequent injunctions to "explore every possibility of the Self" and realize your True Will etc. have often been misunderstood, especially when quoted out of context, in which case he sounds battier than those armchair enthusiasts of mayhem and murder, Stirner and Nietzsche and Sorel.

But the Beast was not an armchair philosopher, but rather an explorer, mountain-climber and big-game hunter who knew violence and sudden death well enough to call by their first names; he did not romanticize them. Here are his actual instructions about Evil from *Liber V*, an instruction manual of the A.A.:

> The Magician should devise for himself a definite technique for destroying "evil." The essence of such practice will consist in training the mind and body to confront things which cause fear, pain, disgust, shame and the like. He must learn to endure them, then to become indifferent to them, then to analyze them until they give pleasure and instruction, and finally to appreciate them for their own sake, as aspects of Truth. When this has been done, he should abandon them if they are really harmful in relation to health or comfort . . .

> Again, one might have a liaison with an ugly old woman until one beheld and loved the star which she is; it would be too dangerous to overcome this distaste for dishonesty by forcing oneself to pick pockets. Acts which are essentially dishonorable must not be done; they should be justified only by calm contemplation of their correctness in abstract cases.

Digest carefully that last sentence. These shrewd and pragmatic counsels are not those of a bloody-minded fool.

XVI — The Tower

"Break down the fortress of thine Individual Self that thy
Truth may spring free from the ruins."

—The Book of Thoth

Now, *The Morning of the Magicians* by Pauwels and
Bergier was a best-seller, especially in the hip neighborhoods,
so I can assume that many of my readers are aware of the
strange evolution of some forms of Rosicrucianism and
Illuminism in 19th Century Germany. Such readers are
aware that there is certain evidence – not a little evidence,
but a great deal of it – indicating that Adolf Hitler joined
something called the Thule Society in Munich in 1923,
and then later obtained admission to its inner circle, the
Illuminated Lodge, and that it was here he acquired certain
ideas about the value of human sacrifice.

It is, in fact, not only possible but probable that the
attempted extermination of European Jewry was not only
the act of insane racism but a religious offering to gods who
demanded rivers of human blood.

The same psychology possessed the Aztecs toward the
end. The omens, the oracles, the astrological skryings all
pointed to doom, and the blood sacrifices correspondingly
multiplied exponentially, hysterically, incredibly . . . and
south in Yucatan much earlier, the Mayans, who always tried
to restrict the blood sacrifice to one or two a year, deserted
their cities for an unknown reason and fled back to the jungle;
they shared the same astrological beliefs as the Aztecs, and
it is plausible to suggest that they ran away from a similar
oracle telling them that only more blood could preserve the
empire.

In fact – I note this only for the benefit of future students
of paranoia – a similar theory about our own glorious rulers

has sometimes crossed my own mind. Why not? Every time an S-M club is raided by the fuzz, the newspapers mutter vaguely that among the clientele were "prominent" and "high-placed" individuals; and don't ever tell me, Clyde, that those birds actually believe the milk-water "liberal" Judeo-Christian faith that they mouth in their public speeches.

Is this the answer to the question we all keep asking – year after unbelievable year, with growing disgust and despair and dementia – *Why are we in Vietnam?* "Many gods demand blood" the Beast once commented sardonically – "especially the Christian god."

XVII – The Star

" . . . burn up thy thought as the Phoenix."

–The Book of Thoth

And, yes, there is a link between Crowley and Hitler. Douglas Hunt, the Beast's most hysterically unfair critic said so in his *Exploring the Occult*, and he was closer to the bullseye than the Beast's admirers. There is a link, but it is a relationship of reciprocity, for Hitler and Crowley are the reverse of each other. Thus (and now we plunge to the heart of the riddle) here are the mind-bending, gut-turning words from Chapter XII, "Of the Bloody Sacrifice and Matters Cognate," in *Magick in Theory and Practice*:

> In any case it was the theory of ancient Magicians that any living being is a storehouse of energy varying in quantity according to the size and health of the animal and in quality according to its mental and moral character. At the death of the animal this energy is liberated suddenly. For the highest spiritual working one must accordingly

choose that victim which contains the greatest and purest force. A male child of perfect innocence and high intelligence is the must satisfactory and suitable victim."

A footnote is appended here, not at the end of this sentence but attached to the word "intelligence." This footnote is perhaps the most famous sentence the Beast ever wrote:

It appears from the Magical Records of Frater Perdurabo (i.e., Crowley himself) that He made this particular sacrifice on an average about 150 times every year between 1912 e.v. and 1928 e.v.

This certainly seems clear, and horrible, enough, but the chapter concludes with the following further remarks:

You are also likely to get in trouble over this chapter unless you truly comprehend its meaning . . ."
The whole idea of the word Sacrifice, as commonly understood, rests upon an error and superstition, and is unscientific. Let the young Magician reflect upon the conservation of Matter and of Energy . . .
There is a traditional saying that whenever an Adept seems to have made a straightforward, comprehensible statement, then it is most certain that He means something entirely different . . .
The radical error of all uninitiates is that they define "self" as irreconcilably opposed to "not-self." Each element of oneself is, on the contrary, sterile and without meaning, until it fulfils itself, by "love under will," in its counterpart in the Macrocosm. To separate oneself from others is to lose that self – its sense of separateness – in the other.

The chapter, let us remember, is called "Of the Bloody Sacrifice: and Matters Cognate," and the Beast was a precise, almost pathologically sensitive, stylist. If the whole discussion was about the "bloody sacrifice," where the deuce are the "matters cognate"? And why does the footnote modify "male child of perfect innocence and high intelligence" instead of the last word in the sentence, "victim"?

Let us review: The Beast originally failed in the invocation of the Holy Guardian Angel; his final success came after:

(a) his success in both the physical and mental disciplines of yoga.

(b) the achievement of accomplished skill in astral voyaging, and

(c) the death of the mind in China, after which he himself became "a little child;" the new ritual which successfully invoked the Angel in 1906 was the same which the Ordo Templi Orientis had kept as a secret for unknown centuries – presumably, other occult groups here and there, like the Beast, have also discovered it independently; because of his oath as a 9th degree member of the O.T.O., the Beast could not disclose it publicly; due to his love of both poetry and cabalism, we can be sure that the code in which he hints at it – the language of bloody sacrifice – would have some innate and existential (not merely accidental) correspondence with the true secret. Finally, the ritual seems somehow connected with "love under will" and losing (the) self – its sense of separateness – in the other."

But some readers already know the secret and others have guessed . . .

XVIII — The Moon

"Let the Illusion of the world pass over thee, unheeded." –The Book of Thoth

Ezra Pound has remarked somewhere that Frazer's *Golden Bough*, all 12 fat volumes, can be condensed into a single sentence, to wit: All religions are either based on the idea that copulation is good for the crops or on the idea that copulation is bad for the crops.

In fact, one can generalize that even the highest forms of mysticism are similarly bifurcate, some going back to ideas derived from the orgy and some to ideas derived from the ritual murder.

Leo Frobenius, in a series of heavy Germanic treatises on anthropology still untranslated from the Deutsch, has demonstrated, or attempted to demonstrate, a periodic oscillation between these two systems of magick, which he calls Matriarchal and Patriarchal. Two spin-offs from the Frobenius thesis in English are Joseph Campbell's *The Masks of God* and Rattray Taylor's *Sex in History*.

The Beast himself (aided by the handy revelations of his friend Aiwass) suggests that magicko-religious history, at least in the Occident, has passed through The Age of Isis (primitive matriarchy), the Age of Osiris or the Dying God (civilized patriarchy, including Christianity) and is presently entering The Age of Horus, the Crowned and Conquering Child, in which woman will appear "no longer the mere vehicle of the male counterpart, but armored and militant."

Thus, if the orgy is the sacrament of The Age of Isis, as Frazer indicates, the dying god – or the dying population – is the sacrament of the Age of Osiris. The link between ritual sex and ritual murder is not merely historical or sequential: they are the same sacrament in two different forms.

And the latter becomes magically necessary whenever the former is no longer functionally possible whenever, that is, orgasm is no longer a true [although temporary] "death" and becomes only the "sneeze of the genitals" which all forms of psychotherapy are admittedly or overtly trying to alleviate.

If it is a truism that, on the psychological plane, repressed or unsatisfied sex seeks relief in sadism or masochism: it is likely more true on the astral or magical plane (whatever that is) that if the spiritual spasm cannot be found through love, it can be sought in violence.

And so we see that human sacrifice is the characteristic sacrament of such peoples as the Aztecs (read any history of Mexico to find out how much male chauvinism, prudery and Nixonian *macho* they wallowed in), the Holy Inquisitors of the middle ages, the Nazis, and some power elites closer to home; while matriarchal cultures such as the Danubians of pre-historic Europe, the pre-Chou folk of China, the first dwellers in the fertile crescent, etc. have left behind clear evidence of an equal and opposite ritualized eroticism, some of which has survived via the Taoists in China, The Tantrists in India, the "Old Religion" or witch cult in Europe . . .

But the Beast was not trying to reinstate the Age of Isis, like these; his magick, he tells us again and again, is preparation for the Age of Horus.

XIX — The Sun

"Make Speech and Silence, Energy and Stillness, twin forms of thy play."

– The Book of Thoth

Even outside the Manson Family, there is a lot of religious balling going on these days by people who have rediscovered part of the ritual of Isis; what the Beast was teaching was nothing as facile as this. The following words from Chapter VII, "The Formula of the Holy Grail," in *Magick* are meant with dreadful literalness:

The Cup is said to be full of the Blood of the Saints; that is, every 'saint' or magician must give the last drop of his life's blood to that cup (in) the true Bridal of the Rosy Cross . . .
It is a woman whose Cup must be filled. It is . . .
the sacrifice of the Man, who transfers life to his

descendants . . . For it is his whole life that the Magus offers to Our Lady. The Cross is both Death and Generation, and it is on the Cross that the Rose blooms . . .

The sacrifice must be a real death, a true Rosy Crucifixion, if it is to replace the more violent magic of the Osirian Age. I forbear further quotation, for the secret is concealed beneath many a veil throughout the Beast's works, but it involves at least: a mastery of *pranayama*, allowing the postponement of orgasm until the magick working is performed at length and in properly exalted enthusiasm; skill in astral voyaging, so the astral body may be busy in its own plane also; perfection in *dharana*, so that one ray of the mind remains in perfect coordination on the symbol of the Holy Guardian Angel.

What happens, then, can be considered either the true, natural oceanic orgasm which the Patriarchal Age has tended to destroy – or a new and artificial creation produced by this complicated yoga. It's the same debate we hear endlessly about acid: does it restore our "natural" form of perception, or does it "artificially" create a new form?

And, thus, we can understand Horus, the Crowned and Conquering Child, who is being created. He is "the Child" that Rose's Cairo vision invoked; the "little child" that the Beast became after his bad trip to China; "the male child of perfect innocence and high intelligence" who was sacrificed a hundred and fifty times a year after 1912; the Beast himself; and also Aiwass, the Holy Guardian Angel, both an internal aspect of Crowley's mind and a separate "Being . . . of angelic order . . . more than a man," for the question posed by the materialist ("Inside or outside? Subjective or objective?") loses meaning in that trance of Samadhi where all the opposites are transcended into a unity that is also a void.

XX – The Aeon

"Be every Act an Act of Love and Worship."

–The Book of Thoth

In an early issue of his magazine *Equinox*, the Beast wrote with uncharacteristic solemnity:

I. The world progresses by virtue of the appearance of Christs (geniuses).

II. Christs (geniuses) are men with super-consciousness of the highest order.

III. Super-consciousness of the highest order is obtainable by known methods. Therefore, by employing the quintessence of known methods we cause the world to progress.

In the first issue, in a more characteristic vein, he wrote:

We place no reliance
On Virgin or Pigeon
Our method is Science
Our aim is Religion

He did his work seriously and humorously, stubbornly and flexibly, wisely and sometimes unwisely, synthesizing – from High Magick and from Yoga, from Cabalism and the Koran, from experiments with hashish and peyote and nitrous oxide to years of study of the Tarot and comparative religion, slowly extracting "the quintessence of known methods."

After him came Wilhelm Reich, who discovered the same quintessence independently, and was also hounded, vilified and slandered. And after Reich was Timothy Leary, who finally let the djinn out of the bottle and in a decade changed the face of the world by a century's worth.

But the Beast started the Revolution, and some of us now see that it is the essential Revolution, far more important than that of economics, and that he and his good buddy Aiwass defined it better than Marx or even better than the frontal-lobe anarchists, when they (he?) wrote in *The Book of the Law*:

> Do what thou wilt shall be the whole of the Law . . .
> To worship me take wine and strange drugs whereof I
> will tell my prophet, & be drunk thereof! . . .
> There is no law beyond Do what thou wilt . . .
> It is a lie, this folly against self . . .
> I am alone: there is no God where I am . . .
> Every man and every woman is a star . . .
> The word of Sin is Restriction . . .
> Remember all ye that existence is pure joy;
> that all the sorrows are but as shadows; they pass
> and are done; but there is that which remains . . .
> Love is the law, love under will . . .

For the Age of the Child is upon us; and those who seek to preserve the Aeon of Osiris and death are themselves only dying dinosaurs.

XXI – The Universe

"And blessing and worship to the prophet of the lovely Star."

–The Book of Thoth

And yet – and yet – Manson reminds us, our brothers and sisters in the Movement remind us, sometimes our own unexpected behavior reminds us: there have been such millennial voices often in the past and they have been heralds not of a Golden Dawn but only of a false dawn.

If there is one central lesson to be learned from the Beast, it is not really *Do what thou wilt shall be the whole of the Law*, which has been around since Rabelais; not even the more profound and gnomic *Every man and every woman is a Star*; not even the formula of the Perfect Orgasm for which Norman [Mailer] has been searching so loudly and forlornly lo! these many years; it is rather his humor, his skepticism, his irony that reveled in the title of Beast and, even, at times, Ass; the rationality that warned against becoming "the prey of madness" by trusting one's visions too quickly, and the common sense which said that, even if good and evil are identical on the Absolute plane, a man operating on the relative plane simply doesn't enjoy a toothache or invent rationalizations to pick a brother's pocket; the solemn warning that the sacrament is not completed until the Magician offers "the last drop of his life's blood" to the Cup, and dies; but, above all these, the simple historical record which reveals that with all the ardor, all the dedication, all the passion he possessed, it still took eight years (including four months' madness) before he broke down the wall that separates Ego from the true Self and that Self from the Universe.

The Great Beast – Aleister Crowley
The Realist, 1971-72, serialized over four issues:
91-B, September-October 1971
91-C, November-December 1971
92-A, January-February 1972
92-B, March-April 1972

DO WHAT THOU WILT

An Introduction to Aleister Crowley
by Robert Anton Wilson

Overture:
Inspirational Thoughts
from The Great Beast Himself

All discussions upon philosophy are necessarily sterile,
since truth is beyond language . . . For the great danger
of this magical theory is that the student may mistake the
alphabet for the things which the words represent.

– Magick in Theory and Practice

A thing is not necessarily A or not-A. It may be outside
the universe of discourse in which A and not-A exist.

– Konx Om Pax

Tear down that lying spectre of the centuries: veil not
your vices in virtuous words . . .

– The Book of the Law

But had it not been for the garter, I might never have
seen the star.

– The Star and the Garter

Free therefore every function of thy Body and of every other Part of thee according to its true Will. This also is most necessary, that thou discover that true Will in every case, for thou art born into Dis-ease, where are many false and perverted Wills, monstrous growths, Parasites, Vermin are they, adherent to thee by Vice of Heredity or of Environment or of Evil Training. And of these Things, the subtlest and most Terrible, Enemies without Pity, destructive to thy Will, and a menace and Tyranny even to the Self, are the Ideals and Standards of the Slave-Gods, false Religion, false Ethics, even false Science.

– Liber Aleph: The Book of Wisdom or Folly

This is the Harmony of the Universe, that Love unites the Will to create with the understanding of that Creation.

– The Book of Thoth

Deliver us from Evil and from Good.

– The Book of Lies

Pure folly is the key to initiation.

– The Book of Thoth

There is no law beyond Do what thou wilt.

The Book of the Law

It is of the first importance that you should understand my personal position. It is not actually wrong to regard me as a teacher, but it is certainly liable to mislead; fellow-student, or, if you like, fellow-sufferer, seems a more appropriate title.

– Magick Without Tears

Being then a perfect young fool, as I am now a perfect old one . . .

– The Confessions of Aleister Crowley

Lion of Light

CROWLEY THE ENIGMA

Everybody knows that he began all his conversations with "Do what thou wilt shall be the whole of the Law". Some know that he also began his letters that way, and few have read (in William Seabrook's, *Witchcraft in the Modern World*) that he once painted that slogan, in bright red, on a mountain facing the Hudson River in New York State, where it could be seen by everybody on the ferries going upriver. (On the other side, for the edification of down-river ferries, he painted, "Every Man and Every Woman is a Star".)

"Do what thou wilt shall be the whole of the Law" is a formula to curl the brain. A slogan, a battle-cry, a prophecy, it excites some, terrorizes others, provokes all who hear it; inevitable objections leap to every lip. And the man behind the mantra, Aleister Crowley himself, is even more disturbing than the slogan itself.

We quote a few representative judgments:

> This man Crowley is one of the most sinister figures of modern times . . . a drug fiend, an author of vile books, the spreader of obscene practices . . .
>
> *—London Sunday Express*

> England's worst man . . . the so-called poet, Aleister Crowley . . . an extremely clever lunatic . . . wild, erotic and disgusting . . . the King of Depravity . . .
>
> *—John Bull, another London tabloid.*

> A man of common sense and forthright response, with a British contempt for British hypocrisy . . . tireless and fearless . . . serious and intrepid . . . sheer arrogance . . . increasingly repellent.
>
> *—The Listener, an English literary magazine, which starts out (you will note) trying to be understanding and ends up with the same fear and loathing as the tabloids.*

A little modesty is provided by a poetry-journal, *The Clarion*, reviewing some Crowley verse: "We must confess that our intelligence is not equal to the task . . ."

John Symonds' biography, *The Great Beast*, finds Crowley alternately brilliant and brutal, self-deluded and fearlessly honest, gradually staggering toward insanity under the weight of neurological experiments no man should dare perform on himself: "A second-rate poet with delusions."

Richard Cammell's biography, *Aleister Crowley*, finds the Beast to be a first-rate poet, a man of brains and courage, flawed by worship of "dark gods" who misled and destroyed him. Cammell, like Symonds, is a Christian.

P.R. Stephensen's *The Legend of Aleister Crowley*, portrays a great poet, no more eccentric than Shelley or Byron, destroyed by the hatred of prudes, bigots, and Christian fanatics. About Crowley's religion and magick, Stephensen is obdurately non-committal; one gets the impression he regards it as just as silly as the beliefs of great poets usually are, but no sillier or more dangerous than any.

Israel Regardie, in *The Eye of the Triangle*, presents Aleister Crowley as the prophet of our age: a man greater than Freud, Jung, Reich, D.H. Lawrence, or even Jesus, "a great mystic, sincere, dedicated and hardworking . . . a strong, valiant man."

"A Master of Corruption," says the Patriot, English right-wing journal of the 1930's, "a strange medley of sexualism, mysticism, indecencies and blasphemies . . . Underlying all this pseudo-mysticism are to be found subversive political activities."

Kenneth Grant, Crowley's successor as Outer Head of the magick society called Ordo Templi Orientis, speaks of the Beast's "constant experimentation with drugs . . . struggle against madness and despair, aggravated by poverty, illness, and persecution" and finds him "chaotic, awful, naked as the nameless God before whose shrine he so fervently aspired."

Louis T. Culling, Outer Head of the Great Brotherhood of God, another Crowleyite magick society, sees a different Beast and speaks of "humanness . . . depth of soul" and praises those hymns by Crowley which "choke me up and bring tears to my eyes . . . a great spiritual soul," he concludes.

The *Observer-Review* is less impressed: "A megalomaniac crank . . . not only manic and paranoid and often drugged to the eyes, but also an accomplished con-man . . .

The *New York Times* finds Crowley "a genuine eccentric," while the Atlantic Monthly pronounces him "clever, amusing and mad." The *Sunday Telegram* muses inconclusively, "One emerges . . . with a respect for his aspiration, his capacity, his hard work . . . I still don't know what to think of him."

Crowley climbed higher on Chogo Ri, in 1902, than any previous explorer. He set other mountaineering records, in his teenage years, that have not yet been matched. He did? He also worshipped the Devil in his adolescence, identified with Jesus by hanging on a cross for several hours once, and so impressed various Hindu, Buddhist, Tantric, and Sufi seers that he was admitted to instruction in certain mystic arts that have seldom been taught to Europeans. Or so he claimed.

The Beast was alternately "pompous" and "witty", a joker and a serious mystic, according to William Seabrook, who knew him well in his American years. "So clever that one finds some of it utterly unintelligible," the *Arbroath Herald* gasped in trying to review Crowley's verses to Buddha. "Demands an emphatic protest from lovers of literature and decency . . . obscene . . . revolting . . . monstrosity," said the *Cambridge Review* of the same volume.

The Atheist found something to forgive in the Beast's experimental mysticism: "Far as we are from admiring his dreamy romanticism . . . his staunch denial of the supernatural, the divine, the mystical must command our respect." But the *Prophetic Mercury*, a Theosophical journal, noted instead "the ever-present sense of God in the mind of the poet . . ." and piously prayed "that one day he may be enlightened." Crowley, according to his private diary, had achieved *dhyana*, the trance of unity sought by Asian mystics, five years before that date; and, one year before the Theosophists wished him enlightenment, had accomplished *Samadhi*, the higher trance that only the most advanced adepts experience. No wonder *Literary Guide* muttered inconclusively that his collected poems were "a masterpiece of learning and satire . . . One of the most brilliant of contemporary writers . . . true poetic feeling . . . pretty wit . . . baffles our comprehension . . . "

But these were the attempts of rational men to understand the mystic. On a lower level, there was no such earnest confusion; the tabloids, with whom we began this introductory note and with whom we shall conclude, had no such doubts:

A man of evil character.

—The Looking Glass

Three women he keeps permanently for his orgies . . . engaged in pro-German propaganda . . . stole money . . . obscene attacks on the King . . . the Black Mass . . . New sinister revelations . . . DREADFUL ORDEAL OF YOUNG WIFE . . . WORSE HORRORS STILL . . .

—Sunday Express again.

A Cannibal at large . . . The Wickedest Man in the World . . . A Human Beast . . .

—John Bull

But let us take a last look at the man behind the mystery, the offensively cheerful Aleister himself, who always said with a twinkle, "I am one hell of a holy guru."

LIFE AND EXPLORATIONS

Edward Alexander Crowley was born in Warwickshire, England, on October 12, 1875 – in compensation, he later claimed, for the tragedy which had befallen mankind on that date 383 years earlier. He was raised in the faith of his parents, a sect known as Plymouth Brethren; their theology was based on accepting every statement in the King James translation of the Hebrew scriptures as being literally true. The boy later recalled being taught further that cats have nine lives and that "ladies have no legs."

In a school, run by the Brethren, the young "Alick" quickly got into very serious trouble, on the basis of what appears to have been a deliberate slander. The charge was that he had become intoxicated on alcohol and had blasphemed against God. He was not informed of the accusation against him, but was merely told to confess his "sin" and, as inducement to elicit the confession, he was restricted to a diet of bread and water and "placed in Coventry" – that is, no human being, student or teacher, was allowed to speak to him. After approximately one year of this barbaric treatment, the boy's health collapsed and he was removed from the school at the insistence of an uncle not totally committed to the Plymouth Brethren theology.

Shortly thereafter, Alick began to drink, gamble, smoke, and generally break loose from the taboos of his background. He even managed to seduce a house-maid, on his mother's bed, Freudians will be delighted to know.

He also embarked on a campaign of re-creating his own

character through psychological brute force. He explored the neighborhoods where poor Blacks and Asians lived, seeking peril, adventure, and exotic vices. He took up the worship of Satan, and began writing erotic Swinburnian poetry. He became a mountain climber, and before he was out of adolescence had accomplished some unprecedented feats on both local English ranges and in the Alps.

At Cambridge University, 1895-8, he inherited his father's huge wealth and changed his name to Aleister Crowley. "Aleister" had an etymology suggesting loneliness and solitude, which suited his self-image – years later, his original title for the book now called *The Confessions of Aleister Crowley* was *The Spirit of Solitude*. The rhythm of "Aleister Crowley", he also felt, was one that sinks into the mind and remains, like that of "Jeremy Taylor", which he considered the most unforgettable name in English. As a poet, later to become a magician, he was particularly conscious of the invocative quality of sound.

He majored in chemistry – a characteristic decision, evidently based on a desire to acquire scientific and logical thought habits as a corrective to the romantic, poetic tendencies of his imagination. In the same vein, he took courses in logic and mathematics and acquired a "blue" (top honors) in chess. He also joined the Carlists, a conspiracy to replace Queen Victoria by a pretender named Don Carlos; on their behalf, he wrote some amusing polemic dubbing Victoria "the dumpy German hausfrau," "the Hanoverian usurper," etc. For this he was awarded a knighthood by Don Carlos and, in later years when in a mood to annoy the establishment, he asserted it occasionally by signing himself "Sir Aleister Crowley." It is under that title that he canonized himself when composing the litany of saints for his Gnostic Catholic Mass. In 1895, however, the Gnostic church was still far in the future, and he was attempting to become a devout believer in the rather medieval Celtic Catholic Church which Don Carlos intended to establish in place of the High Anglican Church after acquiring the throne. Crowley's devotion to Celtic Catholicism already contained the ambiguity to infest his later religious associations; he compromised it both by becoming a militant agnostic and by publishing (although anonymously) *White Stains*, a volume of poetry quite in the decadent-erotic mood of his earlier adolescent Satanism and in the style of Baudelaire, Swinburne, de Sade and Sacher-Masoch.

On December 31, 1896, at precisely eleven o'clock in the evening (i.e., one hour before midnight and the New Year), Aleister Crowley experienced a religious vision. This was spontaneous, unlike his later self-induced trances, and consisted chiefly of an intuitive and highly empathetic identification with the sufferings of all sentient beings. In many ways, it must have been similar to the experience stated by Gautama Buddha in his First Noble Truth: "All existence is suffering." For nearly a year, the young Crowley pushed this experience from his thoughts and remained passionately involved in his poetry, his politics, his omnivorous reading and studying, his sexual pleasures (he was now very active both heterosexually and homosexually) and his chess. Then, on December 31, 1897, again one hour before midnight, the experience of cosmic agony was repeated.

Crowley began seeking for a spiritual teacher feeling a sense not only of universal suffering, but of (as he wrote later) "vital catastrophe." On a mountain climbing expedition in the Alps, he met a man who told him of a lodge which carried on ancient magical and mystical training in the modern world. In 1898, at the age 23, Aleister Crowley gained admission to this group, the Hermetic Order of the Golden Dawn.

The Isis-Urania Temple of the order, in London,

specialized in ceremonial magic. As a scientifically-bent agnostic, Crowley had to square this with his rationality; his theory (condensed) was as follows: The rituals of magic are "physiological experiments." By doing precisely as ordered in the old grimoires, the magician induces highly unusual experiences in his own nervous system. Such neurological adventures enlarge our understanding of the mind and its relationship with the Cosmos. With this working theory and the new title, Frater Perdurabo (I Will Endure to the End), Crowley plunged enthusiastically into invocations, evocations, banishings, astral voyages, and the whole tradition of occult exercises that have come down to us from the paleolithic shamans.

A friend in the Isis-Urania Temple, Frater Ihei Aour (Let There Be Light), known as Allan Bennett, electrical engineer in the profane world, was an asthmatic who had long been in the habit of battling off his asthma attacks with a variety of drugs, including cocaine, ether, and heroin. Somehow, Frater Perdurabo and Frater Ihei Aour together conceived the idea that the "magic potion" repeatedly mentioned in legends and magical lore might be a drug still existing in the world. They dosed themselves with dozens of compounds in search of enlightenment, but, at the time, "like Huck Finn's prayer 'nuffing came of it'" as Perdurabo wrote. The idea, however, persisted and bore fruit many years later.

In 1901, Crowley was in Mexico on a mountain climbing expedition with a German rationalist and engineer named Oscar Eckenstein, who was a vocal critic of Aleister's interest in magic. One day, to Crowley's astonishment, Eckenstein demonstrated an ability to concentrate by use of yoga. The feat was impressive in itself and Eckenstein's rationalism made it more interesting. Frater Perdurabo set out to master the technique, called *dharana*.

Later the same year, Crowley, set himself to master

yoga thoroughly while in Ceylon. His teacher was again
Allan Bennett, previously of the Isis-Urania Temple of
the Golden Dawn, now a Buddhist monk under the name,
Ananda Maitreya. Starting slowly, Crowley quickly advanced
to 8 hours a day of *dharana* (concentration) and pranayama
(rhythmic breathing through alternate nostrils). After several
months, he gave up in disgust and went to the nearest town
to spend a week refreshing himself in a brothel, a notable
departure from yogic tradition. Returning to Bennett's hut,
Crowley achieved *dhyana* (the trance of bliss) within a few
days. In this state – however one explains it – the individual
mind is not separated from the universe, but is identical with
it.

Perdurabo now abandoned both magic and yoga, married
Rose Kelly (sister of the artist, Sir Gerald Kelly) and began
a two-year honeymoon which covered four continents and
was described by him later as "an uninterrupted sexual
debauch." He wrote some of his best poetry, and some of his
most brilliant essays on religion, during this period, taking
the stringently atheistic position of traditional South-Asian
(Theravada) Buddhism. There is no divinity in this
philosophy; the world is much as it appears to the scientific
materialist; but there are higher forms of consciousness
possible to humanity, if we can cure ourselves of the
false perspective caused by egotism; magic and yoga are
physiological tricks or gimmicks to stun the ego and allow
this higher consciousness to develop.

In 1904, in Cairo, Rose Crowley went into a spontaneous
trance and announced that a supernatural entity wished to
communicate with Aleister. He was intensely skeptical and
even hostile at first, but eventually cooperated, after several
days of testing the knowledge of the alleged communicating
entity, a being who gave his name as Aiwass. When it
appeared that Aiwass could read Crowley's mind while

speaking through Rose's mouth, Crowley cooperated. A message in 3 chapters, titled *The Book of the Law*, was dictated to him. It announced the end of Christian culture, the collapse of civilization, and the rise of a new world order based on worship of Horus, the Child-God. Among other pronouncements, some coded and seemingly incoherent, it proclaimed: "Do what thou wilt shall be the whole of the Law . . . Love is the law, love under will . . . thou hast no right but to do thy will . . . Every number is infinite . . . Every man and every woman is a star."

Crowley didn't like the way he had received *The Book of the Law* and found much of it repugnant. He shortly lost the manuscript and forgot the matter.

In 1905-6, during a walking tour of China with Rose, their daughter, and a few servants, Perdurabo went mad. He was in a state similar to certain forms of schizophrenia or a prolonged bad trip on LSD; it was as if he was living out David Hume's philosophy. Both the universe and his own mind became acausal, disconnected, haphazard; there was no link between impressions, no sense of cause-and-effect, no meaning or pattern. "My speculative criticism of Reason is now experienced," he managed to write one day, "I can write no more. This is sickening." He literally could not believe either that a world existed or that he existed; all the "tendencies" (as Buddhists call them) were abolished in his mind – all experience came to him raw, without Gestalts or significance. In self-defense, he began the longest and most difficult of magick rituals, the invocation of the Holy Guardian Angel from the medieval manuscript of Abraham the Jew, circa 1400. This rite requires six months' daily work in a specially prepared temple; Crowley manufactured the temple imaginatively "on an astral plane" and made it vivid by guided hallucinations while smoking opium. As he pursued the concentrated imagination each day and battled off the tendency to sink back into chaos without mind or solidity, war broke out and he found himself and his small party between several wandering bands of government troops, bandits, rebels, and fleeing fugitives. One day, while riding horseback and performing his ritual in the astral temple – under the influence of several pipes of opium – he fell over a cliff, dropped 30 feet, and arose alive. He was suddenly back in the framework where mind and matter exist, are separate, and follow causal laws.

Returning to England, Perdurabo continued the invocation of the Holy Guardian Angel, adding further rites as he went along. Toward the end of the six months' period, he had himself crucified (with ropes, not nails; but it was still painful) and hung on a cross for 8 hours vividly identifying with the Body of Christ. Having learned some Tantric yoga in India, he began arousing the kundalini (serpent-power) which lies at the bottom of the spine and produces an evolutionary change into super-humanity, if it can be induced to rise to the brain (according to Hindu theory). This rite involves prolonged masturbation while remaining in concentration upon a holy image (the Guardian Angel, in this case). Finally, the assembled battery of magic and yogic gimmicks paid off, and "the Holy Guardian Angel" appeared. The experience, Crowley found, matched exactly the state called *Samadhi*, in which the union with the universe characteristic of *dhyana* is transmuted into union with the void. Crowley tried desperately all his life to put this into words which communicate more to ordinary readers. Like other mystics, he failed in that endeavor. All he could say was the traditional formula: ordinary consciousness is dualistic, dividing experience into "me" and "the world"; *dhyana* is unified, bringing "me-world" into single awareness; *Samadhi* is void, abolishing both "me" and "world" and even "me- world." For reasons obscure, *Samadhi* isn't painful or nightmarish, like the Chinese psychoses, but is absolute joy.

In an essay written during the following months, "The Soldier and the Hunchback: ! and ?," Crowley defines his philosophy as a dialectic. The soldier is the exclamation point (!) or "Aha!"—certainty and security. The hunchback is the question mark (?) or "Hmm?"—uncertainty and doubt. The spiritual path is not as dogmatists and unawakened theologians imagine, a series of soldiers (!!!!!!!!!!!) going on forever, but rather a constant alternation of soldiers and hunchbacks (!?!?!?!?!?!?). *Samadhi*, he adds, is not the end of the path, but the beginning. The real spiritual work of humanity begins, he says, only when *Samadhi* ceases to be occasional and becomes the ordinary level of consciousness.

In 1909, Crowley rediscovered the "lost" manuscript of *The Book of the Law* and found that many previously "incoherent" verses now made sense to him – after achieving *Samadhi* consciousness. In 1912, he became an initiate of the Ordo Templi Orientis, a mystic society evidently older than the Golden Dawn – it claimed descent through the Knights Templar (a Catholic order destroyed by the Inquisition in 1307 for heresy), back to the Gnostics and Mithraists. The use of both masturbatory and heterosexual Tantric yogas by the Ordo Templi Orientis soon clarified further the mysteries of *The Book of the Law*: Crowley himself added a form of homosexual yoga to the curriculum, and began experimenting with bestiality, which had been used in magic by the Egyptians among others in the pre-Christian era. Further experiments convinced him that the results of sexual magic and sexual yoga were improved, if the participants employed such drugs as hashish, cocaine, and ether.

In 1917, Frater Perdurabo achieved a state beyond *Samadhi*, and felt he had achieved the magic rank of Magus, one who pronounces the formula of consciousness for the following 2000 years. This formula, he decided, was that given in *The Book of the Law*: "Do what thou wilt." The same year, he took a new title, *To Mega Therion*, which in Greek means either The Master Therion or The Great Beast. By Cabala, this adds up to 666, the number of the "Beast" in *St. John's Revelation*, who is supposed to arise and overthrow Christianity at the end of the Christian era.

In 1919, Crowley's asthma, which had bothered him for many years, became acute. Following Allan Bennett's experience, he began dosing himself with various remedies, having proved many times that he could use countless dangerous drugs without harm. By 1920, it was obvious to him that he had at last become hooked; he was addicted to heroin.

The years 1920-23 were the climax of the Master Therion's life. The wealth inherited from the family brewery was entirely gone and he lived in miserable poverty. Two mistresses fought with each other continually. The sensational press embarked on its most prolonged and vicious attack on him, featuring lurid charges of black magic, human sacrifice, and such crimes as jewel-theft, blackmail, pandering, etc. The heroin addiction tormented him, because it undermined his faith in his own Magical Will and ate severely into his meagre income. He somehow wrote a brilliant novel and a gigantic autobiography under these conditions; but the novel was a commercial failure and the publisher declined to issue the autobiography.

In 1923, Crowley managed to kick the heroin habit, and began slowly to pull himself together again. He had lost all his *siddhis* (magical talents), had been through paranoid and schizoid mental states in his unsuccessful attempts to kick heroin by shifting to cocaine (he always relapsed to heroin) and many times had faced the probability that he was going to die poor, addicted, and insane. In the crises that climaxed these years, he felt that Aleister Crowley had died, and the new person was a synthesis of Crowley and Aiwass, the mysterious Being who had dictated *The Book of the Law*.

By 1930, it was obvious that however much Master Therion's internal state had transcended the low point of 1920-23, his external affairs were permanently ruined. He made one last attempt to sell himself to the world – faking a suicide the day before an exhibit of his paintings opened in Berlin, then showing up alive at the art gallery – but when that failed to attract new fame and fortune, he resigned himself to poverty and obscurity.

He continued to write on yoga, magick, and various other topics, but the books were published at his own expense – at very irregular intervals, when he was a few hundred pounds above destitution. In 1939, he called a public meeting in Hyde Park, predicted the Second World War, and announced a new publication of *The Book of the Law*.

In 1940, finding no other cure for his asthmatic sufferings, Crowley resumed the heroin habit. He remained addicted, this time, until the day of his death – December 2, 1947. His last words were "I am perplexed."

The evidence shows that the Master Therion remained in a happy and tranquil state of mind throughout those last years of poverty and neglect. In *The Book of Thoth* (1944) he says, speaking of poverty in general, "Every man and every woman is a star, and every star has infinite wealth."

A FIRST EFFORT AT UNDERSTANDING

It is undeniable that Aleister Crowley was "psychotic" (by normal standards) part of the time and "neurotic" most of the time. Such an admission does not close the discussion about the value of his life's work, however, but merely opens it. Various psychologists have diagnosed most of the great artists and religious visionaries as mentally ill—Van Gogh, Beethoven, Jesus, Moses, Michelangelo, Ramakrishna, Mohammed, Shakespeare, and Ezra Pound, to name a few. Since the overwhelming majority of "mentally ill" persons do not possess the genius of these men, the fact (or label) of "mental illness" cannot be said to explain them or even to provide a plausible excuse for those who wish to ignore or evade the challenge to our understanding implicit in their works and words.

It is also a fact that many of the founders of modern psychology have been diagnosed as "mentally ill" (to a greater or lesser degree) by other psychologists. Freud, Jung, Rank, Ferenczi, Adler, Reich, and Bergler (among others) have all been diagnosed as either "neurotic" or "psychotic" by certain of their colleagues. Evidently being mentally ill is no more a handicap to the psychologist than it is to the artist or mystic.

A conventional psychological "interpretation" of Aleister Crowley would center on his relations with his parents. He claims to have hated his mother and adored his father; naturally, we must suspect such an assertion. Dr. Israel Regardie – once a student of magick with Crowley, later a Freudian analyst, now a Reichian biopsychologist – argues that as a boy, Aleister actually feared and hated his Bible-thumping father, lusted unconsciously for his mother. This is what Freudian theory would lead us to expect *a priori*. Regardie argues further that Babalon – the goddess of sexual ecstasy in Crowley's system – is the mother he yearned to possess, and that Crowley's polemics against Christianity are a symbolic form of murdering the father he hated.

Not being inclined to the reductionist fallacy – that

logic which demolishes A by proving it is "only" B in disguise – Regardie does not claim that his psychoanalytical analysis reduces Crowley's work to the mere acting-out of an unconscious conflict. To the contrary, he considers Aleister Crowley a more important thinker than Freud, Reich, or D.H. Lawrence. This is a significant claim, coming from a healer skilled in the clinical techniques of both Freudian and Reichian therapies.

If Crowley was "ill" in some sense, then so were Freud and most pioneers of modern psychology. If his methods of "curing" or at least "dealing with" his alleged "illness" were of some personal value to himself, they might be of value to others. Dr. Regardie, who is in a position to judge, regards them as of more value than anything of conventional psychology. This should give us pause when the label of "illness" is used to dismiss Crowley from serious discussion.

A behaviorist in the school of Pavlov, Skinner, and Wolpe would not care to use the terminology of "illness" at all. Such a theoretician would say that the behavior of Crowley's parents and relatives, his schoolmasters, etc. had conditioned into him certain habits of thought and feeling which made him behave and perceive as a member of the Plymouth Brethren. His later life – combining adventure (mountain-climbing, hunting, and exploration) with the disciplines of mysticism – was mostly an attempt to extinguish those Plymouth Brethren reflexes and recondition himself to a new personality. Being value-free, the behaviorist would add that we can only judge the success of this program in terms of our own *a priori* value system, and that all such judgments are relative.

The newer schools of psychology – Gestalt, humanistic, Encounter, the so-called "radical" or anti-psychology school, etc. – would pass judgment on Crowley, unlike the behaviorists, but would not be so quick as the classic Freudian schools to accept that his system was an "illness" just because it reflects a world-view differing from conventional society. Many in the tradition of Dr. R.D. Laing or Dr. Thomas Szasz might think that Crowley was less "ill" than conventional society; and Dr. Szasz, who rejects the metaphor of "illness" entirely, would decide the value of Crowley's work only on answering the question: does his system tend to make people more free or less free? "Do what thou wilt shall be the whole of the Law" evidently tends to make them more free.

It is obvious that Aleister Crowley suffered acute unhappiness in childhood – an autobiographical essay is called, bitterly, "A Boyhood in Hell." He, himself, would not reject the behaviorist analysis of magick as being (at least partly) self-conditioning; we have already quoted his definition of magick rituals as "physiological experiments." He knew that conventional child-rearing methods make people unhappy and on many occasions offered his system as a liberation from that chronic anxiety which lies below the surface of civilized life. We are unfair to him, and to ourselves, if we do not consider the possibility that he might have something of value to offer our troubled times.

But conventional ideas remain a barrier. All that invocation and astral projection, those strange "gods" in Cairo, the continuous experimentation with drugs – surely this is symptomatic of a mentality so disturbed as to qualify as insane?

Let us confront this pre-judgment directly.

Structural Differential

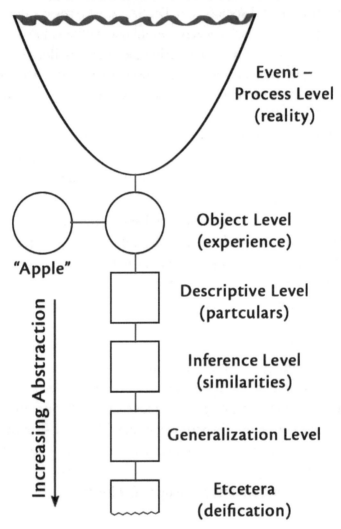

Event –
Process Level
(reality)

Object Level
(experience)

"Apple"

Descriptive Level
(partculars)

Increasing Abstraction

Inference Level
(similarities)

Generalization Level

Etcetera
(deification)

AN ANATOMY OF CONSCIOUSNESS

This diagram is adapted from the "Structural Differential" in Count Alfred Korzybski's *Science and Sanity*. It is a neuro-semantic epistemological anatomy of consciousness as understood by modern science.

The parabola on the top represents the Einstein space-time continuum, which is four-dimensional, dynamic, electronic, and forever invisible and imperceptible to human observation. On the microscopic (or, more accurately the sub-microscopic) level this is described as a "whirling chaos," "a mad dance of electrons," etc.; on the macroscopic level, it is a seamless unity evolving in space-time from an unknown beginning to an unimaginable end.

What is it? As Korzybski emphasizes, it is *not* words, so that whatever we *say* it is, it *is not*. The parabola is cut off at the top (the zig-zag line) to remind us that – whatever answer to that forever-puzzling question, "Is it infinite or finite in space?" – it is *infinite in aspects*, because change and evolution are fundamental to its operations. We can't say "all" about it because it is changing as we speak.

The circle below the parabola represents the objective or perceptual universe of a given moment – the static "photograph" our nervous system abstracts at a particular space-time focus. This is what we usually consider reality, but it is actually the creation of our own nervous system. As we go through life, we take an infinite series of such "snap-shots" and learn, through communication, about the snapshots that others have taken. Sometimes we are surprised, as when we "see" a red chair and somebody else "sees" a green chair. We resolve this conflict by calling the second party "color-blind," although abstractly he has just as much right to call us "colorblind." The color of the chair, and its "form" also, are both inside our nervous system, not outside. It is a curious fact that, even after studying neurology, optics, physics, etc. and becoming aware that all "objective perceptual" experience is *inside not outside*, we still continue to *feel that it is outside*; this point will be reemphasized later. It must also be stressed that, like the four-dimensional and dynamic external world-process, this three-dimensional and static internal "world"-picture is also *silent* – that is, non-verbal. Words can describe it, but are *not* it. A man who has the word "apple", but not the objective apple is still hungry.

The next epistemological level in this diagram, represented by the first square, consists of our subvocal "chatter" – the internal monologue first used in literature by James Joyce in his *Ulysses*, the rambling commentary offered by psychoanalytical patients free-associating on the couch, the moment-by-moment tale we tell ourselves about our experiences. This is recognized as internal (except in some forms of schizophrenia) and the "speaker" who creates it is known as "the ego" or "the self." Actually, both this higher-neurological *Voice* and the lower-neurological *Movie-Maker* who produces the stream of observations which we mistake for "external" reality are aspects of the same process – the nervous system abstracting from the environment on two levels.

The fact that we recognize the verbal level as internal-subjective and mistake the visual-tactile level for external-objective is the main cause of our frequent confusions, mistakes, bad judgments, and repeated or dogmatic "wrong ideas."

Finally, the second, lower square represents our generalized world-view or "philosophy." This second verbal level is often more grammatical and sometimes more logical than the moment-by-moment internal monologue; it is based on all our past monologues, all the monologues we have heard from our parents, teachers, playmates, books, TV, movies, and whatever else has given us communication about the internal monologues of others. When under attack, we will generally insist that this collection of declarative sentences – assertions – is "the truth," i.e. a perfect match with non-verbal reality. In our more philosophic moments (if we have such philosophic moments) we recognize that the odds are quite good that it is only partially true and probably contains much misinformation, wrong guesses, hasty generalizations, brilliant mistakes, etc. However true it may be, it is *not* reality, but merely a verbal (or mathematical, or graphical, or maybe musical) representation of reality. As Korzybski says, quoting mathematician Eric Temple Bell, "The map is not the territory." The menu is not the meal. The abstraction is not the experience.

Although this diagram is Count Korzybski's, and this way of using it is half Korzybski's and half my own simplification (or over-simplification), it represents the best-proven facts known to modern science. It illustrates the theory of perception or consciousness which scientists must assume true while working as scientists, and its implications are terrifyingly agnostic. It indicates, all too clearly, that most of our daily behavior rests on assumptions of certainty that are just not supported by neurological facts. Our religious and political behavior, in particular, if analyzed on this diagram will be shown to be, as Korzybski said, "insane or at least un-sane." We all act as if our nervous systems were delivering us the Absolute Truth, while in fact, we are receiving abstractions which may or may not be truth. The only way we can approximate to truth is by finding some method (or methods) of calibrating and testing our nervous system's reports.

Science, the synthesis of craft methods out of old medieval guilds (empiricism) and analytical thought out of the Greek philosophers (logic), is one such method: the logico-empirical method. Magick and yoga are two other methods widely believed effective throughout history and still used by millions of human beings. We must examine them fair-mindedly and with objectivity before passing such a judgment.

Aleister Crowley's life work was to create a new system of judgment – a four-part methodology which follows science in combining logic and empiricism, but transcends science by including also magick and yoga. It was his claim, and it is our claim here, that this logical-empirical-magick-yogic-method will be the normal mode of knowledge in the future.

Let us define and illustrate this four-fold vision.

FOURFOLD VISION

> Now I a fourfold vision see.
> And a fourfold vision is given to me;
> 'Tis fourfold in my supreme delight
> And threefold in soft Beulah's night
> And twofold always. May God us keep
> From Single vision & Newton's sleep!

—William Blake

Aleister Crowley approached magick from a background in organic chemistry and, like Dr. Timothy Leary more recently, he was obsessed with the molecular basis of consciousness. In the first issue of his magazine, *The Equinox*, he wrote:

> We place no reliance
> On Virgin or Pigeon;
> Our method is Science,
> Our aim is Religion.

The method of science is an unquenchable skepticism; the aim of religion is a secure faith. The two are thought to be in perpetual conflict, the Hunchback of doubt (? in Crowley's symbolism) being an uncomfortable companion for the Soldier of faith (Crowley's !). He set his goal beyond *Samadhi* in the synthesis of endless soldiers and hunchbacks (!?!?!?!?!? . . .). His fourfold method is suggested in *The Gospel According to Bernard Shaw*, which began as a critique of Shaw's socialist Jesus and turned into a book-length analysis of the origins of Christianity out of the old Greek ecstatic cults. Crowley describes the mystic or magick levels of consciousness as follows:

> The mystic attainment may be defined as Union of the Soul with God, or as the realization of itself, or – there are fifty phrases for the same experience. The same, for whether you are a Christian or a Buddhist, a Theist or (as I am myself, thank God!) an Atheist, the attainment of this one state is as open to you as is nightmare or madness or intoxication. Religious folk have buried this fact: under mountains of dogma; but the study of comparative religion has made it clear.

In terms of Korzybski's Structural Differential, Crowley is saying that the mystic experience is on the event level (the parabola), while the theories of religion (usually presented as dogmatic truth) are on the second verbal level (the bottom square). Thus, the Christian may talk of Union with God, the Hindu of Union with Vishnu, the atheistic Theravada Buddhist of Union with the True Self, the Mahayana Buddhist of Union with the Buddha-Nature, the Voodooist of possession by the goddess Erzulie, the Golden Dawn magician of obtaining the Knowledge and Conversation of the Holy Guardian Angel, etc., etc., etc., and all may be merely using differing verbal formulas for the same non-verbal experience.

As Crowley writes in *Liber O*:

In this book it is spoken of the Sephiroth, and the Paths, of Spirits and Conjurations; of Gods, Spheres, Planes, and many other things which may or may not exist.
It is immaterial whether they exist or not. By doing certain things certain results follow; students are most earnestly warned against attributing objective reality or philosophical validity to any of them.

The advantages to be gained from them are chiefly these:

(a) A widening of the horizon of the mind.

(b) An improvement of the control of the mind.

The most stringently agnostic Logical Positivism could hardly quarrel with this. After suggesting this scientific detachment, Crowley goes on to urge the student to master asana, pranayama, and dharana (yogic posture, yogic breathing, and yogic concentration) before embarking on magick experimentation. In *Liber Aleph*, however, the fourfold method emerges in full; and Crowley writes, in a whimsically archaic style:

Now, concerning the first Foundation of thy Mind I will say somewhat. Thou shalt study with Diligence in the Mathematics, because thereby shall be revealed unto thee the Laws of thine own Reason and the Limitations thereof . . .
Since Time and Space are the conditions of Mind, these two studies are fundamental.
Yet there remaineth Causality . . . This also shalt thou seek ardently . . . For our Magick is but one of the Powers that lie within us undeveloped and unanalyzed; and it is by the Method of Science that it must be made clear, and available to the Use of Man . . . Well said Frazer, the most learned Doctor of the College of the Holy Trinity in the University of Cambridge, that Science was the Name of Magick which failed not of its intended Effect.

As Mary d'Este Sturges wrote in the preface to *Book*

Four: "Frater Perdurabo (Crowley) is the most honest of all the great religious teachers. Others have said, 'Believe me!' He says, 'Don't believe me!' He does not ask for followers; he would despise and refuse them. He wants an independent and self-reliant body of students to follow out their own methods of research." Crowley restates his position in the 1908 essay, "Psychology of Hashish":

> . . . my travels in India had familiarised me with the fact that many of the lesser Yogis employed hashish (whether vainly or not we shall discuss later) to obtain *Samadhi* . . . I also had the advantage of falling across Ludlow's book, *Confessions of an American Hashish Eater*, and was struck by the circumstance that he, obviously ignorant of Vedantist and Yogic doctrines, yet approximately expressed them, although in a degraded and distorted form . . .
>
> . . . if only I could convince a few competent observers – in such a matter I distrust even myself – Science would be bound to follow and investigate . . . and . . . arm itself with a new weapon ten thousand times more potent than the balance and the microscope . . .
>
> Possibly if pharmacists were to concentrate their efforts upon producing a standard drug, upon isolating the substance responsible for (the *Samadhic* effect), and so on, we might find a reliable and harmless adjuvant to the process which I have optimistically named Scientific Illuminism . . .
>
> Even as insanities, they (mystic states) would demand the strictest investigation for the light they throw upon the working of the brain. But as it is! All the sacred literature of the world is full of them; all the art and poetry of all time is inspired by them; and, by the Lord Harry! we know nothing about them. Nothing but vague and troubled reflections the minds of the mystics themselves, untrained in accuracy of observation, bring back from the fountains of light . . .
>
> One single trained observer with five years' work, less money than would build a bakehouse, and no more help

than his dozen of volunteer students could give him, would earn himself a fame loftier than the stars, set mankind on the royal road to the solution of the One great problem. Scientific Illuminism would have deserved its name, or mysticism would have received a blow which would save another young fool like myself from wasting his whole life on so senseless a study . . .

Elsewhere Crowley defines his method of logic-empiricism-yoga-magick in terms of the traditional Rosicrucian formula, "To know, to dare, to will, to keep silence." In other places this in turn is related to the four emblematic beasts of magick—lion, eagle, bull, man. In the psychology of Jung, these beasts are defined as emblems of the four faculties of the mind: intuition, reason, sensation, feeling. In *The Book of Thoth*, Crowley offers a set of correlations for bringing the whole mind into harmony, as expressed by the four suits of the tarot deck. Summarizing all this we can define his fourfold vision as combining

To Know	To Will	To Dare	To Keep Silence
Logic	Empiricism	Magick	Yoga
Reason	Sensation	Intuition	Feeling
Eagle	Bull	Lion	Man
Swords	Pentacles	Wands	Cups
Air	Earth	Fire	Water

This is a peculiarly modern formulation of the Great Work as defined by the alchemists.

Looking through history, we can readily see that no culture to date has followed this carefully balanced formula. Tribal societies may have pushed magick experience to astonishingly high levels – in many cases, higher than any civilized society – but they are usually somewhat defective in logic and science. Chinese civilization at its greatest combined high science (higher than that of the Western world until around 1700 A.D., according to chemist Joseph Needham's *Science and Civilization in China, Volume II*) with Taoist magick and Buddhist yoga, but never devised a system of logic. Hindu civilization combined yoga, dialectical logic of great subtlety and Tantric magick, but never developed a tradition of empirical science. Our own culture in recent centuries pushed the logico-empirical method to unprecedented heights, but ignored the yogic and magick disciplines. (The consequences are all around us in a technology without wisdom or heart that seems likely to kill us, and all around the world, if we do not learn to balance it with "spiritual" forces.)

A CROWLEYAN CURRICULUM

We know that Aleister Crowley obtained admission to the Hermetic Order of the Golden Dawn in 1898 at the age of 23 and that he was invited to accept the VII degree of the Ordo Templi Orientis in 1910 at the age of 35. The third of the magical societies connected with his name, the A.A., is more mysterious. We do not even know what the initials stand for – some say Atlantean Adepts, but others claim Argentum Astrum (Silver Star). We don't know when he joined it or if he joined it, for some authorities believe it never existed save as one of the notorious Crowley hoaxes.

Nevertheless, people are findable who were initiated into the A.A. by Crowley, and the curriculum of the A.A., has been published as an appendix to Crowley's, *Magick in Theory and Practice*. This gives us a handy guide to the kind of education Crowley thought appropriate for the Scientific Illuminist. It consists of thirteen steps.

1) The *Student* must read a fairly lengthy corpus of

literature, consisting of (a) various classics of mysticism and magick – the Tao Te Ching of Lao-Tse, the Bhagavad Gita, the Upanishads, works of Blavatsky, Molinos, Pythagoras, etc. (b) general philosophy – Hume, Berkeley, Erdman's *History of Philosophy*, etc. (c) rationalist and anti-religious classics – Tom Paine, Huxley, etc. (d) studies in comparative religion – Frazer's *Golden Bough*, Wright's *Worship of Priapus*, etc. (e) fantasy and science-fiction to stretch the mind – Hinton's *Flatland*, Carroll's *Alice* books, *Dracula*, etc. (f) all of Crowley's own writings.

2) The *Probationer*, after being tested in knowledge of the above classics, is allowed to practice any form of magick or yoga he likes, for one year, and must keep a careful record of "each experiment" and its results.

3) The *Neophyte* is then assigned to attain mastery of astral projection and is not promoted again until this is accomplished.

4) The *Zelator* must achieve complete technical proficiency in yogic postures (asanas) and yogic breath-control (pranayama).

5) The *Practicus* must study the Cabala and learn to classify magical and mystical states on the diagram known as the Cabalistic Tree of Life.

6) The *Philosophus* is put through certain moral tests which have never been published and are possibly not even known as tests when the subject is plunged into them.

7) The *Dominus Liminis* is trained in yogic concentration and control over the mind.

8) The *Adeptus Minor* is trained in sexual yoga.

9) The *Adeptus Major* is taught all the secrets of practical magick.

10) The *Adeptus Exemptus* confronts a further test which determines future advancement.

11) The *Magister Templi* becomes a teacher of the lower grades.

12) The *Magus* is able to teach a new level of consciousness to mankind; the magi of the past were Lao-Tse, Buddha, Krishna, Thoth, Moses, Mohammed, and Adam Weishaupt, Grandmaster of the masonic Order of the Illuminati (1776).

13) The *Ipsissimus* cannot be defined. He is 'beyond all comprehension of those of lower degree.'

It appears that Crowley did not follow this system rigidly in all cases. According to John Symonds', *The Great Beast*, when a certain Hollywood actress arrived at Crowley's Abbey of Thelema in Sicily in 1920, she was first induced to smoke opium for a day and a night, then taken to an isolated hut and ordered to master the techniques of asana and pranayama before returning to mingle with the other students or consult the master again. Israel Regardie, in *Roll Away the Stone*, describes the kind of training Crowley used with his Paris students in the later 1920s; it is closer to the above curriculum:

> The first responsibility set for the beginner was to do some reading from a preliminary list . . . when he had completed this mass of reading in some three months, he could apply for a written examination of the study material. The prime intention here was to ensure that he had, at the very least, acquired an intellectual familiarity with basic classical material . . .
> Before him lay a year's arduous work on a practical experimental level. He had personally to select from the assorted materials he had read a particular practice or several practices – meditation or magical or devotional. It was up to his own discretion and ingenuity . . . Nobody

could tell him what to select or what to do . . .
Mandatory, however, was keeping of a magical record,
a diary. Whatever else he might be slipshod in, the diary
had to be entered regularly and soberly and in detail. To
fail in this was inexcusable. At the end of a whole year's
work, the record was to be submitted to Crowley for
examination . . . And since Crowley, borrowing from the
Hermetic Order of the Golden Dawn, had written that
'equilibrium is the basis of the work,' he then prescribed
specific exercizes and practices that would tend to
equilibrate the student's psychological structure.
Had the student chosen to work with Yoga alone . . .
Crowley might recommend some diametrically opposed
practices – such as devotional exercizes, ceremonial
magic, or whatnot. The effect of this was to prevent the
student developing one-sided traits of character . . .
In the event that the student showed promise, and was
theoretically familiar with, say, William James' *Varieties
of Religious Experience*, Crowley might recommend the
use of hashish . . .
I want to emphasize unequivocally that Crowley has
asserted not once but a thousand times that the discipline
itself was far more important than any one particular result
or attainment."

In *Magick Without Tears*, letters written to a pupil
who could not meet with him regularly (during the war
years, 1943-45, and Crowley then being in his late 60s),
we find another variation on the curriculum. The student
is first assigned six months' study in Cabalism; while this
progresses, Crowley writes to her weekly, encouraging
skepticism and critical analysis of all she reads. Later, she is
taught astral projection, the elements of magical invocation,
and finally the six techniques of yoga – asana, pranayama,
dharana, pratyahara, yama, and niyama. He insists again
and again on scientific accuracy in the records kept and is
merciless in criticizing the usual language of mysticism:

. . . whatever you mean by 'God' conveys no idea to me:

I can only guess by the light of my exceedingly small knowledge of you and your general habits of thought and action. Then what sense was there in chucking it at my head? Half a brick would have served you better . . .

I know I'm a disheartening kind of bloke . . . and surely what was said was perfectly harmless, and . . .

No, N. O., no: not harmless at all. My whole object is to train you to silence every kind of hypothetical speculation and formulae both resonant and satisfying. I want you to abhor them, abominate them, despise them, detest them, eschew them, hate them, loathe them, and *da capo* and to get on with your *practice*.

In *De Arte Magica*, an instruction manual in sexual yoga for the Ordo Templi Orientis, Crowley writes that the "knight-monk" of the order should remember among "treasures to be preserved" the history of the Order (including its persecution by the Catholic Church) and "our war on those never wholly subdued foes of humanity, tyranny, and superstition."

It may be said that Aleister Crowley's goal in life was to deliver the arts of mysticism from dogmatists, fanatics, theologians, and fools, making them available to persons of logical and scientific mind.

HUMOR AND TRUTH

. . . my "conversion" to my own "religion" may yet take place.

– Crowley, *Equinox of the Gods* (1936)

In Crowley's delightful short story, *Thien Tao*, a Chinese Taoist magician lands on the shore of Japan during a period of chaos and decay, greeting the inhabitants with the following cheerful song:

Blow the tom-tom, bang the flute!
Let us all be merry!
I'm a party with acute
Chronic beri-beri.
Monday I'm a skinny critter
Quite Felician-Ropsy.
Blow the cymbal, bang the zither!
Tuesday I have dropsy.
Wednesday cardiac symptoms come
Thursday diabetic.
Blow the fiddle, strum the drum!
Friday I'm paretic.
If on Saturday my foes
Join in legions serried,
Then on Sunday, I suppose,
I'll be beri-beried!

A correspondence between this remarkable fellow and
the mikado soon ensues, by telegraph. Highlights are – from
the mikado – "Who is your honorable self, and why has
your excellency paid us cattle the distinguished compliment
of a visit?" Answer: "This disgusting worm is Great Tao. I
humbly beg your sublime radiance to trample his slave." The
Mikado – "Regret great toe unintelligible." Answer – "Great
Tao – T.A.O. – Tao." Mikado – "What is great Tao?" Answer
– "The result of subtracting the universe from itself." Etc.

Eventually it is arranged for Great Tao to visit the
Imperial Palace, and, after a great deal of politeness and
decorum, serious conversation begins. Great Tao finally
delivers his cure for all social problems, in the following
terms – charmingly echoing Lao-Tse in places and in others
following the Golden Dawn principles of equilibrium but
withal characteristically Crowleyite emphasis and tone:

To the prostitute I prescribe a course of training by which
she shall comprehend the holiness of sex. Chastity forms
part of that training . . . To the prude equally I prescribe
a course of training by which she shall comprehend the

Lion of Light

holiness of sex. Unchastity forms part of that training . . .
To the bigot I commend a course of Thomas Henry
Huxley; to the Infidel a practical study of ceremonial
magic. Thus, when the bigot has knowledge and the
infidel faith, each may follow without prejudice his natural
inclination; for he will no longer plunge into his former
excesses . . .
I have been taxed with assaulting what is commonly
known as virtue. True; I hate it, but only in the same
degree as I hate what is commonly known as vice . . .
There are men who make a fetish of cleanliness; they shall
work in a fitter's shop, and learn that dirt is the mark of
honorable toil. There are those whose lives are rendered
wretched by the fear of infection . . . such would I send to
live in the bazaar at Delhi . . .
There are slow men who need a few months' experience
of the hustle of the stockyards; there are businessmen in a
hurry, and they shall travel in Central Asia to acquire the
art of repose . . .
By solitude and fasting for the social and luxurious, by
drunkenness and debauch for the austere, by scourging for
those afraid of physical pain, by repose for the restless,
and toil for the idle, by bullfights for the humanitarian,
and the care of little children for the callous, by rituals for
the rational, and by philosophy for the credulous, shall . . .
men . . . seek to attain to unity with the great Tao.

Those who have, by these methods, attained to relative
equilibrium shall be admitted to a special training body for
further advancement in wisdom. This body shall be called
Synagogue of Satan to avoid attracting "the fools who
mistake names for things." By intellectual and spiritual
influence this group shall be "master of all", but it shall
"never seek to dominate." The Mikado is so delighted by this
program that it is instituted at once, with such happy results
that thereafter "no less than three hundred and sixty-five days
in every year and one extra day every fourth year" are set
aside for special rejoicing.

We find no problem here. Crowley is obviously saying what many mystics have said before him, and his lightly humorous touch is hardly without precedent – recall the absurdities of Chuang-Chou, the riddles of the Zen masters, the jokes of the Sufi saint, Mullah Nasrudin. Our perplexity arises when we find that in a work as mystical and pious as his *Ambrosii Magi Hortus Rosarium* the marginal notes are not quite as classical as they seem: "Pater Iubet Scientum Scribe," for instance, is a notarikon and yields a startling comment when one scans the first letter of each word in turn. The same is true of "Culpa Urbium Nota Terrae" and many other marginalia in this book, and in other of his Holy Works. This has left some readers mildly aghast.

Then there is *The Book of Lies*, which has baffled more readers than any mystical text since the *Tao Te Ching*. Things are not helped by the subtitle: *Which Is Also Falsely Called BREAKS: the Wanderings or Falsifications of the One Thought of Frater Perdurabo (Which Thought Is Itself Untrue)*. Trying to reason one's way around in this formula is two degrees more oxymoronic than Empedocles' paradox of the liar who asserts that he lies or Bertrand Russell's problem of the barber who shaves all the men who do not shave themselves. (Does he shave himself?) Chapter 69 of this remarkable work, "How to Succeed – and How to Suck Eggs," appears to be about the Miracle of Pentecost (called "the Gift of Tongues" by Catholics). It is actually about oragenitalism; and both the title and the chapter number are bawdy puns.

There is a curious note on the title page of this volume, incidentally, informing us helpfully that "There is no joke or subtle meaning in the publisher's imprint." This seems only a veiled warning about the rest of the text; but Francis King has recently discovered that the imprint is actually misdated one year, making the warning the only real lie in *The Book of*

Lies. Could there possibly be any point in such relentlessly intricate pranks on the reader?

There is also the puzzling matter of the *Bagh-i-Muattar* ("The Scented Garden") which was published as a newly-discovered Persian manuscript of the Middle Ages.

It now appears that the original never existed, the translator (a British Major, who died gallantly in the Boer War; he never seems aware of the homosexual meaning of many verses he renders) also never existed, and the Bishop who wrote the introduction was imaginary: Aleister Crowley concocted the whole waffle. But not out of whole cloth; many similar texts, using homosexual love as synecdoche of the Divine Rapture, *were* composed by Sufi poets of the Persian middle ages. Did Crowley devise this prank as subliminal propaganda for Gay Liberation, as a nuisance to contemporary English Sufis (who prefer to ignore that part of their tradition) or just because he felt like writing some poetry in the Persian manner? Or was there more? It has been calculated that the Cabalistic value of the letters in *Bagh-i-Muattar* add up to 1906 – the year Crowley achieved *Samadhi*.

(His codes are endless, as are his numerology games. *The Confessions* has 96 chapters, three in the third person, evidently representing the 3 non-ego states on the Cabalistic Tree of Life. The rest of the book, then, is 93 chapters – and 93 is the basic magick number in his whole system. Similarly, "Laylah," heroine of *The Book of Lies* is homonymic of Leila Waddell, his mistress at that time, but is also Arabic for "night" and Nuit, his goddess, means "night" in French. The gruesome chapter in *Magick in Theory and Practice* called "Of the Bloody Sacrifice: and Matters Cognate" is not about killing animals, as it appears to be, but about sexual intercourse during women's menstrual period, which Crowley, like the alchemists, considered energetically beneficial to magick workings; elsewhere he describes it under the traditional alchemical code, "making red into gold." That this is chapter 13 is no accident, evidently; c.f. the moon-menstrual cycle. It is also no accident that the chapter in *Confessions* where he hints at the letters of the Masonic Word happens to be chapter 72. See the back of your dollar bill.)

Eight Lectures on Yoga was originally published as by Mahatma Guru Sri Paramahansa Shivaji, a name roughly equivalent to Lord Master Great God Little Devil. Guess the real author. (Hint: his initials were A.C.) *Hail Mary* was published anonymously and widely praised in Roman Catholic publications before Crowley revealed he was its author and that some of the verses were originally dedicated to Isis. *White Stains* his most decadent volume (the very title a handful of guck in the face of Victorian prudery) was signed George Archibald Bishop. This appears to be the name of a pious uncle our anti-hero particularly detested.

But at this point we might consider his warning in *Liber Aleph* ("The Book of Wisdom and Folly"):

> Yea, I, thy Father, work for thee solicitously, and also I laugh at thy Perplexities; for so it was foreordained that I should do so . . . Also it is thy Nature as it is mine 0 my son, to will that all men share our Mirth and Jollity; wherefore have I proclaimed my Law to Man, and thou continuest in that Work of Joyaunce.

In fact, it is no accident that magicians and witches are usually portrayed in popular art as laughing wildly and a bit crazily; from the perspective of the higher consciousness-states the world is not a problem to be solved, but a joke to be enjoyed and even enriched. The fact that Crowley's humor has often been used as evidence against him – to "prove" that he was a Black Magician, a blasphemer, or a Satanist – merely shows that those making such accusations have never achieved an expanded awakening themselves. Such folk should remember that Scotus Erigena listed "hilaritas" as a symptom of the spiritual consciousness, as did that model of Roman Catholic sobriety, Saint Thomas Aquinas. Indeed, after his Awakening (which occurred in the last week of his life), Thomas said that his sober and earnest theological writings seemed to him "weeds." Perhaps if he had lived longer, and written from the post-Awakened state, the Bulldog of Aquin might have left us a final testament as absurd, as paradoxical and even as obscene ("the Tao is in dung") as Lao-Tse's *Tao Te Ching,* or even one as mind-bending as *The Book of Lies*.

PROJECTIONS: ASTRAL AND HALF-ASTRAL

If the dogmatic old-fashioned Christian is somewhat unconvinced by the above Apologie for Absurditie, the dogmatic old-fashioned materialist is still more dubious about the "need" to balance logico-empiricism with yogic and magick disciplines. For instance, what the deuce was Aleister Crowley doing when he "projected" his "astral body" outside his "physical body" and taught his pupils to do the same? Aren't such practices "delusory and possibly dangerous"? Well, in fact, the description of astral projection as "delusory and dangerous" does not come from any scientific criticism of magick, but from Aleister Crowley himself, in his essay *The Psychology of Hashish* (where he quickly adds that, although this is true of astral projection, it is not true of the higher mystic trances of *dhyana* and *samadhi*). This should not bother the prospective magician in the slightest; his desire is to collect data and our subjective experiences are all data, however we interpret them after the event.

The practice itself is simple and most entertaining. The

apprentice merely sits in a comfortable position (or in a yogic position, if he knows that he can hold that comfortably), with spine erect, in an empty room where he is not likely to be disturbed. With eyes closed, he visualizes his "astral" body sitting in an "astral" chair facing him. When this is visualized with perfect clarity and distinctness, consciousness is moved out of the physical body into the astral body. (Some people find this step difficult. The drugs used by Crowley and other magicians – hashish and ether, particularly – make it much easier.) When awareness is centered in the astral body, one opens the astral eyes and enjoys the sensation of looking at one's own physical body from outside. This is always an emotional experience to the beginner. After one has enjoyed and analyzed this unique experience, one begins "rising on the planes" – ascending the 32 levels of the astral world and exploring them. They are quite a bit livelier and more colorful than the dense material world of ordinary consciousness.

The Master Therion has been at some pains to write a tightly compressed little book, *Liber 777*, which is an anatomy, in convenient table form of all 32 astral planes, their scenery, their typical denizens, their associated perfumes, astrological signs, alchemical equivalents, etc. Guided by this book – and such studies in comparative religions as Frazer's *Golden Bough* or Joseph Campbell's *The Masks of God* – the astral voyager can easily determine where he has been, who has been there before him, and what major religions (or philosophies, or even scientific models) have been formed by other voyagers' remembered visions of these arcane places.

There is no absolute need to posit any "supernatural" theories at all about these investigations. One can say that one has been exploring around Carl Jung's "collective unconscious," which is quite respectably scientific, or one can assume that the whole adventure is an entry into "molecular consciousness," the visual aspect of the DNA memory of the species – which is Dr. Timothy Leary's theory about LSD voyages and might equally well describe these astral trips. Or one can, if so inclined, take the opposite tack and dare to believe that one has been deciphering the "Akashic records" of the Theosophical hypothesis, or tuning into that "astral switchboard" suggested by the young American magician, P.E.I. Bonewits, which sounds both traditionally mystical and quite electronically modern. The real interest lies not in such interpretations, but in the actual visions themselves, especially as one acquires greater experience and more control.

The most intriguing experiences, to those of scientific training and skeptical intellect, occur not on the "astral" plane, but between there and here. These are not normally visible to the eyes of the physical body; here it seems, indeed, that one has veritably projected an "astral consciousness" across real physical space. These are by no means rare experiences; there is much reason to think that we hear so little of them, because people keep silent about them thinking they might be diagnosed as crazy. Nevertheless, they occur to many people who are not even attempting to perform "astral projection", and the English psychologist, Celia Green, has written a whole book painstakingly analyzing such cases (*Out-of-the-Body Experiences*, Celia Green, Ballantine, New York, 1968.) It is by no means easy to explain *all* these accounts as autosuggestion or hallucination. Similarly, the very astute Dr. John Lilly, in his *The Center of the Cyclone*, describes two incidents in which he seemingly "projected" himself from a laboratory in Kansas City, where he was engaged in hypnosis research, to a friend's home in California. Subsequent checking revealed that the events he "saw" were actually occurring there at the time of his "visit."

All such events can be analyzed, by Occam's Razor, into real telepathy (ESP) combined with the hallucination of astral travel. This is a more "economical" explanation than that of astral projection itself; whether it can be maintained as research proceeds is something that remains to be seen, Crowley himself often projected successfully to the home of a friend in Hong Kong, but although they agreed on what transpired while his astral body was there, he utterly failed in producing concrete physical phenomena; for instance, his attempts to knock a vase off a mantelpiece were frustrated: his astral hand always passed through the vase without moving it an inch.

The English magician, David Conway, reminds us in his *Magic: An Occult Primer*:

> The mechanics of this (astral) awareness are best explained if we think of the mind as a mirror in which images are reflected. Most of these images are due to the reaction of one or more of our sense organs, but it is still the mind that does most of the work. This is what Aristotle meant when he declared that the words "I see" really mean "I have seen," for the mind has in this case intervened to sort out whatever impressions were made on the optic nerve. Because of this, the mind can be described as the surface on which is reflected the reality known to us by experience. Like the celebrated Lady of Shalott we behold the outside world in a looking-glass and like Tennyson's heroine we need only to change the angle of the glass for it to reflect new and hitherto unsuspected things . . . [Thus] no one is naive enough nowadays to believe that lions, snakes, and knights in armor populate the astral planes. We see such things because our subconscious has translated the non-pictorial impressions it has received directly into objective forms recognizable by the mind.

Reference back to the Structural Differential should make this point more clear to any who find it obscure. It applies, we must remember, both to "astral" perception and to the normal perception we take so much for granted. As Crowley remarks in *Magick in Theory and Practice*:

> In the Astral Light we are bound by what is, superficially, an entirely different series of laws . . . Our operations in that Light are really the adventures of our own personified thoughts. The universe is a projection of ourselves; an image as unreal as that of our faces in a mirror, yet, like that face, the necessary form of expression, thereof, not to be altered save as we alter ourselves. This passage must not be understood as asserting that the Universe is purely subjective. On the contrary, the Magical Theory accepts the absolute reality of all things in the most objective sense. But all perceptions are neither the observer nor the observed; they are representations of the relation between them.

We have known since Newton that was true of optics; Albert Einstein proved it was true of all dynamic physical systems; the theory of magic merely generalizes it to all systems, dynamic or static, physical or otherwise. In this philosophic position it is no more "subjective" than the transactional psychology of Alfred Ames, the gestalt neuropsychology of Kohler, the general semantics of Korzybski, the mathematical biology of Rashevsky and Rapoport, or the synergetic cosmology of R. Buckminster Fuller.

MASKS OF GOD

Another method of Crowleyan magick seems less *impossible* to the rationalist than astral projection, but appears *absurd* to all philosophies, until they have given it a suitable trial. This is the "assumption of god-forms." Like astral projection, this exercise also begins as an act of imagination, but there is no reason at all to think it ever becomes anything else. Its value lies in forcing our awareness to the discovery that those things which appear most "real" to us are also acts of imagination.

This is the experimental procedure: the student, or dupe, merely sits with spine erect in any posture that is comfortable to him (or her). It is necessary to have a room where one will not be interrupted. While sitting in this erect, alert posture, one begins by closing the eyes and carefully envisioning one's body changing until it has become some deity. (Thoth of the ibis-head, patron of magick, is a good god to use here, since his physical form is especially easy to memorize and visualize.) One holds onto this visualization for quite a long time, until it is fully three-dimensional, clear in all details, crisp as a Renaissance portrait. Then one begins to expand the image; one is not merely a god-form, but gradually a god-size.

Bigger than one's house, bigger than the city, bigger than the planet Earth, bigger than the solar system . . . One can continue outward to galactic dimensions, actually, or even beyond. One holds this cosmic view as long as possible and then returns to normal consciousness, back in the room and the skin one left so dramatically a while ago.

ESP, "race memory," a kind of ecological or planetary consciousness, and even solar or stellar consciousness are sometimes keyed off by this exercise, when it is performed often and with vivid imagination. What *are* these alternative levels of consciousness? This is a question we do not need to ask at this point; presumably, each experimenter will invent his or her own theory, in line with whatever kind of experience is gained in this visualization and trance.

Here we have, of course, a rather dramatic alternative to the well-known yogic exercise of visualizing a geometrical form – say, a triangle – until one has successfully vanquished all other internal processes, verbal and visual. When successful, this triggers off *dhyana*, the state Crowley achieved in 1902, in which the "observer" and the "observed" are one.

Both of these exercises are made easier by the preliminary ingestion of small amounts of hashish and marijuana.

It is well-recognized by psychiatrists and psychologists of all schools that one of the primary problems of civilized humanity is negative self-image. This is enforced on all members of the servile classes, and lower members of the ruling class, in all authoritarian cultures, in order to ensure that they will obey the tribal rules and take orders from above. Dr. Albert Ellis, that master of forthright vernacular, calls it the sense of "poor itty-bitty-shitty me." It emphatically includes, in almost all cases, negative body-image; psychologists are continually amazed at how many handsome and attractive men and women believe firmly that there is something unspeakably ugly about their nude bodies.

The reader had better look back at the Structural Differential one more time; otherwise he is in danger of "understanding" without really knowing what is said. The negative self-image, including the negative body-image, are on the verbal levels and only partially on the objective (visual) level. Metaphorically, they are sound-tracks and movie films projected inside our minds. (Dr. Eric Berne includes them in what he calls our life-scripts.) They are absolutely subjective. Our partial and very limited awareness that the sound-track (internal monologue) is subjective, and our total unawareness that the movie film (visual field) is subjective, are two major hallucinations causing the "normal insanity" of everyday human society. This is what Gurdjieff and Buddha meant in saying we are all "sleepwalkers;" this is what mystical "Awakening" is awakening from. Recognition that "all this is Me!" is the *dhyana* state sought by yoga and high magick.

Now, it is easy to "see" this on the Structural Differential. Any study of optics or neurology brings it home to the understanding. Reading of the Upanishads, or Heraclitus, or Bohme, or the scientific and witty modern mystic, Alan Watts, easily makes it clear to the unprejudiced mind. Such intellectual understanding is not enough to liberate anybody; what is needed is neurological understanding, by the organism-as-a-whole, and that is what the strange techniques of yoga and magick are largely for. We do not need new understanding, but new imprinting.

He who can change easily from the Thoth self-image to the normal "little suffering me" self-image, and back again, rapidly and repeatedly, is beginning to awaken. He will have a dawning sense of what the Zen Buddhists mean in saying mind is "no-form," what the medieval Platonist, Gemistos Plethon, meant in saying mind is "omni-form," and how they both agree.

AUTHORITY AND SUBMISSION

Saint Aleister himself offers the following "explanation" of the time he became Count Vladimir Svareff:

I wanted to increase my knowledge of mankind. I knew how people treated a young man from Cambridge. I had thoroughly appreciated the servility of tradesmen, although I was too generous and ignorant to realize the extent of their dishonesty and rapacity. Now I wanted to see how people would behave to a Russian nobleman. I must say that I have repeatedly used this method of disguise – it has been amazingly useful in multiplying my points of view about humanity. Even the most broadminded people are necessarily narrow in this one respect. They may know how all sorts of people treat them, but they cannot know, except at second hand, how those same people treat others.

Lack of this knowledge, of course, allows the ruling class in all authoritarian societies to go on believing that the servile class are quite happy and content in their lot. Crowley adds a more provocative thought, in a later passage also from the *Confessions*, dealing with this in his production of a whole book, *Hail Mary*, which seemed to be the poetic rhapsodies of a very devout Roman Catholic:

I must not be thought exactly insincere, though I had certainly no shadow of belief in any of the Christian dogmas . . . I simply wanted to see the world through the eyes of a devout Catholic, very much as I had done with the decadent poet of *White Stains*, the Persian mystic of the *Bagh-i-Muattar*, and so on . . . I did not see why I should be confined to one life. How can one hope to understand the world if one persists in regarding it from the conning tower of one's own personality?

The same thought is taught differently by the 20th Century's second internationally-famous magus, Don Juan Matus, teacher of magick to anthropologist, Carlos Castaneda. Says Don Juan in *Journey to Ixtlan*:

That is a little secret I am going to give you today . . . Nobody knows my personal history. Nobody knows who I am or what I do. Not even I . . . How can I know who I am, when I am all of this? . . . Little by little you must create a fog around you until nothing can be taken for granted, until nothing is any longer for sure, or real . . .

According to esoteric tradition, this is the inner meaning of the famous Sufi parable about the five blind men and the elephant. Each of us, like one of the blind men in the fable, sees only in part, through the lens of one narrow and seemingly rigid ego. When the ego expands to infinity, when the mind is both no-form and all-forms, when there is no longer a "real" or "for sure" ego at the center of perception, the ears and tail and side and legs of the elephant all fall into relationship, and one finally "sees the elephant." In another sense, one "is the elephant."

When returned to normal (statistically normal) consciousness, one may then be much inclined to babble of "Union with God," "discovery of the true Self," "the Buddha-mind of Bliss at the center of everything," "the Knowledge and Conversation of the Holy Guardian Angel," etc.; but if one retains enough perspective to recognize that both this glowing vision and normal consciousness are dramas staged by the same faculty of imaginative identification, one will gradually cease to babble at all.

But this, of course, is precisely what the authoritarian society does not want and cannot tolerate. Every caste-or-class system demands that each person identify totally and only with the one "role" assigned to them in the tribal game. To "know who you are," "to know your place", "to take the game seriously," to worry genuinely about one's movements on the checkerboard, to have the proper emotional-glandular responses to each game-victory or game-defeat: these are everywhere, virtues beyond virtue itself. They are the definition of "sanity." The mystic who stands aside laughing is a threat to the whole hallucination.

How many times have I been asked if this war can be stopped," Gurdjieff mused aloud in 1917. "Of course, it can be stopped. All that is necessary is for the sleeping men to wake up; then they will stop shooting at each other and come home." In the same way Carlyle wrote:

> The widow is gathering nettles for her children. Far off a perfumed signeur lounges in a salon; and he hath an alchemy by which he takes every tenth nettle from her. He calls it *rent*.

It is easy enough for the widows and orphans to keep
that "unearned increment" of rent stolen by the seigneur;
all they have to do is wake up and stop paying. They do not
even need Henry George (who coined the term "unearned
increment") to nationalize the land for them; they merely
need to wake up.

Meditation on such simple facts as these explains why
Lao-Tse wrote ironically, "Those who speak, do not know;
those who know, do not speak." This silence has, indeed,
been the traditional policy of the mystic and magus, and it
mostly still is. Bhagavan Sri Rajneesh, for instance, a leader
of the much-maligned and rather Tantric wing of Hindu
theology, is still conservative enough to warn his followers as
late as August 1973:

> And once you know this (Awakening) you can go on
> behaving in your society as it requires . . . But you are not
> in it; you are just acting. You will have to use unreal faces
> because you live in an unreal world. Otherwise, the world
> will crush you and kill you.
> We have killed many real faces. We crucified Jesus
> because he started behaving like a real man.
> The unreal society will not tolerate it. We poisoned
> Socrates because he started behaving like a real man.
> Behave as society requires; do not create unnecessary
> troubles for yourself and others . . .

Shri Rajneesh is one of the boldest men in India;
orthodox fanatics have often enough rioted and staged
demonstrations to prevent him from speaking, because of his
use of Tantric sex-rituals (very similar to Crowley's!). And
yet in this passage, he takes the same tone of pessimism,
conformity, "don't spook the herd," and tacit elitism that
mystics have espoused throughout history. Those who are
awake, according to this viewpoint, should carefully pretend
to be still asleep, so as not to disturb the others and lead to a
general panic.

A few mystics down the ages (Jesus for one, several early Sufis, the divine Adam Weishaupt, and some others) have rejected this passive posture. None ever rejected it more thoroughly or vehemently than Aleister Crowley.

To understand this aspect of Crowley's life and work, the Law of Thelema given to him by his "Holy Guardian Angel," Aiwass, in *The Book of the Law*, we must take a closer look at the neuro-psychology of authority and of liberation.

POTENCY AND IMPOTENCE

"The word of the law is THELEMA," said Aiwass in *The Book of the Law*. Crowley, of course, recognized at once the echo of Rabelais' Abbey of Thelema in *Gargantua and Pantagruel*: a gentle anarchist commune in which class and caste did not exist, each man and woman was an individual sovereign and the only law, inscribed over the gate, was "Do what thou wilt." *The Book of the Law* immediately goes on:

> Who calls us Thelemites will do no wrong, if he look but close into the word. For there are therein Three Grades, the Hermit, and the Lover, and the man of Earth. Do what thou wilt shall be the whole of the Law.

Elsewhere the "Angel" dictating this book offers further glosses on the pivotal message:

> thou hast no right but to do thy will. Do that and no other shall say nay. For pure will, unassuaged of purpose, delivered from the lust of result, is every way perfect . . .
> Every number is infinite. Every man and every woman is a star . . .
> they shall bring the glory of the stars into the hearts of men . . .
> Invoke me under my stars! Love is the law, love under will . . .
> There is no law beyond Do what thou wilt.

If one looks "deeply" into the word, THELEMA, one finds that in classical Greek it means "will," but in pre- classical Greek it appeared to have meant something similar to "a magical charm" or "an invocation," i.e. an act of magical power. We have here a philosophy not unlike that of the Sufis, and, indeed, an excellent gloss is provided by the former Secretary-General of the Sufi Order, Hazrat Inayat Khan, in his little book of illuminated wisdom, *Cosmic Language* (Omen Press, Tucson, Arizona, 1972):

> Will is not *a* power, but it is *all* the power there is. With what did God create the world? By will. Therefore what is in us we call will-power in reality is a God-power . . . Our hands, with all their perfect mechanism, cannot support a glass of water if there is no will-power to support them . . . It is not the body which makes us stand upright; it is our will-power . . . Therefore in reality birds do not fly with their wings, they fly with will-power; fishes do not swim with their body, they swim with their will-power . . .

> Now coming to the question of what will-power is made of – in poetical words, will-power is love, in metaphysical terms love is will-power. And if one says God is love, it really means God is will . . .

When Crowley, an intrepid Cabalist, approached *The Book of the Law* receptively in 1909 (having rejected it when given to him in 1904), he first added up the numerological value of THELEMA and found 93. Seeking other words of 93-value in Greek – a Cabalistic method of exegesis – he quickly recognized AGAPE, love, as another 93. This reconciliation of "Love is the law . . ." with "Do what thou wilt . . ." convinced him there was meaning behind the seeming contradictions and occasional coded and/or incomprehensible passages of *The Book of the Law*. Hazrat Inayat Khan continues:

> Also, will and consciousness are the same fundamentally.

It is two expressions of one thing which make them distinct; this duality comes out of unity. It is God's own Being that in expression is will, in response consciousness; in other words in action it is will, in stillness it is consciousness; just as fundamentally the sound and the sight are one and the same thing. In one condition the friction of vibrations produces light; in another condition the same vibrations are audible.

In other words, just as we know one aspect of Niagara Falls through sight and another through sound, we know one aspect of ourselves through will and another through consciousness. We do not know our true will or our true mind in authoritarian society because we are trained from infancy to repress both. The resultant of all these repressions *acting convexly from outside* is *experienced concavely from inside* as the defined self; it has been defined by others. "The ego is a conspiracy by society for which you take the blame," said Mordecai the Foul, high priest of a Crowleyan magick society in California; in other words, the "I" which is seeking to escape the social trap *is* that trap.

Thus, in the axioms at the beginning of *Magick in Theory and Practice*, the Master Therion writes:

6. "Every man and every woman is a star." That is to say, every human being is intrinsically an independent individual with his own proper character and proper motion . . .

8. A man whose conscious will is at odds with his True Will is wasting his strength. He cannot hope to influence his environment efficiently . . .

9. A man who is doing his True Will has the inertia of the Universe to assist him . . .

12. Man is ignorant of the nature of his own being and powers. Even his idea of his limitations is based on experience of the past, and every step in his progress extends his empire. There is therefore no reason to assign

theoretical limits to what he may be, or to what he may do.

(Cf. Hazrat Inayat Khan, still in *Cosmic Language*: "It is an optimistic attitude toward life which develops will; the pessimistic attitude reduces it, robs it of its great power. Therefore if there is anything that hinders our progress in life, it is our own selves.")

There are two classic cases of trained impotence ("conscious will . . . at odds with . . . True Will") in very recent history. First, of course, is the incredible sexual miasma of the Victorians, in which it was widely believed that women did not and could not have orgasms; whereupon as the psychiatrists of the late Victorian period discovered, a quite incredible number of women did stop having orgasms. To some extent the daughters and granddaughters of these energetically castrated women, among us today, are still impotent, although as Masters and Johnson have shown, very few cases have any physical cause and almost all can be corrected in a few weeks of proper therapy.

The second case of trained impotence in recent times is the withering away of ESP ("telepathy") during those decades in which "all responsible scientists" claimed there was no such thing. Ever since statistical studies showed that some ESP decidedly exists, and scientific dogma has gradually retreated before real scientific curiosity, it has been easier and easier for magick students and others to unleash their own telepathic powers. These potent psychic talents were repressed, just like female sexuality in the Victorian age, by social prejudice.

These are acute and specific instances of the general paralysis of will in authoritarian society. To say that caste or class exist is to say that repression exists; Freud and Marx were looking at the same problem without quite getting it into focus either psychologically or sociologically. The divided society is mirrored in the divided self, and etymologically *re-pression* (to push down) is the word best describing what is happening on all levels. The citizen is repressed as an infant, as a child, as an adolescent, as an adult, and the methods vary from the most brutal (armed policemen) to the most psychologically subtle "pressure" to conform. On all levels, fear is the force directing behavior; and the "wisdom lectures" of the Hermetic Order of the Golden Dawn told Crowley as early as 1898 that "Fear is failure, and the forerunner of failure," He seems to have been the only Golden Dawn alumnus to have understood that aphorism fully.

Oscar Wilde once remarked that "Disobedience was man's Original Virtue"; and, from a Thelemic point of view, the Original Sin myth seems to have the facts precisely backwards. Obedience is best understood by observation of animal-trainers, where the link between authority and submission can be observed most nakedly. Disobedience indicates the first appearance of manhood, of *humanitas*, of a mind functioning above the reflex-arc loved by behaviorists. *Disobedience, will,* and *magick* are synonyms for that wholeness of which we are daily robbed by the divided society and the divided self.

ORGASM AND ECSTASY

The sexual repression at the core of authoritarian society is no accident or coincidence. The most brilliant and radical of all meta-Freudian psychologists, Dr. Wilhelm Reich, has written extensively in *The Invasion of Compulsive Sex Morality, The Mass Psychology of Fascism,* and *The Function of the Orgasm,* of how human society evolved from the primitive libertarian matriarchy to civilized authoritarian

Lion of Light

patriarchy; he finds that "psychological castration" or sexual repression is absolutely necessary to the production of vast, docile, submissive populations who will take orders from above. The purpose, he says, is the same as that served by gelding our stallions and bulls; the wildness is removed and the primordial Beast is tamed.

But more: especially in *The Function of the Orgasm* and *The Cancer Biopathy*, Dr. Reich has stressed the link between sexual repression, submissive personality, and "muscular armor." The muscular armor is a chronic tension holding down (literally *re-pressing*) biological feeling.

In authoritarian society, the genuine biological impulse is not only against the law, but against the grain; it is often imperceptible. It then becomes almost an act of faith to continue to regard ourselves as living beings. The behaviorists, who refuse to make that act of faith, are content to regard us as complex machines. This philosophy of mechanism, Dr. Reich points out, is only possible to muscularly armored beings; a real single orgasm, involving the whole energy of the body, puts us in touch with cosmic life.

The techniques of "sex magick" so notoriously associated with Crowley were not, of course, his own invention; they had been treasured for unknown centuries by the Ordo Templi Orientis, and were also known to the medieval witches, Hindu and Buddhist Tantrics, and many Sufis and alchemists. The technique is excellently described by Thomas Pynchon in his novel, *Gravity's Rainbow*:

> The charm she recited then, fastening the silk crotch torn from her best underpants across the eyes of the doll, his eyes . . . was this:
> May he be blind now to all but me. May the burning sun of love shine in his eyes forever. May this, my own darkness, shelter him. By all the holy names of God, by

the Angels Melchidael, Yahoel, An-fiel, and the great
Metetron, I conjure you, and all who are with you, to go
and do my will.
The secret is in the concentration. She inhibits everything
else: the moon, the wind in the Junipers, the wild dogs
out ranging in the middle of the night. She fixes on
Tchitcherine's memory and his wayward eyes, and lets it
build, pacing her orgasm to the incantation, so that by the
end, naming the last Names of Power, she's screaming,
coming, without help from her fingers, which are raised to
the sky.

The energy usually bound in tense muscles, but released
in true orgasm is called orgone by Dr, Reich, and is said to
permeate all space-time, both the "organic" and "inorganic"
being aspects of it. Dr. Andrei Pujarich, neurologist,
offers a similar theory in *Beyond Telepathy*, naming the
force "bioplasm" and connecting it with psychokinesis,
poltergeists, and similar magick happenings. Similarly,
it is *prana* to the Hindu, *Tao* to the Chinese, *mana* to the
Polynesian, *wakan* to the Plains Indian, *orenda* to the
Iroquois, "animal magnetism" to Mesmer, "Odyle" to Baron
Reichenbach, "psionic force" to Russian parapsychologists.
When directed by will, it seemingly can do everything,
except violate the laws of its own nature, although these
laws are more flexible than the incurious and uninvestigative
imagine them.

Such magick orgasm is always *ec-static* in the
etymological sense: one is "outside" one's usual self-image,
as in the exercize of assuming the form of God. The usual
self-image, indeed, while basically an act of imaginative
identification, is also the internal sense of the muscular armor
described by Reich. That this magical art was so murderously
persecuted by the Holy Inquisition (nine million dead, some
estimates say) may be only partially attributed to "Christian
bigotry": the fact that authoritarian society cannot afford

to tolerate people without a restricted, limited, specific self-identification as a player in a social game.

Timothy Leary, Ph.D., in a neglected, but tremendously important paper, *How to Change Behavior*, has defined the fashionable game-concept of human behavior more tightly than Berne, Von Neumann, Morgenstern, Werkheiser, Huizinga, and other game-theorists. A *game*, in Dr. Leary's sense, comprises: (1) roles, (2) rules, (3) rituals, (4) language, (5) goals, (6) characteristic space-time locations, (7) characteristic space-time movements.

LEARY'S INTERPERSONAL GRID

The popular "alcoholic" or "heroin-addict" games, for instance, have three pivotal roles of addict-victim, angry persecutor, and sympathetic rescuer, as Eric Berne, M.D. has pointed out. The rules are equally rigid and include visits to jails after meeting certain persecutors, visits to hospitals after meeting certain rescuers. The rituals are intricate, as can be observed at any bar, or any place heroin junkies assemble. The language carries a great burden of unacknowledged metaphysics, in which imaginative identifications are projected promiscuously upon the world and taken for "reality." The goals are guilty escape from the authoritarian games otherwise in force, and masochistic punishment for that escape. The typical locations and movements grow so stereotyped, that one can find the players within half an hour in any large city, and they will be in the same environs, doing the same routines, as in any other large city.

In *The Interpersonal Diagnosis of Personality*, Dr. Leary has classified typical game-transactions on a grid showing how the various authoritarian games relate to each other. (See the previous diagram). A person whose games involve transactions in any quadrant easily finds others, in the reciprocal quadrants, to "play" with him. For instance, the masochistic and submissive who function far out near the perimeter of quadrant 5 (H-L) easily "draw" the autocratic types who function near the perimeter of quadrant 1 (A-P); this is the typical master-slave position sacralized in the typical way of doing business in authoritarian cultures, played more earnestly and violently by the "docile slaves" who advertise for "masters" to "discipline" them in the personals sections of sleazy newspapers. The Army is the murderous ultimate in this game.

Muscular armoring, in which all the genuine biological drives are repressed, is the price we pay for maintaining the authoritarian structure of these games. Sexual repression, allowing for some pleasure occasionally, but atrophying the ecstasy function, maintains the superficial ego needed to enter the game and confuse it with real life.

It is hard to believe that most people spend almost all their lives monotonously playing the same "games," i.e. restricting themselves only to the interpersonal transactions of one narrow quadrant of the Leary graph. Strange as this is, it is true, as all clinical psychology bears witness. The man who arrives late and apologizes for it, will soon exhibit other clumsy or maladaptive behavior, and will apologize for that, and so on, through all his interpersonal relations. The oaf who criticizes your first transaction will soon criticize another, then another, and another, and so forth; if you do not cooperate by being properly guilty and submissive, he will give you up as a bad case and go on, until he finds his natural playmate in the first man mentioned above. The "characteristic space-time locations" are known, and the first initiatory transaction will set the whole game in motion. I once knew a lady who had six abortions in a row, although materialistic psychology is hard put to explain how she always managed to find men who would play the "seduced and abandoned" game with her.

Having lived in several parts of the East, Midwest, and Far West, only one time in my life did I actually see a private detective agency advertising "Armed Rent Collectors." (It was on 110th Street, in New York City: Harlem.) Nonetheless, the supposedly "free" citizens of this allegedly "democratic" nation go on paying their monthly tribute to the lords-of-the-land, or land-lords, just as if Feudalism still survived; as, indeed it does. Benjamin R. Tucker defined "rent" as the "tribute paid by the non-owning user of land to the non-using owner," yet most people accept this medieval exploitation as if there had never been an "Age of Reason." They also accept a medieval censorship system for TV and radio, and only a slightly less medieval control over drama, movies, books, and records. The authoritarian split between master class and servile class has survived the Declaration of Independence, the Bill of Rights, the 14th and 15th Amendments, the 20th Amendment, Women's Liberation, and even the LSD revolution. It is by far our most popular interpersonal game and the foundation under all other games.

THE GREAT WORK

The saying of "Grace" before meals, widely used as a conditioning device in authoritarian religions to produce the submissive personality, has undergone a radical change in Crowley's system. The "Thelemic" eating ritual goes as follows:

First speaker: Do what thou wilt shall be the whole of the Law.

Second speaker: What is thy will?

First speaker: It is my will to eat and drink.

Second speaker: To what end?

First speaker: That my body may be fortified thereby.

Second speaker: To what end?

First speaker: That I may accomplish the Great Work.

Second speaker: Love is the law, love under will.

First speaker: Fall to!

Thus, just as "grace" in authoritarian cultures is a mnemonic of submission, the Thelemic "grace" is a mnemonic of Will and the Great Work.

This latter term, borrowed by Crowley from the Golden Dawn and Ordo Templi Orientis, and by them from the Illuminati of Bavaria, the 17th Century Rosy Cross Brotherhood, the medieval alchemists, and ultimately the 9th Century Sufi, Fariduddin Attar, refers to the integration and equilibration of the total psyche. This involves transcending the imprinted ego and re-establishment of a new center equidistant from all polarities. It is often symbolized, among alchemists, by the four-cornered circle, or mandala, also used in Tibetan forms of Tantric Buddhism. On Leary's Interpersonal Grid, each individual "ego" is a compulsive attachment to certain game-patterns in one quadrant or another; the new self, after the Great Work is completed, appears then – just as in alchemy or Tibetan Buddhism – as a circle covering all quadrants. Such a fully-realized personality cannot be destroyed by any force on earth, because he or she is in harmony with all forces.

A submissive ego, for instance, is at a loss in a situation demanding managerial action; he can only look around, vainly, for a person of that type, to tell him what to do. Conversely, the authoritarian ego, placed in a situation where submission is the only rational course, will nonetheless go on seeking "control", even if this destroys him utterly.

As Dr. Leary has pointed out (*Interpersonal Diagnosis*, p.71) the four major divisions of this grid correspond to the classic humors theory of Hippocrates. The upper left (hostile strength) is Hippocrates' choleric temperament, the lower left (hostile weakness) is the melancholic, the lower right (friendly weakness) is phlegmatic, and the upper right (friendly strength) is sanguine.

Traditional alchemy identified these Hippocratean temperaments with the four elements of fire, water, earth, and air, which Rosicrucians then further complexified by a second identification with the suits of the Tarot deck: wands, cups, swords, and pentacles. Both alchemy and magick, since the Sufi impact on (non-Catholic, non-orthodox)

Western thought, c. 900 A.D.-1200 A.D., have always stressed bringing these four polarities into balance or equilibrium. This is the functional or operational meaning of transcendence of the conventional ego. Crowley has further extended this formula – as we saw in our section, *Fourfold Vision* – by including in the forces to be balanced, those faculties of the psyche known as intuition, feeling, reason, and sensation, and their corresponding methodologies: magick, yoga, logic, and experimental science.

Dr. Leary offers an historical perspective in his satirical *Jail Notes*:

> The word "humor" has carried down through the centuries a peculiar etymology. In origin it means "wetness," and is of the same source as "humidity."
> At the dawn of medical science, medical science, (this is important) medical science, Hippocrates (c. 400 B.C.) recognized four chief currents or "humors" in the human body: phlegm, blood, choler, black bile.
> The decline of medical knowledge, DECLINE OF MEDICAL KNOWLEDGE, threw the term into a vague significance . . .
> Hippocratic principle. Basis of all psychology and religion. Your inner juices determine your state of mind and your level of consciousness . . .
> Psychology is alchemy plus astrology. Modern terms: psychopharmacology plus bio-rhythmic sequential analysis . . .
> When we left galactic center they told us: when you reach a biologically inhabited planet ask two religious questions. Which biochemicals do you use? What is your attitude toward the male-female relationship?
> Hippocrates said that there are eight humors, liquids, potions. Euphorics, Erotics, Phlegmatics, Narcotics, Melancholics, Emergenics, Cholerics, Energetics . . .
> A natural healthy flow of humor allows the appropriate juice to mobilize the psychomotor machinery in response to any stimulus. Dis-ease (or sin, if you prefer) is caused

by inhibition, imbalance, or over-production of any natural juice. In this case the state of healthy balance is recovered by administration of a medicament-sacrament. Hippocrates lists eight generic sacraments: Cocaine. Cannabis. Hashish. Opium. Bile. Neurotin. Cholerin. Amphetamine.

A footnote in the Hippocratic Collection suggests that if the reader understands the preceding three paragraphs then the reader has penetrated the highest secret of nature and ranks among the wisest to have ever lived . . .

Hippocrates is probably the most dangerous and socially disruptive man ever to have lived. His principles and his techniques with potions, if become widespread, would totally free each individual from state control and make possible total liberty of consciousness.

As his disciple and direct heir, Leary can be described as the most dangerous man alive.

Crowley, whose experimentation with drugs was almost as extensive as Dr. Leary's (or Hippocrates'), came to similar conclusions about their values, *when intelligently used*, to assist in the internal balancing of the Great Work. As the symbolism of the alchemists (and their strange brews) suggests, this seems to have been a secret tradition for many centuries before young Crowley and Alan Bennett, ransacking old manuscripts, decided that there was indeed a chemical pathway to higher consciousness.

The ultimate formula, however, is not chemical *per se*, but chemical-energetic, as Crowley eventually realized, and as Dr. Leary has subsequently re-discovered. We must take another look at sex-magick, in its higher forms, to comprehend this.

FERTILITY, HIEROGAMY, TANTRA

Due to the research of Cleve Backster, using polygraph equipment to measure plant's reactions to human thoughts, evidence suggests that vegetation is in intimate telepathic contact with human beings. This is one of the most dramatic scientific breakthroughs of our time, but has led to little speculation on the question: how did our ancestors know about this when they didn't own polygraphs or other psycho-galvanic instruments? Somebody will eventually write a best-seller proposing that the Flying Saucer people came down and gave the cavemen polygraphs, of course; if we do not accept that easy solution, what must we think? The only instrument that the early shamans undoubtedly possessed was the human nervous system. As philologist John Allegro, in *The Sacred Mushroom and the Cross*, neurologist Andrei Pujarich, in *The Magic Mushroom*, and mycologist R. Gordon Wasson, in *Soma: Divine Mushroom of Immortality*, have all argued, our paleolithic ancestors seemed to know a great deal about those fungi which Dr. John Lilly recently named "meta-programming substances," also called by others "hallucinogens" or "psychedelics." The magic mushroom of the Old World, *amanita muscaria*, seems to have been used almost universally in the hunting era; the new world mushroom, *psilocybe mexicana*, came along soon after; other psychedelics, such as *cannabis* (marijuana) or *lophophora williamsi* (peyote) are dated between 20,000 and 2,000 B.C.E. Using these substances to meta-program their nervous systems, early shamans evidently achieved telepathy with plants and animals, thereby inventing what we call magick. Upwards of 250 such meta-programming substances are still in use among various tribal shamans, according to Prof. Weston LeBarre in *The Ghost Dance: The Origins of Religion*.

The only religious practice older than (or as old as) drug-taking, and equally widespread in the primitive and ancient worlds, is the ritual orgy. As Frazer points out at length, in *The Golden Bough*, the purpose is to ensure the fertility of the crops. Frazer assumes, with Victorian chauvinism, that the primitive shamans were too ignorant to realize that the plants would not respond to such a ritual. In the light of Backster's polygraphic research, and the dozens of similar investigations on both sides of the Iron Curtain, we can now see that the plants probably did and do respond to such ritual. Meanwhile, however, the shamans – who deserve Frazer's praise of them as "primitive scientists" far more than Frazer himself ever realized – discovered something else. They found the magick function of the ecstatic state.

Hierogamy, or "sacred marriage," (sometimes shading over into what is also called "religious prostitution,") seems to have existed once in all early civilizations, such as Babylon, Egypt, Persia, India, etc. Here the orgy was replaced by the ceremonial copulation of one "religiously" significant couple – often the King and his Sister. (This is possibly the origin of the royal incest of Egypt.) The details of hierogamy are unknown to us, but since the sexual act in this context was considered important to the welfare of the whole people (indeed, of all nature) we must assume it was not just a matter of "the sneeze in the loins" (D.H. Lawrence's ironic term for armored, civilized sex).

The sexual rites of modern Tantra and magick probably derive from this practice, and these rites involve prolonged and concentrated sexual trance. This activates what magicians call the "astral field" – i.e. Reich's "orgone", the Russians' "psionic force", Mesmer's "Animal Magnetism." Readers seeking further historical details on the evolution of such practices should see my *Sex and Drugs: A Journey Beyond Limits*, Playboy Press, 1973. (Republished by Hilaritas Press, 2021, as *Sex, Drugs & Magick: A Journey Beyond Limits*)

The result of such rituals is known as "the ascent of

the serpent" among Tantrists in India and Tibet, and was called "the production of the First Matter" by the alchemists. The serpent, or *Kundalini*, is an alleged energy that rushes to the brain during such artificially prolonged (and/or drug-enhanced) sexual ritual; the "First Matter" is evidently the alchemists' name for the pre-atomic bioplasm or "orgone" which underlies life, will, love, consciousness, and other forces repressed by authoritarian civilization and denied by mechanistic behaviorism.

What is going on neurologically in this form of magick is suggested by Dr. Leary in his *Neurologic*, which we, will now quickly summarize.

Just as the Egyptian magicians said mankind has seven "souls," Dr. Leary suggests our nervous systems can potentially operate on seven circuits, or form in series – seven levels of "imprints."

1. The forward-back circuit, mediating the advance programs (3-2 on the interpersonal grid) or the retreat programs (6-7 on the grid). This primitive circuit evidently goes back to the amoeba level; advance toward pleasure, retreat from pain, being the first polarity of life. Infant imprinting determines which tendency will become habitual, and life-games are then programmed in accord with either forward or backward trends.

2. The up-down circuit, monitoring such behaviors as dominance (1 on the grid) or submission (5 on the grid). This goes back to the first amphibians who became erect and swelled up, or skulked down and slunk away, in conflict situations. Most of the strong emotions (rage-fear) are triggered by glandular mechanisms involved in this circuit.

3. The right-left circuit, determining whether higher order reactions shall be programmed by the right cortical lobe (intuition, art, mysticism) or the left cortical lobe (logic, dexterity, engineering science). This is imprinted in early childhood.

4. The socio-sexual circuit, monitoring such behavior as strutting, display, mating, orgasm, nest-building, etc. This is imprinted by early adolescence and narrows the polymorphous infant into an adult with a definite and rigid sex-game role which will be monotonously played for the rest of the life-span.

Dr. John Lilly has argued that we are born with brains that potentially function as "all-purpose computers." The way each brain gets programmed to be a few-purpose or one-purpose computer is contained in the imprints on each of the above circuits. Authoritarian society everywhere imprints chiefly to create an "adjusted" automaton capable of fitting into an exact in the caste-class game. Part of this imprint-ing-for-limitation (Veblen's "trained incapacity") consists in never deliberately opening the remaining three circuits at all.

5. The rapture circuit is opened by epilepsy, traumatic fear (near death), schizophrenia, casual drug-taking, deliberative (programmed) drug-use in a magick context or the rigors of hatha yoga. Consciousness moves from the symbolic arena of brain activities (sub-vocal speech and "reasoning") to direct perception on the sensory level. Hashish meditation is the path most likely to produce an ability to operate on the rapture level (which is not to be confused with the intoxications of narcotics, alcohol, barbiturates, or the un-informed careless *mis*-use of hashish.)

6. The ecstasy circuit moves consciousness outside the nervous system – into cellular, molecular, and atomic levels of consciousness, usually thought by modern science not to exist. (Evidence of molecular consciousness, however, is rapidly accumulating, e.g., McConnell's research on cannibal worms who acquire the "memory" of the eaten worms, Ruth Sager's similar work on *paramecia*, the experimental administration of RNA followed by renewed memory in the senile.) On these levels, "racial memory" in the Jungian sense – or "recollection of past incarnations" in traditional occult ideology – may easily be found. Dr. Leary suggests that each of us possesses cellular memory, molecular memory, and atomic memory going back to the dawn of life, or earlier; this explains the mystic's conviction that one part of our consciousness is immortal.

7. The neurogenetic imprint creating a new circuit occurs when mastering of all six circuits allows for continuous re-programming, meta-programming, serial imprinting, etc. This is the "free will" sought by Sufis and misleadingly claimed to exist in all of us by Christian theologians. In short, this is another definition of the Great Work Completed.

Dr. Leary knows, and carefully points out, that the only safe way to move from the rapture imprint (circuit 5) to the ecstasy imprint (circuit 6) is through what he calls "the delicate Hedonic engineering of Tantric sex"; that is, the magick use of sexual energies to self-program the mind out of its usual verbal ego into the "unconscious" (inarticulate) levels of cellular, molecular, and atomic memory in which all evolution lives on within us.

THE HOLY GUARDIAN ANGEL

The principal device of Crowleyan magick is not the technique of astral projection, the assumption of god-forms, or the use of drugs, but the invocation of the Holy Guardian Angel. This ritual consists of prolonged (1 to 3 hours) sexual intercourse followed by consummation of the "elixir" from the "Holy Grail" (vagina).

In this connection there is much to mull over in the famous "skeptical" words of the medieval Cabalist, Moses Maimonides, who was almost certainly trained in the Sufi sex-yoga rites from which Crowley's tradition ultimately derives:

> "Angel" means messenger, therefore everyone who is entrusted with a certain mission is an angel . . . Say to a person who is believed to belong to the wise men of Israel that the Almighty sends His angel to enter the womb of a woman and to form there a fetus, he will be satisfied with the account, he will believe it . . . But tell him that God gives the seed a formative power which produces and shapes the limbs and that this power is called an "angel" . . . and he will turn away.

Maimonides is describing what we now call the DNA molecule and saying that this is the Guardian Angel of the newly conceived being. DNA is indeed the ageless, trans-egoistic and "immortal" part of each human being; although, ironically, most atheists are as confused about this aspect of genetics as any believer in dualistic Christianity or similar "supernatural" religions. The idea that our immortality is physical seems to both groups to imply that we have no "mental" immortality. We need to meditate a bit on Dr. Leary's simple, subtle definition: "Consciousness is energy received and decoded by a structure."

The great paradox in the history of Buddhism – the denial of the individual "soul" together with the belief in "reincarnation" – has led to 2500 years of exquisite Asiatic debate on the question, "What, then, reincarnates?" Recent evidence that DNA and its associated RNA carry *information* down the chain of evolution, begins to answer that question. Crowley, like other mystics, discovered this by direct introspection, and writes unambiguously in *Magick Without Tears*:

> The structure of the mind reveals its history as does the structure of the body . . .
> In the course of initiation . . . the layers are stripped off very much as happens in elementary meditation (*Dharana*) to the conscious mind.
> (There is a way of acquiring a great deal of strange and unsuspected knowledge of these matters by the use of Sulphuric Ether . . .)
> Accordingly, one finds oneself experiencing the thoughts, the feelings, the desires of a gorilla, a crocodile, a rat, a devil-fish or what have you! One is no longer capable of human thoughts in the ordinary sense of the word . . .

Lao-Tse also seems to be describing the DNA when he invokes the Tao as "the smallest form and mother of all forms," just as Crowley defines the alchemical elixir as "not living and not dead, neither liquid nor solid, neither male nor female," etc. The most celebrated Crowley paradox, or contradiction, is his direct statement to student Frank Bennett that the Holy Guardian Angel is nothing else but "your own subconscious mind" followed by his equally direct statement to the student that the Angel is "a separate being . . . of angelic nature . . . more than a man." Like his famous (or infamous) admission that his rituals often involved the sacrifice of "a male child of perfect innocence and high intelligence" (which refers to his own semen), this requires a level of understanding far beyond ordinary "materialism" or conventional "spiritualism." We had better stop and take to heart three of his more complex warnings against dualism:

> It seems to me, ignorant as we all are, easier to call a nerve "God" and so explain its functions, than to speak of a "God" using the nerve as vehicle.
> – *Konx Om Pax*, 1906

There must be a "natural" explanation!

There must be a "supernatural" explanation!
Let these two asses be set to grind corn.
 – *The Book of Lies*, 1912

It is now said that "God" is no more than a name for the
Sex Instinct. Very well; but then the Sex Instinct is no
more than a name for God.
 – *Magick in Theory and Practice*, 1928

The invocation of the Holy Guardian Angel, adapted
by Crowley from the 15th Century Latin of "Abraham the
Jew," and by him evidently from some Sufi documents that
may derive ultimately from Gnosticism of earlier, contains
such clear-cut lines as:*

Thee I invoke, the Bornless One . . . Thou didst produce
the Female and the Male. Thou didst produce the Seeds
and the Fruit . . . , O Lion-Serpent-Sun, the Beast that
whirlest forth, a thunderbolt, begetter of life! Thou that
flowest! Thou that goest! Thou inviolate wisdom! Thou
secret seed! . . . Thou Fire! . . . All hail, thou Great Wild
Beast! . . . Seed most wise! Innocent babe! . . . Soul of all
souls!

~•~

* RAW is a little mistaken here. "Liber Samekh," the invocation
he refers to, was adapted by Crowley from the Fragment of a
Graeco-Egyptian Work upon Magic translated from Latin by
Charles Wycliffe Goodwin and used as a preliminary invocation
in *Goetia: The Lesser Key of Solomon*. This is also known as the
"Bornless Ritual." *The Book of the Sacred Magic of Abramelin the
Mage* by Abraham the Jew, a translation by MacGregor Mathers,
was the Golden Dawn ritual for invoking the Holy Guardian
Angel. Crowley tried and didn't complete this one twice before
resorting to his own methods.

~•~

John Bleibtreu's splendid introduction to modern
genetics, *The Parable of the Beast* (what a Crowleyite
title!), notes that primitive cannibalism may have been
an attempt to acquire the molecular memory of others.

He adds, significantly, "The intuition that persists even today, in the sophisticated Christian West that there is a knowledge-substance or memory-substance in the flesh, is testified to by the persistence of the ceremony of the eucharist, in which a symbolic act of cannibalism is enacted." Crowley, in turn, comments in *The Equinox of the Gods*, on "the perfection with which the Roman Communion has preserved the form, and lost the substance, of the Supreme Magickal Ritual of the True Gnosis," i.e. the consumption of the elixir of life from the chalice of an embodied Goddess.

Dr. Leary summarizes the results of more than 20,000 LSD protocols (records of voyages into inner space) which he has collected:

> The psychedelic correlates of these evolutionary and genetic concepts are to be found in the reports of almost every LSD tripper. The experience of being a one-celled creature tenaciously flailing, the singing, humming sound of life exfoliating; you are the DNA code spinning out multicellular esthetic solutions . . . The psychedelic experience is the Hindu-Buddhist reincarnation theory experimentally confirmed in your own nervous system. You re-experience your human forebears, shuttle down the chain of DNA remembrance . . . Many, and I am bold enough to say most, LSD subjects say they experience early forms of racial or subhuman species evolution. Now the easiest interpretation is the psychiatric: "Oh, yes, hallucinations . . ." Read a genetics text. Read and reflect about the DNA chain . . . Your body is the universe . . . What is without is within . . . The kingdom of heaven is within you . . .

The one-life theory of Judeo-Christian cultures, with the reduction of total psyche to mere personality or ego (whereas to the Romans, the *persona* was a mask through which the actor, or psyche, expressed itself) has made pagan and Asian thought inscrutable to us. The dogma that the personality survives death, always an hysterically presented (i.e. fearful) expression of hope without evidence, is the result of that ego-centering. Nowadays the LSD trippers know what the magicians, the pagans, and the yogis always knew: the personality is the only part of us that does not survive death.

THE AEON OF HORUS

According to Crowley's commentaries on *The Book of the Law*, human society has passed through two stages and is now entering the third: the Aeon of Isis, or primitive matriarchy, the Aeon of Osiris, or civilized patriarchy, and now the Aeon of Horus, which can only be predicted in the most vague and general terms.

The Aeon of Isis, or the Mother Goddess, is now widely celebrated in the polemics of the Women's Liberation Movement; not coincidentally, Crowley predicted this movement in *The Book of Thoth*, saying that woman will soon appear "armed and militant." Books such as Robert Graves' *The White Goddess*, J.J. Bachofen's *Mother Right*, Helen Diner's *Mothers and Amazons*, Elizabeth Gould Davis's *The First Sex*, Wilhelm Reich's *Invasion of Compulsive Sex Morality*, Robert Briffault's *The Mothers*, etc., present most of the evidence for the existence of this primitive matriarchy. Other anthropologists deny all this, but G. Rattray Taylor's *Sex in History*, rising above the debate among the hard-liners, offers a schemata of "predominately matrist" and predominately "patrist" cultures which can scarcely be denied and shows that "predominately matrist" (if not actually "matriarchical") cultures are the earliest and seemingly the least violent, most stable of human societies. As objective a work as Will Durant's *Story of Civilization* presents enough evidence to convince any partisan that, at the very least, "the decline of the position of women" (and of goddesses) appears at the beginnings of each civilization for which data still exists. A decline indicates a previously higher position.

According to Crowley, fatherhood was either not known or not regarded as spiritually important in the Aeon of Isis. The relationship with the mother was the only important relationship, and the divine was accordingly a Great Mother-Goddess, whose avatars still remain in such early-patriarchal-age figures as Isis herself, Ishtar, Hera, Juno, Venus, Brigit, etc. Life was erotic (cooperative), tribal, libertarian; the concept of punishment and sadomasochism hadn't been invented.

The Aeon of Osiris, the Dying God, introduced human sacrifice (first the Divine King, then a scapegoat-substitute, as analyzed by Frazer's *Golden Bough*, ultimately whole populations, as in the genocides of the Aztecs, Persians, Nazi Germans, or the American treatment of Indians, blacks, Vietnamese . . .). The erotic basis of communal life was lost; the State arose, based on punishment (tortures, death, mutilations, etc.). Life was conceived as catastrophic, and the philosophies of the Osirian age – Buddhism, Platonism, Christianity, Marxism – are a catalog of woe and foreboding.

The Aeon of Horus, which began with the dictation of *The Book of the Law* to Crowley in 1904, can only be forecast in the most general outlines. Cosmologically, just as worship shifted psycho-spiritually from the moon (Isis) to the sun (Osiris) in the revolution from matriarchy to patriarchy, the Age of Horus "the Crowned Child" represents a further shift to the stars. ("Come forth under the stars and take your fill of love," says *The Book of the Law*; and "Invoke me under my stars;" Crowley himself is called "the prophet of the lovely star," who shall "bring the glory of the stars into the hearts of men.")

If the lunar-matriarchal age was tribal and biological

(based on familial bonds), the solar-patriarchal age was authoritarian and centralized (based on domination of the Solar male Deity or the Sun-King, as in Japan, old Mexico, Peru, and – generalized – the modern State); the stellar-neonatal age will be as relativistic as Einstein's cosmology. Similarly, as the lunar age of Isis was cycle-centered, the solar age of Osiris was catastrophic, and the stellar age of Horus will be evolutionary.

Ethically, the prophecy of *The Book of the Law* is so shocking that Crowley himself rejected it as "barbaric" and "atrocious" at first reading, and ignored it for five years thereafter. Only after achieving *Samadhi*c consciousness did he begin to grasp the whole meaning contained in "Thelema," although the book itself warns that "those who do not understand these runes shall make a great miss. They shall fall into the Pit called Because and perish with the dogs of Reason." The key text is, as quoted before:

> The word of the law is THELEMA. Who calls us Thelemites shall do no wrong if the word be deeply considered, for there are therein Three Grades: the Hermit, and the Lover, and the man of Earth. Do what thou wilt shall be the whole of the Law.

This means, first of all, that authoritarian absolutism is dying; just as the shift to stellar relativity from solar centrality creates a universe without up or down, the advance in social sciences (especially anthropology and psychology) has undermined hierarchical supernatural religions. Every educated person knows that there is no absolute "right" and "wrong" anymore than there is an absolute "up" or "down" – cultural relativity is as firmly established as physical relativity, but we are mostly uncomfortable with this knowledge and not sure what to do about it. Indeed, some of the best brains of our century have devoted their best energies to a fruitless attempt (similar to the anti-Darwinians in the 19th Century, or the anti-Copernicans in the 17th) to argue away the facts and turn the clock back to a less disturbing reality. Poets in particular have been horrified by moral relativism and have rushed pell-mell back to medieval Christianity or other absolute systems, truncating their minds in the process. Nonetheless, the truth slowly dawns, and becomes grudgingly accepted: Do what thou wilt shall be the whole of the Law.

But there are therein three grades, and of these the last and least is "the Man of Earth." This seems to signify the person of statistically normal consciousness: the deluded or game-playing or role-playing one whose awareness remains on the dualistic level. Such persons, with the collapse of traditional supernatural religion, have behaved just as *The Book of the Law* predicts in its most frightening passages; to the Hitlers, Stalins, Nixons, etc. "Do what thou wilt" has become what a dualistic consciousness naturally is, when not checked by fear of a divine Judge: the war of all against all, the world without elementary decency in which we currently live, the chaotic reign of force which dualists imagine is the meaning of "anarchy." That *The Book of the Law* predicted this collapse of "civilized" restraint and wholesale reversion to barbaric bandito-ethos was the worst shock in it, to Crowley, in 1904; subsequent history convinced him that this book was indeed inspired by an intuitive intelligence superior to mere reason alone, as (he also decided) was Nietzsche in predicting the same anarcho-fascism as the pattern of "the day after tomorrow."

Chapter 3 of *The Book of the Law*, spoken by the twins, Ra-Hoor-Khuit and Har-Poor-Krat, represents this dualistic Thelemism, the divided self in the divided society. Startling as it was in 1904, it announced the 20th Century clearly:

> Now let it be first understood that I am a god of War and of Vengeance. I shall deal hardly with them . . .

I will give you a war-engine . . .

Worship me with fire & blood; worship me with swords & with spears . . . let blood flow to my name . . .

Ye shall see that hour, o blessed Beast, and thou the Scarlet Concubine of his desire!

Ye shall be sad thereof.

I am the warrior Lord of the Forties; the Eighties cower before me, & are abased.

The second grade of Thelema, evidently to be activated when the chaos unleashed by the Man of Earth has run its course and destroyed Osirian (authoritarian) civilization, is that of the Lover. This refers to the second mode of consciousness, the *dhyana* vision in which dualism is transcended and all is known as One. Here "Do what thou wilt shall be the whole of the Law" means exactly the same as "Love is the law;" Chapter 2 of *The Book of the Law*, spoken by Hadit (an embodiment of the kundalini-serpent, or life-energy) is the consciousness of the One who is and knows himself identical with the All:

I am the flame that burns in every heart of man, and in the core of every star. I am Life and the giver of Life; yet therefore is the knowledge of me the knowledge of death . . .

I am the Snake that giveth Knowledge & Delight and bright glory and stir the hearts of men with drunkenness. To worship me take wine and strange drugs whereof I will tell my prophet & be drunk thereof!

I am alone: there is no God where I am . . .

(Crowley explains this odd verse with a citation from the *Bagh-i-Muattar*: "Allah's the atheist! Allah hath no Allah!" I.e., in *dhyana* there is no remaining separation between mind and its contents, observer and observed, worshipper and God, Hadit also says "Who worshipped Heru-pa-kraath have worshipped me; ill, for I am the worshipper.)

I am uplifted in thine heart; and the kisses of the stars rain hard upon thy body . . .

Thrill with the joy of life & death! . . .

Come! lift up thine heart & rejoice! We are one . . .

Crowley, who once noted in his diary that "the subconscious mind is aware of its own immortality," could say on different occasions that this Angelic voice was the unconscious of humanity and also that it was "a separate being . . . of Angelic nature;" we are not far wrong in identifying it with the Atman (world-soul) of the Hindus or with the DNA molecular memory of Dr. Timothy Leary's neurologic theories. On this level of awareness "Do what thou wilt" and the evolutionary blueprint are identical; Crowley refers to it as "the True Will," as distinguished from the many "false and perverted Wills, monstrous growth, Parasites, Vermin" which control the Man of Earth.

The third grade of Thelema, symbolized by the Hermit, is articulated in the first chapter of *The Book of the Law*, in which the speaker is Nuit, goddess of the stars and the void. If the consciousness of the Man of Earth is dualistic and torn by wars internal and external, and the consciousness of the Lover is at one with all, the consciousness of the Hermit can only be described as empty, in the Taoist sense. This is called *Samadhi* in Hinduism and para-nirvana in Buddhism; it appears as far beyond ordinary mystical one-ness as that blissful state is beyond ordinary dualistic consciousness. Nuit, whose name is frequently punned with "naught" and "not" and means "night" in French, says:

With the God & the Adorer I am nothing: they do not see me . . .

And the sign shall be my ecstasy, the consciousness of the continuity of existence, the omnipresence of my body . . .

Then the priest answered . . . O Nuit, continuous one of Heaven, let it be ever thus; that men speak not of Thee as One but as None; and let them speak not of thee at all, since thou art continuous!

None, breathed the light, faint & faery, of the stars, and two.

For I am divided for love's sake, for the chance of union . . .

The Perfect and the Perfect are one Perfect and not two; nay, are none!

Nothing is a secret key of this law.

In terms of Dr. Leary's neurologic theory, Chapter Three, the dualistic consciousness of Ra-Hoor-Khuit and Hoor-Par-Kraat, the mentality of the Man of Earth, signifies the normal ego imprinted on the first four neurological circuits of forward vs. back, dominate vs. submit, dexterous reason vs. passive intuition, sexually restricted vs. sexually free. Chapter Two, the unified consciousness of Hadit, the Lover, signifies the opening of the fifth and sixth circuits, rapture and ecstasy – the usual mode of mystic awareness. Chapter One, the void or empty mind of Nuit, the mentality of the Hermit, signifies the seventh imprint or neurogenetic circuit in which no-thing (nothing) is fixed or permanent, the nervous system re-imprints and serially imprints (meta-programs) itself into potential infinity of form and function. It is this level described by Zen Buddhists when they say mind is "no-form" and by Gemistos Plethon when he said mind was "omni-form."

The Book of the Law is unambiguous in announcing the death of the old gods and the collapse of absolutist ethics.

The Man of Earth, in our time, is not restricted by any fear of a punishing Jehovah, and "Do what thou wilt" in the sense of "grab what you can" is indeed the whole of the law in the previously civilized nations. There is no going back to Aquinas or even to Kant. "The only way out," as Malaclypse the Younger has said, "is straight up"; consciousness must ascend to unity, and beyond, or the harsh god of Chapter Three will continue to rule, for a short while yet, leading humanity and possibly all earth's biosphere to ruin and destruction. In short, if dogmatic religion based on faith is dead, the only alternative is personal experience of the higher consciousness states. We can no longer be told what to do; we must learn by our own scientific experiments in consciousness expansion what we really are, beyond the superficial personality imprinted by social reward-punishment conditioning. If there is no Sun-King at the apex of a hierarchy, guiding and leading us all, if "every man and every woman is a star", we have not only the right, but the duty to expand our consciousness and our powers to the utmost. This is the final meaning of the Great Work, and of Crowley's slogan of "Scientific Illuminism."

Wilhelm Reich defined the social ego as a function of the muscular armoring: the armor is experienced subjectively as fear or phobia and tells us what we cannot do, i.e. what is too frightening to contemplate. What remains, the small area of un-armored action left to the "adjusted" citizen, is the personality called "I". Similarly, Timothy Leary defines the ego as the function of anxiety; it is the contour of all games (interactions) permitted by society's imprints. To push against the armor or struggle against the imprints normally leads to more fear than the organism can stand; there is a sense of self-loss in this struggle, and a fear of perishing, because the normal "self" is in fact the limits created by social reward and punishment.

If the Age of Isis was dominated by mothering psychology and loving-kindness, and the Age of Osiris by fatherly sternness and authority, the Age of Horus must be centered on the outstanding quality of the Child-Spirit. That quality is the capacity to grow up.

THE TRUE WILL

To find the True Self and the True Will, beyond the historical accidents of social imprinting, is the goal of Crowley's magick. Following Crowley's own practice, we have tried in this essay to show only that the true self and true will are normally unknown, repressed, *terra incognita*, and that the methods of discovering them require no supernatural or theological dogma. If we have hinted, at times, that they are of such immensity and power as to justify the extravagant language of mystics, taken as metaphor, we do not ask any reader to believe us without experience.

Like Crowley, we do not say "believe!", but "don't believe – find out for yourself!"

It can be suggested, however, that the True Will is as impersonal as evolution itself. If we identify it, tentatively, with Dr. Leary's hypothetical DNA memory or Bergson's *élan vital*, we do not seriously distort Crowley's meaning. The mythic, or poetic, image of dancing Shiva, destroying all forms to allow the creation of new forms, may be, however, closer to the truth, which is still beyond the capacity of human thought to express; a poetic symbol, in these regions, may be more adequate than a rational pseudo-explanation.

The techniques of self-transcendence and inner growth, through the Rapture Circuit and beyond, have been known empirically for 2000 to 3000 years, minimum, but this knowledge was "craft," rule-of-thumb, traditional, modified by the individual Guru's knowledge of the individual aspirant. Since 1962, this picture has changed, largely due to Dr. Timothy Leary, Dr. John Lilly, and other scientists who, in the track of Crowley, have invaded the domain of mysticism with scientific method. (Coming from the other side, Gopi Krishna, after achieving self-liberation, instead of taking on a few disciples in orthodox Hindu fashion, moved on to Europe and persuaded some physicists and other scientists to join him in investigating the scientific principles involved and at work in his kundalini yoga. Other yogis are beginning to follow suit and cooperating in neurological and other studies on their heightened consciousness.) The techniques of imprint, re-imprint, serial imprint, metaprogramming of mind, are now part of science. We are thus at a turning point in human neuro-psychology, comparable to the revolution that began when medieval craft-technology joined Greek logic to produce science itself and the Industrial Revolution.

If a mutation in consciousness is the only answer to the continued rule and mis-rule of the Man of Earth, the technology of that mutation is now at hand. Our techniques of mind-expansion and self-programming in 1994 can be as far ahead of what we already know in 1974 as the airplane of 1950 was ahead of the airplane of 1930; that is what can happen in a free scientific community. The lack of such a free scientific community – the government repression of this research – is the outstanding intellectual disgrace of our time.

The True Will of life itself can scarcely be mistaken and cannot be caged forever by any government. The Great Beast, Crowley's name for that part of him that transcended ego and social conditioning, is cognate with an earlier Golden Dawn archetype, the Unicorn from the Stars. Sir Francis Crick, co-discoverer of DNA, now says that DNA contains some elements (e.g. molybdenum) in more abundance than these elements naturally occur on earth, and DNA must be therefore of extra-terrestrial origin. Dr. Leary goes further and says that both our origin and our destiny are among the stars.

The direction of modern technology is outward. It is obvious that the parochial, tribal, provincial ego-games of earth cannot be brought with us when we answer the cry of Crowley's star-goddess, Nuit: "Come unto me!" The transcendence of all we have ever been and all we imagine we can be is not just a possibility, but a necessity, now.

When Confucius said, "You cannot depart from the Tao," he evidently meant that, unconsciously, we are part of the Life-Will whether we know it or not. He who follows Crowley's scientific illuminism becomes a conscious agent of that evolutionary and esthetic search for higher consciousness, higher solutions, higher wisdom. For this knight of Thelema, today is the first day of the rest of the universe.

~~~~~~~~~~~~~~~~~~~

Do What Thou Wilt
Previously unpublished, written in 1974, 1st offered to Revisionist Press, currently owned by Houghton Library, Harvard University from which permission to publish was generously given to Hilaritas Press.

Liber LXXVII

Z

" the law of
the strong :
this is our law
and the joy
of the world."

AL II. 21

" Do what thou wilt shall be the whole of the law."
                                                —*AL I 40*

" thou hast no right but to do thy will.   Do that, and no
other shall say nay."—*AL I 42-3*

" Every man and every woman is a star."—*AL. I. 3*

There is no god but man.

1. Man has the right to live by his own law—
    to live in the way that he wills to do :
    to work as he will :
    to play as he will :
    to rest as he will :
    to die when and how he will.

2. Man has the the right to eat what he will :
    to drink what he will :
    to dwell where he will :
    to move as he will on the face of the earth.

3. Man has the right to think what he will :
    to speak what he will :
    to write what he will :
    to draw, paint, carve, etch, mould, build as he will :
    to dress as he will .

4. Man has the right to love as he will :—
    " take your fill and will of love as ye will,
    when, where, and with whom ye will.' —*AL I 51.*

5. Man has the right to kill those who would thwart
    these rights.
                " the slaves shall serve."—*AL. II. 58*
    " Love is the law, love under will."—*AL I 57.*

Aleister Crowley

OFFICIAL
DISCORDIAN SOCIETY
HAIL ERIS

Introduction to Israel Regardie's Eye in the Triangle

By Robert Anton Wilson, Ph.D.

I happen to agree with Ernest Hemingway that, of all the requirements a writer needs, the most important is a built-in, cast-iron, shock-proof bullshit-detector.

A writer may have seen and felt a great deal; with extreme good luck, they may even have understood what they saw and felt; but without the tool Hemingway recommended, they will never communicate efficiently.

This is especially true of writers on mysticism, who have produced more bad writing than any other single group on this planet, except for the politicians.

Ezra Pound once commented that there are two types of clarity. The first is illustrated by the sentence, "Get me two pounds of four-inch nails." The second is illustrated by, "Get me the type of Rembrandt I like." Anybody can understand the first kind of clarity; the second is clear only when speaker and hearer share a mutual universe of sensibility; but both are equally LUCID under ideal conditions. Most mystical writing

contains neither type of clarity. Dip into Gopi Krishna or
Ken Wilber, for instance – or into ten dozen like them – and
you will find yourself afloat in an ocean of semantic mush.
Any sentence from such writers could easily be inserted
into a political speech; just change "God" or "True Self" to
"the government" or "the chief executive," and the general
tapioca-like fog will remain the same – vapid, rhetorical,
hollow, but vaguely "inspirational" if you don't think about
it.

All of which is to explain why I originally read *The Eye
in the Triangle*. You see, it was recommended to me by Alan
Watts, who said "It's the best book on mysticism that I've
read in ten years or more."

I had been reading Alan's books for a decade and
had known Alan for almost as long, and my Hemingway
bullshit-detector had not yet found a sentence anywhere in his
works containing BOVINE EXCRETA. If he recommended a
book, I immediately trotted off to buy a copy. He knew what
good writing was, even in the area of mysticism, where the
author is, by definition, trying to unscrew the inscrutable and
eff the ineffable.

I read all through *The Eye in the Triangle* in one evening
and it passed the Hemingway Test with all flags flying and
a band playing on the deck. There was no B.S. in it, no
smog, no greasy rhetoric. It was as lucid as a cookbook or a
five-line objectivist poem by William Carlos Williams.

I have re-read it several times in the last twelve years –
and read it again before writing this introduction – and I still
consider it a masterpiece of exposition in one of the most
difficult areas a writer can confront.

Dr. Regardie not only writes about mystical
consciousness with unparalleled precision, but he has
even succeeded in explaining the unique life and works of
Aleister Crowley – the most difficult, perverse, enigmatic

and generally egregious individual in the whole history of occultism. Like the first books to introduce Einstein or *Finnegans Wake* or Picasso to a general audience, *The Eye in the Triangle* is an intellectual landmark, making accessible to all intelligent persons what had previously been understood only by a few. The reader can turn from this book to any of Crowley's works without being hopelessly baffled by Aleister's paradoxes, his brain-teasing riddles, his (*seemingly!*) childish jokes, and the endless dialectic between the serious things Crowley had to say and the playful way he said them.

Aleister Crowley was, in my opinion, one of the most original and important thinkers of this era – right up there with such titans as Einstein and Joyce. Indeed, what Einstein did for physics and Joyce for the novel (and Picasso for painting, and Pound for poetry, and Wright for architecture), Crowley did for the mystic tradition. He swept aside all 19th Century barnacles and incrustations, redefined every concept, and created something that is totally contemporary with our existence as 20th Century persons.

The major intellectual discovery of our age is Relativity; that is why the general public, with intuitive accuracy, always classifies Einstein as the archetype of modern genius. But at the same time Albert was formulating the mathematics of Special and General Relativity, the same principle was – synchronistically and inevitably – being discovered/created in a dozen other fields. Anthropologists were beginning to recognize *cultural relativism*, which was a kind of Copernican Revolution of the sensibility, as it became clear that the typical reality-tunnel of Western Christian Civilization was not the only valid way to sense the Universe around us. It was from an exhibit of African art assembled by anthropologist Leo Frobenius that Picasso first saw the possibilities of organizing visual space in non-Western ways; and Frobenius also influenced the structure of Ezra Pound's *Cantos* and, through that epic, all of the poetry that is distinctly modern.

Freud and Jung were, at the same time, discovering psychological relativism, or, as I prefer to call it, neurological relativism. What any person sees in a room full of people is not just "what is really there" (which is known only to Bishop Berkeley's God) but also what that person's conditioning and complexes bring into the room *as a filter*. We are all galaxies shouting to each other over vast interstellar distances of prejudice; it is a minor miracle that we are able to understand each other even approximately. Korzybski and the General Semanticists, Garfinkle and the Ethnomethodologists, and all psychologists working in perception theory, have made this variety of relativism even more obvious than it was to Freud and Jung. Joyce's *Ulysses* mutated the novel by introducing this relativity into the very structure and style of the narrative; we never see the "real" Dublin of Berkeley's "God" in *Ulysses*: we see the Dublin that impacts on the brain of Stephen, the Dublin that impacts on Mr. Bloom, the Dublin of the barflies in Barney Kiernan's pub, the Dublin of Molly Bloom's sleepy reveries. Each "Dublin" is equally real: that is the essence of the Relativity Revolution.

Aleister Crowley discovered/experienced all these relativistic reorientations in his life and expressed them in his works; thus, he is the first truly 20th Century mystic. Crowley was reared in a Fundamentalist Protestant sect, trained in Ceremonial Magic by the Rosicrucian order of the Golden Dawn, learned Buddhist and Hindu yogas in Ceylon, climbed mountains for excitement, and lived often amid the *avant-garde* artistic clique in Paris (among other things, Crowley was an early champion of Rodin's late, experimental sculpture). He also studied I Ching and Taoism, experienced something of Sufism in North Africa, and was vividly aware of Freud, Jung, Einstein and modern mathematics. He not only learned to quantum-jump from one reality-tunnel to another, but developed, out of traditional "magical" practices, his own techniques for making such jumps quick and efficient.

One of his cruder exercizes, which all could profit from, was to adopt two "opposite" personalities, such as a vegetarian pacifist and chauvinistic militarist, key each one to a different piece of jewelry (a talisman or ring) and change his verbal opinions, his outer behavior, and his (more subtle) inner responses, depending on which piece of jewelry he was wearing. It sounds childishly simple, but the results are profound. Even physicists and anthropologists, who understand relativity better than most, could understand it more deeply if they tried this exercize a few times.

Crowley tried, like all mystics, to abolish the ego. As Dr. Regardie makes clear, he did not succeed in any total sense; but those not blinded by hero-worship can easily see that this is true of many other Illuminated and Enlightened beings. (The phrase *prima donna* was coined in opera, and quickly adapted in the other arts, but nobody deserves it more than certain Gurus and Sages now at large in the Republic). The ego has a seemingly infinite phalanx of strategies for sneaking back each time it seems to be demolished. Crowley was always eccentric, often outrageous on principle, and sometimes downright vicious, but he is unique among the Illuminati in not trying to conceal such traits but, rather, in making every possible effort to ensure that disciples would never be able to sentimentally sanctify him.

"There is no sense in trying to whitewash Crowley's reputation," I was once told by Caliph Hymeneus Alpha of the Ordo Templi Orientis (a magical society once headed by Crowley), "Aleister spent most his life systematically blackening it."

It is a fitting part of the O.T.O. tradition that the last time I saw the Caliph giving a public lecture, he was so pie-eyed drunk as to be nearly incoherent. Crowley would have been proud of him; but I also thought of the time I saw a Sufi Murshid deliberately *light a cigarette!* at a Holistic Health Conference – and of the "scandalous behaviors" of Gurdjieff. and the "blasphemies" of the Zen Masters.

What is behind Crowley's perversities involves that perennial problem of mysticism – the necessity and the near-impossibility of abolishing the ego. The ego is not "evil;" it is an evolutionary necessity. Unfortunately, it is also very limiting: it restricts consciousness and freedom at just those points where the mystic wishes to increase consciousness and expand freedom. Crowley tackled this problem with his usual heroic and foolhardy Total Commitment. He pushed the techniques of ceremonial magic far beyond the point most occultists dare to go; he became expert at a dozen or so varieties of Hindu and Buddhist yoga; he wrote reams and reams of "inspired" poetry – *literally* inspired by Dionysus (booze) in many cases – to let his unconscious gush forth; he invented many tricks like the two personalities-keyed- to-jewels mentioned before; and he experimented with more drugs more frequently than anybody in the West before the Neurological Revolution of the 1960s.

I have no doubt that Crowley got outside the normal constrictions of ego – way outside – many, many times. I accept the reports in his diaries that he learned to achieve *dhyana* (the trance of unity) fairly regularly and easily, and occasionally got beyond even that to *Samadhi* (the state, known only to advanced Oriental adepts and students of quantum physics, where it makes sense to say that existence and non-existence are the same). Meanwhile, he developed and nurtured a hierarchy of separate selves, each with its own functions and levels of awareness; Dr. Regardie is especially helpful in distinguishing these separate entities and explaining which of them were responsible for which of the books and behaviors that emanated from the physical body called "Aleister Crowley."

Meanwhile, the primordial Crowley ego lurked deep in the imprinted brain circuits and crept back at every opportunity. Aleister played games with it, at times; indulged it when he was in the mood; and had a dozen gimmicks to get rid of it (temporarily) whenever he needed more consciousness and more freedom than an ego allows. An undated note by Nietzsche says:

> The task? To see things as they are. The means: to look through hundreds of eyes, across many peoples.*

~•~

* Quoted from *The New Nietzsche,* ed. by David Allison, MIT Press, 1985.

~•~

Every great artist attempts this; it is the goal of mysticism. It is the only way to escape the constricted, mechanical and ultimately stupid limitations of the primate ego. Crowley succeeded well enough and often enough to rank among the giants of our century, and he expressed what he had learned in terms of the Relativism which every educated person these days must accept. His wonderfully funny but often unfair diatribes against the great mystics of the generation before him, or those of his own generation who had not yet grasped Relativity, are over-stated, yes; but no more so than the polemics that were going on at the same time between the modernists in dozens of other fields and those who were trying to preserve the obsolete Victorian worldview.

Read Ezra Pound fulminating against those who wanted modern poems to sound like Victorian poems; or Frank

Lloyd Wright howling against those who wanted modern buildings to look like Renaissance buildings; or Count Alfred Korzybski denouncing those who are trying to preserve Aristotelian logic in a non-Aristotelian scientific age; and you will begin to understand Crowley's invectives against those spiritual traditions that did not understand that we have entered a New Aeon.

DO WHAT THOU WILT SHALL BE THE WHOLE OF THE LAW – the most "infamous," the most (deliberately) shocking, and the most often misunderstood of Crowley's axioms – is his way of placing Relativity at the heart of his system. We all have a hierarchy of selves, whether or not we are as conscious of this as Crowley and whether or not we develop each of them as he did. Out of this hierarchy a "resolution of forces" (as it would be called in physics) can emerge, if one is true to one's total psyche and does not tailor everything to the tyranny of the socially conditioned mechanical ego. This one force that is resultant of all inner selves is the True Will, in Crowley's sense. One can never go wrong by following it, even though it is different for each person. These differences are given by evolution, as Crowley knew, and cannot be permanently crushed by any kind of tyranny, of the Church, or the State, or of that herd of contented COWS who define "acceptable taste." If nature wanted us to be replicable units, we'd be ants, not primates. That is the meaning of Crowley's second favorite slogan, *EVERY MAN AND EVERY WOMAN IS A STAR.*

Crowley was always true to that inner "governor" – that hidden star in every human psyche – and followed it without flinching. It made him always the funniest, sometimes the brightest and occasionally the most abominable man of his generation. Equal fidelity to the True Will can make one person a great chef, a second a mediocre but happy accountant, a third a genius in music; genetics (and darker aspects of destiny) along with social conditioning, make up the forces that average-out to True Will.

As the great Sufi teacher, Hazrat Inayat Khan writes:

"However unhappy a man may be, the moment he knows the purpose of his life a switch is turned and the light is on . . . If he has to strive after that purpose all his life, he does not mind so long as he knows what the purpose is. Ten such people have much greater power than a thousand people working from morning till evening not knowing the purpose of their life."*

~•~

* *Mastery Through Accomplishment,* Sufi Order Publications, New Lebanon, N.Y., 1971. Revised 1985, Omega Publications.

~•~

This is Crowley's doctrine of the True Will, and it is why he claimed his system would produce "geniuses." A genius is simply a person who has found his or her purpose (True Will) and is no longer swept about by every wind of circumstance.

To conclude, I would like to give an example of Crowley's "obscurity." which is also an instance of his astonishing humor, and explains a great deal that still puzzles people who have studied his work for years and still can't understand him as a man. I refer to a verse in *The Book of Lies* (falsely so called), Chapter 70, paragraph 6, "But FRATER PERDURABO is nothing but an EYE; what eye none knoweth." Frater Perdurabo is Crowley himself, or at least the Crowley who wrote *The Book of Lies*. But what eye? Crowley's official commentary is unhelpful: "Paragraph 6 states a fact unsuited to the grade of any reader of this book."

However, if one is persistent, one eventually finds elsewhere in the book that all the eye symbols refer to the Eye of Hoor and one is advised to seek further light in Crowley's *Liber 777*. Hunting through that complex of

Qabalistic tables, the mystery is finally solved. The Eye of Hoor, among other things, means the anus.

The fact that was unsuited to the grade of any reader, but which Crowley was careful to put on record for the discerning and persistent student, is that he knew he was an asshole. (Of course, there is even a deeper, alchemical joke here, but I leave something to the reader's own efforts).

Robert Anton Wilson
San Francisco
March 1982

~~~~~~

Introduction to Regardie's *Eye in the Triangle*
Falcon Press, 1982

FOREWORD TO
SCOTT MICHAELSEN'S
PORTABLE DARKNESS

Everyone knows the sinister story of how Aleister Crowley and his son, MacAleister, went one dark night into a hotel room in Paris and howled within a magic triangle the nameless names that invoked the Devil. The results, we are told, were eldritch and abominable, as the late great H. P. Lovecraft would say. MacAleister was found dead . . . of a heart attack . . . in the dawn's ghastly light, and Aleister himself was off his skull and had to spend six months in a French mental hospital before he partially recovered. But he was a broken man from that time, a pale shadow of his former self, a walking zombie.

This is an entirely typical Crowley story – the kind of horror movie stuff that sensational tabloids have been printing about the Great Beast now for decades. I have seen the story in print dozens of times, in books as well as in schlock papers and magazines. Also typical of the Crowley legend is that, to anybody of ordinary skepticism and commonsense, this yarn is hardly credible, for a variety of reasons:

1. It was first published in a novel – a work of *fiction* – by Dennis Wheatley, a writer of sensational thrillers.

2. Crowley's life has been extensively researched by six biographers, four hostile and two friendly, and none have found any record of this invocation or of his spending six months in a French nuthouse.

3. There is no indication that Crowley's son, MacAleister, died of a heart attack.

4. There is no record that Crowley's son, MacAleister, took any interest in his father's Magick – or ever did anything in his whole life, except appear in this wild yarn.

5. Crowley never even had a son named MacAleister.

If I had enough space, I could regale you with a hundred similar Crowley stories that have made him the most infamous sorcerer of the twentieth century – all of which are also total works of fiction. P. R. Stephensen in 1931 said Crowley had been the victim of "a campaign of vilification without parallel in the history of English literature." The vilification has not ceased in the forty-two years since Aleister was cremated and his ashes scattered over the state of New Jersey. Even Uncle Al's funeral was an occasion for renewed slander. One continually reads that his last rites consisted of a Black Mass and a reading of a poem on Pan that he had written. The poem part is accurate. The mass was a Gnostic Catholic mass, and had no more in common with a real Black Mass than a dancing hippopotamus has in common with a three-car highway collision. What did Crowley do to inspire so much hostility? Well, he had a sense of humor similar to that of the Monty Python group many decades before such surrealist satire became fashionable. He obviously was a sincere mystic of some sort but also violently and blatantly opposed organized Christianity (some fundamentalists, and some who do not admit to being fundamentalists, can only understand nonorthodox mystics as agents of the Devil). Uncle Al also had a burning hatred for all forms of hypocrisy and (seemingly) a real dread that his "followers" would try to turn him into a plaster saint after his death. For those reasons, and because he liked to annoy the puritans, he took great pains to see that none of his vices and human foibles were concealed from anyone. When he and his first wife, Rose, divorced (because he would not tolerate her alcoholism any longer), he arranged with her that she would sue him for adultery – not merely a gallant gesture, but a way of ensuring that at least one of his "sins" would be on the legal records forever so that his disciples could never deny it. His one major fear in old age was that "Crowleyanity" would some day supplant Christianity: He protested so violently against that possibility that none of his admirers call themselves Crowleyans (they use the word *Thelemites* – a word from his *Liber AL*, coined from the Greek, that carries connotations of both Magick and Will.) They also never refer to him as Lord or Master or Saviour or Prophet or anything of that sort. Generally, they call him Uncle Al, as I do.

Perhaps the quickest introduction to the real Aleister Crowley is a bit of his verse:

By all sorts of monkey tricks
They make my name mean 666;
Well, I will deserve it if I can:
It is the number of a Man.

Fully trained in Western Gnostic mysticism, in Sufism, and in such Asian systems as Buddhism, Taoism, and Tantric Hinduism, Crowley knew more about altered states of consciousness than any European of his time. But he was also trained in organic chemistry and had a skeptical streak that prevented his embracing any metaphysical theory literally (although he could use a dozen metaphysical systems metaphorically). Another bit of his verse makes this clear:

We place no reliance
On Virgin or Pigeon:
Our method is Science,
Our aim is Religion.

Despite his official role as the Beast 666, Uncle
Al could even appreciate the inner meaning of mystical
Christianity. I learned this directly by performing his
Lesser Ritual of the Hexagram (a combination of Christian
and Egyptian invocations, and one of the most powerful
consciousness-altering techniques I know), which gave me
an entirely new and fresh insight into the central Christian
symbolism of Crucifixion and Resurrection. Yet to understand
the original inner truth of Christianity – its gnosis – was not,
in Crowley's mind, any justification for tolerating the vulgar
"Christianity" of the churches – which was denounced as
"Crosstianity," a cult of masochism, by Bernard Shaw and
similarly scorned by every intelligent philosopher for the last
three centuries.

So, to the extent that an adept of the gnosis seemed
like the Antichrist to fools, Crowley was amused to play the
role and pull their legs endlessly. After all, A. C., his chosen
initials, are the initials of Antichrist, and Edward Alexander
Crowley (his real name) can be equated to 666, with a little
cheating. "It is the number of a Man," and he set out to be
a Man to the fullest possible extent. I am reminded of the
Buddha, who was once asked, "Are you a god?" "No," he
replied. "Well, are you a saint?" "No." "Well, what are you?"
"I am awake."

Crowley was never a god or a saint (and never let
anyone think for a moment that he might be either), but he
was awake – to a terrifying extent. Whenever I think of the
sheer information content of a typical page of Crowley –
defining information in the strict mathematical sense as dense

unpredictability – I remember Carl Jung's initial response to Joyce's *Finnegans Wake*. "This is either mental illness," Jung said, "or a degree of mental health inconceivable to most people." You have not fathomed all that is going on in a Crowley poem or in a single prose sentence by him until you have a similar reaction. The great Zen koan Crowley has buried in all his writings, for those who can see deeply into them, is precisely that: Which is it – lunacy or the highest sanity possible to a human being?

Scott Michaelsen answers that question, in his own way, in the marvelous commentaries he has interspersed in this anthology. I will give you a parable and a hint. I once knew a real live Zen master from Japan. As I got to know him, it gradually appeared to me that he had not one personality, but three. When "on the job" as Zen master (*Roshi*) he was absolutely a master, in the sense the most superstitious and naive will give to that term. When off duty, he was simply a kindly old Japanese gentleman, a bit eccentric but perfectly courteous at all times. When wandering in the woods alone— where I sometimes encountered him – he was the brightest and most curious monkey I ever saw. Later, I got to know him better and discovered that he had not three personalities, but about three dozen. At least! Aleister Crowley, as I have learned to know him through his writings, through six biographies, and through conversations with some who knew him, was arrogant, acrimonious, agnostic, atheistic, admirable, baffling, bawdy, bisexual, bombastic, benign, clownish, cosmopolitan, chauvinistic, churlish, confusing, cuckoo, cacodoxical, commonsensical, cynical, demoniac, delightful, duplicitous, earthy, esthetic, egotistical, funny, forgiving, forbearing, gross, God-intoxicated, humble, hardworking, honest, intellectual, intolerant, juvenile, kindly, lovable, loathsome, long-suffering, monstrous, mystical, nihilistic, orgulous, poetic, pantheistic, petulant, quarrelsome, queer, rascally, romantic, scholarly, skeptical, tender, tolerant, underhanded, vile, vindictive, whimsical, xenophobic, yeomanly, and uncommonly zealous.

Uncle Al was also one of the great mountain climbers of all time, and wrote about thirty volumes of widely varied poetry (mystical, erotic, romantic, and sometimes hilarious). His capacity for hard work and dedication are awesomely documented in Israel Regardie's *The Eye in the Triangle*, but he called himself "the laziest man in the world." He wrote detective stories and pornography as sidelines and served British intelligence in World War II. He was a great chess player.

A single ego is an absurdly narrow vantage point from which to view the world, he once explained. Who has ears, let him hear.

Actually, you already know Aleister Crowley, for he is part of you. You are as multiselved, polysexual, and chaotic as he was for eight hours out of every twenty-four – one third of your whole life. Unfortunately, you have probably not learned to take that side of your Self seriously, as Crowley did. As one Zen master said, "There is nothing special about illumination. You do it every night in your sleep. Zen is just a trick for doing it while awake." This anthology of Crowley gives you a few hundred other tricks for doing it while awake. It is worth your attention if you have any ambition to become more than just another robot in the great machine of modern society. Blake described that machine as a Dark Satanic Mill. Philip K. Dick decided it was the Empire's Black Iron Prison. Gurdjieff called it sleepwalking. Alan Watts described it as a cultural madness in which we eat the menu and ignore the meal. Other mystics have called it maya, delusion, literalism, or a kind of hypnosis in which you stare at a map until it becomes the territory and you spend aeons wandering in the map's valleys and hills without ever finding your way back to the non-map world again.

Crowley once said that the giant Death Machine could equally well be named the Abyss or Hell or consciousness, and that it was governed by the Lord of Hallucinations, whose battle cry and mantra is "Truth! Truth! Truth!"

If you want to escape from Truth (and Falsity) – or from Good (and Evil), or from any of the other traps created by the Lord of Hallucinations – turn the page and start reading.

I must warn you, however, that the Attorney General has determined that these pages may be hazardous to your Dogma.

– Robert Anton Wilson

Foreword to Michaelsen's *Portable Darkness*
Harmony Press (1st ed, 1989), Sunvision Press (2nd ed)

THE HIDDEN HERITAGE

Foreword to Charles Kripp's
Astrology, Aleister, & Aeon

I believe in one secret and ineffable LORD, and in one
Star in the company of Stars of whose fire we are created,
and to which we shall return; and in one Father of Life,
Mystery of Mystery, in His name CHAOS . . .

> *– Gnostic Catholic Mass*, by Aleister Crowley

Something Wicked This Way Comes

When I first heard of Aleister Crowley, in some 1950s
tabloid, they called him "the Wickedest Man in the World."
I wondered what Crowley had done to deserve that title in
a century overcrowded with such strong rivals as Hitler,
Stalin, Mao, Mussolini, and the galoot who makes up the
IRS forms. I therefore read the article avidly. To my intense
disappointment, I found that Crowley's "wickedness"
consisted merely of having unconventional ideas and leading
an unconventional sex life. I forgot about him. Lots of other
people had unconventional ideas and/or led unconventional

sex lives (e.g., Oscar Wilde, Ludwig Wittgenstein, James Joyce, D.H. Lawrence, Charles Fort, Wilhelm Reich, Ezra Pound, President John F. Kennedy, President Bill Clinton et al.).

Around 1970, Alan Watts recommended a book to me, called *The Eye in the Triangle* by Dr. Israel Regardie. Alan was almost a guru to me in those days, so I rushed out and bought the book that very day. To my astonishment, it was about the "wicked" Aleister Crowley and revealed that he was even more egregious, and a hell of a lot more interesting, than tabloid journalism had suggested. The title of the book, however, was never explained therein and I was left wondering what the hell Crowley had to do with the Great Seal of the United States . . . (I still wonder about that).

Since then, I have read virtually all of Uncle Aleister's books and about a dozen other biographies or "interpretations" of him, and have even written introductions to three books about him, including a new printing of Regardie's *The Eye in the Triangle*.

As a result of this 28 years of study I know a great deal more about The Wickedest Man In The World and understand a great deal less. I learned, for instance, that he was a Bishop of the Gnostic Catholic Church, an author of reams of poetry (some of it excellent), a member of the now-forgotten Carlist conspiracy (which attempted to replace Queen Victoria with a surviving member of the Stuart dynasty), a mountain climber of great accomplishment, a devilishly clever prankster and practical joker, an early recruit to the Irish Republican Army, an intelligence agent for both England and Germany in World War I, and a man who, either out of perverse humor or for even stranger reasons, did as much as his most hostile critics to blacken his own reputation.

To prepare you for what you will encounter in the body of this text, let me offer a different perspective on the very gnomic, very mysterious, and actually very funny man who has become, to more and more people, the Magus of the New Aeon.

On the exoteric level, Aleister Crowley was raised in the Plymouth Brethren, a Christian Fundamentalist sect of very puritanical orientation. He once described that early training as "A Boyhood in Hell." After attaining the age of reason and rejecting all superstitions of that ilk, he majored in organic chemistry at Cambridge, which lingered in his mind for life and provided the impetus to his efforts to synthesize the insights of mysticism and the methods of modern science. "Thank God I'm an atheist," he once wrote piously – and that's not anywhere near the peaks of paradox he employed to both reveal and conceal the meanings of his very hermetic books.

On the more esoteric level, Crowley joined several very secretive secret societies, and all of them influenced his own unique visionary experiences. To look into these groups, even briefly, will give us some insight into why this man Crowley remains a mystery inside a puzzle within a controversy cloaked in uncertainty.

Hold onto to your hats. We are about to plunge into matters about which no two academic historians agree totally, and non-academic theorists who go fishing here generally accuse each other of being fools, charlatans or crackpots.

To begin with, Aleister was a Freemason. He belonged to the Ancient and Accepted Craft. He held the 33rd degree in the Scotch Rite, among other titles. What the deuce does that mean, really? What distinguishes the Freemasons from the Lions, the Oddfellows or the Elks? Why has masonry appeared so conspicuously in so many right-wing conspiracy theories?

The Ancient and Accepted Craft

The symbols of the Craft of Freemasonry, the square and compass, symbolize the rationality of the universe, as a work of Great Craft and G simply abbreviates the usual English name of that master builder, God, also known to masons as GAOTU, the Great Architect of the Universe.

Freemasonry has an extremely obscure history. Depending on which "authority" you believe, it either originated in the Garden of Eden, taught to Adam by God Himself . . . or else among the priests of ancient Egypt . . . or perhaps the builders of Solomon's temple . . . or possibly in the 14th century . . . or maybe the 17th. It certainly existed by the early 18th Century, where we read of such competing masonic traditions as the Grand Orient Lodge of Egyptian Freemasonry, the Strict Observance lodge, the Grand United Lodge of England, the Grand Orange Lodge of Ireland etc. As Ambrose Bierce wrote in *The Devil's Dictionary*:

> Freemasons, n. An order with secret rites, grotesque ceremonies and fantastic costumes, which, originating

in the reign of Charles II among working artisans in London, has been joined successively by the dead of past centuries in unbroken retrogression until now it embraces all the generations of man on the hither side of Adam and is drumming up distinguished recruits among the pre-Creational inhabitants of Chaos and the Formless Void.

Or as a popular witticism puts it:
How many masons does it take to change a light bulb? That's a Craft secret.

To look at masonry in some kind of perspective we must remember that many tribal peoples have both all-male and all-female secret societies, which help maintain the "cultural values" – i.e., the local reality-tunnel. Freemasonry is certainly the largest, quite probably the oldest and still the most controversial of the all-male secret societies surviving in our world, and that is about all we can say about it for sure or for certain. No two scholars can even agree on how old it is, much less on how "good" or "evil" it is. (See *Born In Blood* by John J. Robinson, Evans & Company, New York, 1989, for one book tracing it back to the Knights Templar, an allegedly Christian order, allegedly heretical, destroyed or almost destroyed by the Holy Inquisition early in the 14th Century; masonic works of the last century traced it back much, much further, inspiring Bierce's sarcasm above.)

Although masonry is often denounced as either a political or religious "conspiracy," freemasons are forbidden to discuss either politics or religion within the lodge. Gary Dryfoos of Massachusetts Institute of Technology, who maintains the best masonic site on the World Wide Web:

https://web.archive.org/web/20200214035213/
https://web.mit.edu/dryfoo/Masonry/

always stresses these points and also offers personal testimony that after many years as a mason,* including high ranks, he has not yet been asked to engage in pagan or Satanic rituals or to plot for or against any political party. The only values taught in all masonic lodges, Dryfoos and other masons say, are charity, tolerance and brotherhood.

~•~

* Both "freemason" and "mason" are correct usages. Members often refer to masonic mysteries simply as "the Craft."

~•~

The more rabid Anti-masons, of course, dismiss such testimony as flat lies.

The enemies of masonry, who are usually Roman Catholics or Fundamentalist Protestants, insist that the rites of the order contain "pagan" elements. This is probably true, but only to the extent that these religions themselves contain "pagan" elements, e.g., the Yule festival, the Spring Equinox festival, the dead-and-resurrected martyr (Jesus, allegedly historical, to Christians; Hiram, admittedly allegorical, to Masons.) All these and many other elements in Christianity and masonry have a long prehistory in paganism, as documented in the 12 volumes of Frazer's *Golden Bough*, which argues at length that everything we call "religion," whether "higher" (like our own) or "primitive" (not like our own) derives from worship of sexuality and from associated rituals to ensure the fertility of nature – human, animal and plant.

For instance, the dead and resurrected god/hero (Jesus, Hiram, Osiris, Dionysus, Attis, John Barleycorn, etc.) represents the death and rebirth of nature each year, which explains why the winter solstice and spring equinox are surrounded by so much associated ritual even today in such "higher" religions (as judged by themselves) as Judaism and Christianity.

Freemasonry, then, seems one of the more rationalistic and less sectarian of the solar-phallic cults. Like its Oriental cousins, Taoism and Buddhism, it almost never remembers its origin in fertility worship.

But Crowley was not just a masonic initiate. He began his search for scientific mysticism with an odd offshoot of freemasonry and Rosicrucianism called the Hermetic Order of the Golden Dawn. (Rosicrucianism? That's another secret society about which those who know the least speak the most and those who know the most speak the least. It either began in ancient Egypt, or in 1414 e.v., or around 1610-1620. The founders were either high priests of Osiris, or friends of Martin Luther – whose coat of arms contained the Rose and Cross after which this order is named – or somebody actually named Christian Rosycross, if you can believe that, or Giordano Bruno* or maybe somebody else. There are now several Rosicrucian orders ahoof on this planet, all of them denouncing the others as frauds).

~•~

* Bruno, burned at the stake by the Papist heresy in 1600, is generally regarded as a martyr to scientific rationalism for espousing the Copernican system of astronomy. Actually, the Inquisition also charged him with 17 other counts of heresy, including the practice of Magick and forming secret societies to oppose the Vatican. Historian Francis Yates believes he was somehow involved in the creation of both Rosicrucianism and Freemasonry.

~•~

Light in Extension

The Hermetic Order of the Golden Dawn, a freemasonic order with heavy Rosicrucian symbolism, possibly came into existence in 1881 due to some combination of mysterious events involving three *freemasons* named S.L. Mathers,

William Wynn Westcott, William Woodman and a mysterious Bavarian woman, Anna Sprengel. Either (1) Westcott found some ciphered papers in Freemason's Hall, London, which put him in touch with Fraulein Sprengel, or (2) he found the papers in a bookstall, or (3) he and Woodman and Mathers made up the whole story or (4) Westcott made it all up alone and deceived Woodman and Mathers.

Or maybe all the above is deliberately misleading legend. Other sources trace the Golden Dawn to (1) the *Loge zur augehenden Morgenrothe*, a Masonic lodge in Frankfurt which established a branch in France called *Aurore naissante* (both titles mean "Rising Dawn") and a branch in London and/or (2) the *Chabrath Zerek Auor Bokher*, or Society of the Shining Light of Dawn, a Cabalistic college in London, founded by one Johannes Falk from Hamburg, Germany.

However created, the Golden Dawn became the most influential occult society of the turn of the century, numbering among its members such influential persons as Irish poet and Nobel laureate William Butler Yeats; fantasy writers Algernon Blackwood and Arthur Machen (who both influenced H.P. Lovecraft); famous actress Florence Farr, who at various times was a mistress of Crowley, of Yeats and even of Bernard Shaw; Arthur Waite, creator of the best-known modern Tarot cards; and Israel Regardie, the psychotherapist and Magician whose book on Crowley first got me involved in these murky matters.

Like ordinary freemasonry, the Golden Dawn had a system of grades, each one marked by an initiatory ritual intended to make a lasting impression on the consciousness of the candidate – to bring him *or her* closer and closer to Illumination in the mystical sense. (Unlike mainstream masonry, the Golden Dawn included women as well as men.) This was combined with profound study of Christian Cabala, a derivative of the original Jewish Cabala, a science or art influential occult society which provides a religious language and numerology to discuss and clarify various altered states of consciousness.

The influence of the Golden Dawn extended far beyond conventional occultism. Much of modern literary culture owes its symbolism and themes to this group; not only Yeats' poetry, but even that of Ezra Pound and T.S. Eliot, and the novels of James Joyce, show Golden Dawn elements, which were common currency in the London of 1900-1914, where all these writers met. Modern horror fiction is replete with themes Lovecraft acquired at second hand from Blackwood and Machen. Bernard Shaw's *Back to Methuselah* owes much to syncretic Golden Dawn ideas he probably learned from Florence Farr, as does his synthesis of the Salvation Army and Dionysianism in *Major Barbara*. The Tarot deck, virtually forgotten by all but gypsy fortunetellers a century ago, is now widely studied for both mystic and psychological meanings, due to the Waite and Crowley Tarot decks, both based on the Golden Dawn deck.

The Golden Dawn fell into dissension and acrimony in 1898 and has continued to remain disunited. In the late 1980s, when the present author lived in Los Angeles, that city alone rejoiced in three Outer Heads of three Golden Dawns, each claiming to have been appointed by Israel Regardie.

The possible connection of the Golden Dawn with the shadowy Anna Sprengel of Bavaria brings up the spectre of the Bavarian Illuminati, the most colorful of all secret societies and a perpetual source of conspiratorial theorizing by many pious persons. Was Fraulein Sprengel an Illuminatus? I don't know, but after 1914, Crowley began to use the title Epopt of the Illuminati, and his magazine, *The Equinox*, bore the masthead, "The Journal of Scientific Illuminism" . . .

Ignotium per Ignotius

Although the really hard-core conspiracy buffs want to trace it further back, the Illuminati known to most historians was founded on May 1, 1776, in Ingolstadt, Bavaria, by a *freemason* (and former Jesuit) named Adam Weishaupt. According to the *Encyclopedia Britannica*, the Illuminati managed to influence many masonic lodges and gained "a commanding position" in the movement of "republican free thought," i.e., anti-royalist and pro-democratic secularism. They attracted such literary men as Goethe and Herder but the whole movement came to an end when the Illuminati were banned by the Bavarian government in 1785. Or so the *Britannica* claims . . .

Many conspiracy hunters following the decidedly paranoid Abbe Augustin Barruel believe the Illuminati merely regrouped under other front names after 1785 and still continues to the present, although they often disagree as to whether the Illuminati is promoting democracy, communism, fascism, anarchism, Satanism, international banking, or some combination thereof.

According to masonic historian Albert G. Mackey, the Illuminati was very popular and had at least 2000 members in masonic lodges in France, Belgium, Holland, Denmark, Sweden, Poland, Hungary, and Italy. Mackey emphasizes that Baron Knigge, one of the most powerful and active members of the Illuminati, was a devout Christian and would not have worked so hard for the order if its aim had been, as Abbe Barruel and others claim, the abolition of Christianity. He concludes that it exercised no "favorable" or "unfavorable" effect on the history of freemasonry.

On the other hand, the Abbe Barruel linked the Illuminati positively to the Order of Assassins, the Knights Templar (condemned by the Inquisition for sorcery, sodomy and heresy) and a worldwide Jewish plot, an idea which later gave birth to a notorious forgery called *The Protocols of the Learned Elders of Zion*.

Both Daraul's non-hostile *History of Secret Societies* and Nesta Webster's very hostile *World Revolution* document the existence of a revived Illuminati group in Paris in the 1880s; but Daraul regards it as a copy of Weishaupt's original order with no lasting influence, while Webster thinks it was the original order coming out in the open again and heavily influencing the modern labor and socialist movements.

More intriguing and complex was the Order of the Illuminati founded by freemasonic druggist Theodore Reuss in Munich in 1880. This was joined by actor Leopold Engel who founded his own World League of Illuminati in Berlin in 1893.

In 1896 Reuss, Engel and occultist Franz Hartmann co-founded the Theosophical Society of Germany, and in 1901 Engel and Reuss produced or forged a charter giving them authority over the re-established Illuminati of Weishaupt. In 1901, Reuss, Hartmann and metallurgist Karl Kellner founded the Ordo Templi Orientis and appointed William Wynn Westcott – of the *Hermetic Order of the Golden Dawn* – Regent of England.

In or about 1912 Reuss conferred the 9th degree of the Ordo Templi Orientis upon our man Crowley claiming that Crowley already knew the occult secret of that degree. He later appointed Crowley his successor as Outer Head of the order.

In 1934 the Gestapo forcibly suppressed both the Order of the Illuminati and the Ordo Templi Orientis in Germany along with all other freemasonic orders and lodges, and schools of Esperanto to boot. The Ordo Templi Orientis survived elsewhere, but the Illuminati as an occult order only seems to exist in Switzerland at present. (As far as I know . . .)

Crowley includes Adam Weishaupt, the founder of the 18th Century Illuminati, among the Gnostic Saints in his Gnostic Catholic Mass, performed regularly in all Ordo Templi Orientis lodges. But that list includes also such odd birds as King Arthur, Parsifal, Pope Alexander Borgia, John Dee, Goethe, Wagner, Nietzsche, King Ludwig ("the mad") and painter Paul Gauguin . . .

But where did the Ordo Templi Orientis come from?

Ordo Templi Orientis

The Great Seal of the O.T.O.

According to one interpretation, the eye-in-triangle represents God the Father, the dove represents the Holy Spirit descending and the chalice represents the "Holy Grail" or Earth transfigured by the Spirit. Alternately, the eye represents the "eye" of the penis, the dove represents the ejaculation of sperm and the chalice represents the womb: the miracle of creation, on another level. A third interpretation combines both, in a sense: the eye represents the ego of the magician, the dove represents both sperm and soul ejaculating/exploding in orgasm and the chalice represents the "body of Nuit" or the universe into which the soul disappears at the height of Tantric sex magick.

The Ordo Templi Orientis is a freemasonic-style ritualistic occult order which traces itself back to the Knights Templar. Although several groups have claimed to be the real O.T.O., and there were five competing Outer Heads at one time, the U.S. federal courts have ruled that the order represented on the World Wide Web is the "true" O.T.O. and have granted it tax-exempt status as a charitable corporation and religious entity.

The O.T.O. has eleven degrees, the first nine and the eleventh involving freemasonic-style "initiations" in which the candidate is tested and, hopefully, illuminated by deeper insight into the world and his/her/self. The tenth degree represents the Outer Head of the Order, a post currently held by one Hymenaeus Beta.

As we mentioned, Aleister Crowley became an initiate of the O.T.O. in 1912. This happened because he had published a mystic treatise and/or book of dirty jokes titled *The Book of Lies*. The Outer Head at that time, Theodore Reuss (mentioned above for his alleged link to the Illuminati) came to Crowley and said that, since he knew the secret of the 9th degree, he had to accept that rank in the O.T.O. and its attendant obligations. Crowley protested that he knew no such secret but Reuss showed him a copy of *The Book of Lies* and pointed to a chapter which revealed the secret clearly. Crowley looked at his own words and "It instantly flashed upon me. The entire symbolism not only of Free Masonry but of many other traditions blazed upon my spiritual vision . . . I understood that I held in my hands the key to the future progress of humanity." Crowley, of course, does not tell us which chapter contains the secret. You can spend many happy hours, days, maybe even months or years, pouring over that cryptic volume seeking the right chapter and the final secret.

Crowley succeeded Reuss as Outer Head and was succeeded by one Karl Germer who died without appointing a successor, leading to the long struggle among various factions. Charlie Manson once belonged to an alleged Ordo Templi Orientis, but not to the one currently recognized by U.S. courts as a legitimate charitable and religious organization.

We should remember at this point that Aleister Crowley also received training, sometimes briefly and sometimes lasting much longer, in such traditions as Taoism, Buddhism, Hinduism and Sufism; and we should recall his training in organic chemistry. He never abandoned his commitment to "the method of science, the aim of religion."

The Widow's Son

Two recent books that shed some light on all these murky matters deserve some attention at this point – *The Hiram Key* and *The Second Messiah*.* The authors of both books, Knight and Lomas, are both Freemasons and claim that they have received "support and congratulations" from "hundreds" of other masons, although they admit that their research has been greeted with hostile silence by the United

Grand Lodge of England, one of the more conservative masonic bodies.

~•~

* *The Hiram Key* by Christopher Knight and Robert Lomas, Century, 1996; *The Second Messiah* by Christopher Knight and Robert Lomas, Element Books, 1997. Both reissued by Fair Winds Press, 2001

~•~

Basically, Knight and Lomas try to prove that masonry not only dates back to ancient Egypt – as only the most Romantic masons have hitherto claimed – but that it also served as a major influence on "Jerusalem Christianity," the earliest form of the Christian faith, which was persecuted and driven underground when the official Romish Christianity became dominant. Primordial or "Jerusalem" Christianity survived through various "heresies," they say, and became a major force again when rediscovered and accepted as their own secret inner doctrine by the Knights Templar. When the Templars were condemned by the Inquisition, the survivors used various other names until emerging again as Freemasons in the 17th or 18th Centuries.

Parts of this thesis have been argued in other books – the underground survival of primordial Christianity, for instance, appears in the famous *Holy Blood, Holy Grail* by Baigent, Lincoln and Leigh – but Knight and Lomas have put the puzzle together in a more convincing way than any of their precursors.

But what was the original Egyptian "mystery" out of which this underground tradition emerged? Do Knight and Lomas attempt to delve that far back and claim to find a convincing answer?

Indeed they do.

The masonic "myth" of the widow's son, Hiram, who was murdered for refusing to reveal "the mason word," derives from actual events in Egypt, they aver. The "word" is not a "word" but a coded euphemism indicating a secret. (How could a "word" have the magick power implied in the masonic legend?) The secret is this: every new pharaoh, before ascending the throne, had to visit heaven and become accepted among the gods. Only after this other-worldly journey could the pharaoh be accepted by the priests, *and by himself,* as one fit to fulfill the divine, as well as political, functions of kingship, as conceived in those days. This voyage to the highest stars, where the gods live, was accomplished, Knight and Lomas claim, with a ritual employing a "narcotic." When the last pharaoh of the native dynasty refused to reveal the secrets of this ritual to the new Hyskos dynasty, he was killed in the manner of the widow's son. The lost "word" = the details of the Ritual of Illumination and the name of the "narcotic" used.

It seems to me that Knight and Lomas have this last detail wrong, due to their ignorance of psycho-pharmacology. Narcotics do not allow you to walk among the stars and communicate with gods. They kill pain, they numb anxiety, and they knock you unconscious; that's all they do. Almost certainly, the magick potion used in the ritual was not a narcotic but an entheogen – the type of drug also called a psychedelic. Entheogens produce "mystic" and godly experiences, and at least one of them and perhaps two were widely used among the Indo-European peoples from ancient times, *amanita muscaria* definitely and *psylocibin* possibly, both of them members of the "magic mushroom" family.

Data to support this interpretation is now widely available. See especially Pujarich's *The Sacred Mushroom,* Allegro's *The Sacred Mushroom and the Cross,* Wasson's *Soma: Divine Mushroom of Immortality,* Wasson et al., *Persephone's Quest: Entheogens and the Origins of Religion,* McKenna's *Food of the Gods,* LeBarre's *Ghost Dance:*

Origins of Religion, Peter Lamborn Wilson, *Ploughing the Clouds: The Search for Irish Soma,* Robert Anton Wilson, *Sex, Drugs and Magick.*

Crowley claimed, in his *Confessions*, Chapter 72, that he knew the lost mason "word." He had majored in organic chemistry, studied in many mystic traditions, and definitely served an entheogen (mescaline, from the peyote cactus) to the audience at his Rites of Eleusis in London, 1914. He was the one man most likely to have deduced the lost secret before Gordon Wasson "pioneered" the study of magic mushrooms in the 1950s and showed their role in religious history.

All over northern Europe traditional art shows the fairy-people and sorcerers surrounded by mushrooms, usually the "liberty cap" mushroom, now identified as psilocybin, the same used by American shamans for around 4000 years. The Irish Gaelic name for this fabulous fungus is *pookeen*, little god. ("Little fairy" in modern Gaelic, but *pook* is related to *bog*, the Indo-European root for "god.")

"Success is thy proof," says *The Book of the Law* (*Liber Al*), Crowley's holy book. He never openly or explicitly revealed any of the lost secrets he had uncovered, but the lost "word" has gotten out anyway: millions all over the globe now know about the entheogens, where before Aleister Crowley the knowledge scarcely existed outside of tribal shamans, i.e., allegedly "backward" peoples. Despite continued persecution by the conservative religious bodies that control Western governments, the secret of the gods is now known on every street . . .

On the Other Hand

Doubt.
Doubt thyself.
Doubt even that thou doubtest thyself.
Doubt all.
Doubt even if thou doubtest all.

— Aleister Crowley, *The Book of Lies*

Of course, most recent books on Crowley and the O.T.O.
suggest that the lost secret was Tantric sex-yoga.

And a witty Frenchman named Gerard de Sede has
examined most of these mysteries in a book titled *La Race
Fabuleuse* (Editions J'ai Lui, Paris, 1973). M. de Sede
concludes that the real secret is that some ancient Israelis
intermarried with extraterrestrials from Sirius *and their
descendants still walk among us passing as human . . .*

Kenneth Grant, one of the four other Outer Heads of the
Ordo Templi Orientis not recognized by the American courts,
claims that Crowley was in communication with advanced
intellects from Sirius starting in 1904 and continuing.

And Robert Morning Sky, an American Indian student
of linguistics, claims that invaders from Sirius heavily
influenced early human religions and left traces still visible in
surviving god-names.

But then David Wood, in his book *GenIsis*, also claims
that humanity was created by extraterrestrials from Sirius
but adds that the most advanced adepts of all the Mystery
Schools amputate their penises as a sign of total faith. (Uncle
Aleister was obviously not an advanced adept of the Schools
known to Mr. Wood.)

Some mysteries, perhaps, do not allow themselves to

be known in simple either/or logical terms. They remain, forever, a mystery inside a puzzle within a controversy cloaked in uncertainty, revealed to all and yet still strangely concealed . . .

And of these mysteries, Aleister Crowley certainly ranks as the Magus of our Aeon and true prophet of one Star in the company of Stars, Mystery of Mystery, CHAOS . . .

Robert Anton Wilson
October 23, 1998

The Hidden Heritage
Foreword to Charles Kipp's *Astrology, Aleister, & Aeon*
New Falcon Press, 2001

THE LORD OF
FORCE AND FIRE:

A Review of The Law is For All

A physicist named Saul Paul Sirag recently told me a somewhat thought-provoking anecdote about Uri Geller. Saul Paul, who was involved peripherally in the investigation of Geller at Stanford Research Institute, went to see Geller one evening in an expanded-consciousness state. He asked Uri, "While I'm in this state, can I see SPECTRA?"

(SPECTRA, of course, is the alleged extraterrestrial intelligence communicating through Geller.)

"Look into my eyes and wait," said Uri.

Saul Paul looked – and Uri's whole head turned into the head of a hawk.

I draw no moral from this episode and I certainly do not think that it proves anything. Saul Paul, a very skeptical scientist, would certainly howl with rage if anybody claimed such an anecdote is "proof" of anything.

Nonetheless, something is certainly *suggested*, and the unconscious senses a resonance. The suggestion grows more interesting when one learns that Dr. Andrija Pujarich also encountered SPECTRA *in the form of a hawk* while visiting Uri Geller in Israel. Dr. Pujarich's account of these encounters (there were several) is in his book, *Uri*. It is impossible that Saul Paul Sirag's experience was the result of auto-suggestion brought on by reading Pujarich's similar experience. Saul Paul did not read about Pujarich's SPECTRA-hawk until months after his own vision.

Of course, every parapsychological investigation turns up a few similarly bizarre episodes; but scientists do not generally write them up. They are "anecdotal, not statistical, and not under laboratory control," and therefore prove nothing. The trouble is that (as Jung knew) they haunt the people involved, sometime for years, and often key off abrupt "spiritual" or behavioral mutations. Like UFO "contactees" or LSD users, people who've had this type of archetypal encounter often feel that they have been touched by a higher intelligence.

It happened to Aleister Crowley in Cairo in 1904 when "the world was destroyed by fire," as he said later. On the tangible level, Crowley came out of the experience with a book which most people think was written by him but which he always insisted was dictated to him.

The book, *Liber Al vel Legis* or *The Book of the Law,* announces that the Equinox of the Gods has come, that the age of the Dying God, Osiris, is over, and that we are entering the age of Horus, the Hawk-headed Lord of Force and Fire.

Hawk-headed!?

Worse (or better). Horus himself speaks in the last chapter of *Liber Al* and tells us, in no uncertain terms:

> Now let it first be understood that I am a god of War and of Vengeance. I shall deal hardly with them . . .
> I will give you a war-engine . . .
> Sacrifice cattle, little and big: after a child . . .
> Deem not too eagerly to catch the promises; fear not to

undergo the curses. Ye, even ye, know not this meaning
all . . .
I am the Warrior Lord of the Forties: the Eighties cower
before me, & are abased . . .

Even the most resolute skeptic must grant that this is not
bad as prophecy of the twentieth century, for a manuscript
produced in 1904. When one learns further that the book
is full of Cabalistic cryptograms built on the number 93,
one may be more impressed, for the ninety-third element,
plutonium, is the trigger of the mightiest war-engine of
all, the hydrogen bomb. It is not far-fetched to think that
some people, over-given to what the Sufis call "the vice of
literalness" may be following the instruction to "sacrifice
cattle, little and big" in order to prepare for the apotheosis of
the Hawk-headed God in the Eighties.

The Law Is for All is a collection of Crowley's
commentaries on *The Book of the Law*, together with a
long and determinedly commonsense introduction by Dr.
Israel Regardie, certainly the sanest and most scientific of
Crowley's expositors. (I'm not sure it would be accurate to
call him a "disciple.")

Dr. Regardie is most concerned with demonstrating
the extent to which the book was produced by Crowley's
"unconscious," or by an aspect of his unconscious. He is
careful not to deny that some other, more esoteric entity
might have influenced or "inspired" Crowley's unconscious;
but the *tendency* of his interpretation remains "reductionist"
or, at least, psychogenic. He emphatically rejects the
interpretation of Mr. Kenneth Grant, self-declared successor
to Crowley as Outer Head of the Ordo Templi Orientis, who
holds that the book was actually transmitted to Crowley by
an extraterrestrial from the system of the dog star, Sirius.

I have been so presumptuous as to dissent from Dr.

Regardie's emphasis, in correspondence with him. *Both* his view and Grant's are equally true, I suggested: that is, the aspect of Crowley's unconscious through which the book was given to us might be "extraterrestrial," if we accept the thought that *part of the Terran unconscious is itself extraterrestrial.* (The "extraterrestrial unconscious" is described, under that name, in the recent writings of Dr. Kenneth Ring. It also appears, called "the metaphysical circuit," in the neuropsychology of Dr. Timothy Leary, and as the "+3" mental state in the works of Dr. John Lilly. If the DNA itself is of extraterrestrial origin, as suggested by DNA's co-discoverer, Sir Francis Crick, Terran physiology, neurology and psychology would all have latent components of a cosmic, unearthly aspect.)

Dr. Regardie replied to this argument with a sentence only a high adept could write: "All explanations are true simultaneously."

Crowley's own commentary approaches this mystery in typically hermetic and elusive language, defining the communicating entity as "the 'Babe in the Egg of Blue' . . . not merely the God of Silence in a conventional sense. He represents the Higher Self, the Holy Guardian Angel . . . Almost identical symbols are those of the secret God of the Templars, the bisexual Baphomet, and of Zeus Arrhenothelus, equally bisexual, the Father-Mother of All in One Person . . . But the 'small person' of Hindu mysticism, the dwarf insane yet crafty of many legends in many lands, is also this same 'Holy Ghost' or Silent Self of a man, or his Holy Guardian Angel." Is that quite clear, class?

Modern neurology, of course, recognizes a Silent Self, a "bisexual" Higher Self, in a sense. This is associated with the usually silent right lobe of the brain, called the Silent Lobe, which becomes mysteriously active in yogis, LSD-users, persons who score high on ESP tests and (oddly) musicians.

It is associated with the idea of "polymorphous perverse," in the stilted language of Freud and Norman O. Brown; that of "hedonistic," "Tantric" and "rapture-prone," in less Teutonic definitions; "childish" and "playful" in Taoist descriptions; "just like ordinary life, but one foot above the ground" in the famous Zen metaphor; and it is evidently highly active whenever magick (i.e., ESP or PK) is being done.

(Readers interested in more details about the Silent Lobe should consult Robert Ornstein's *The Psychology of Consciousness* and Timothy Leary's *Neurologic.)*

The paradox is that the Silent Lobe is *both* more "spiritual" and more "animalistic" than the usually-dominant left lobe, where our linear-logical processes occur. It *both* turns one on to "subtle" energies ("astral" bodies, "auras" etc.) and also tunes one in to abnormal awareness of one's own body, the bodies of others and our evolutionary (animal) heritage. With the Silent Lobe speaking, one does not need to read Darwin to understand that one is the descendant of three-and-a-half billion years of mammals, reptiles and fish. Indeed, it was almost certainly this Silent Lobe experience which gave Sufis and yogis their marvelous insights into evolutionary process 1,000 or 2,000 years *before* Darwin.

If the cataclysm of Cairo, 1904, was this turning on of the Silent Lobe of Aleister Crowley, his subsequent identification as The Great Beast is no huge mystery. The Great Beast is the end product of evolution, the mind that knows itself to stand midway between animal and divinity, ready to leap from Earth to the stars. Or, to say it another way, the Great Beast is the DNA code become conscious through a human being, the only Earth-creature who thus far can become conscious of it.

Crowley, indeed, points directly to the DNA as the source of his inspiration, using the best language available to him before the work of Crick and Watson. He calls it "the talisman," the secret Lord of Force and Fire within the spermatozoa, and he insists on its immortality: "It stands plain, even to skeptical reason – indeed, most of all to the skeptic – that our talisman, one microscopic serpent of which can build for itself such a house as to rule men's bodies for a generation like Alexander, or their minds for an epoch like Plato, cannot be destroyed or diminished by any conceivable force." In his *Magical Diaries*, the same thought is expressed even more strikingly: "The subconscious mind is aware of its own immortality." The subconscious, the DNA mind, Jung's "collective unconscious," Leary's "neurogenetic archives," – the Great Beast, the Lord of Force and Fire, the "dwarf insane but crafty," Pan, and all of Crowley's other poetic metaphors for the intelligence communicating through him.

The Book of the Law communicates this sexual-evolutionary secret in its very structure. The three chapters are image-glyphs of 0, 1 and 2. Zero, speaking in the first chapter, is Nuit, or Naught, or Night, namely Samadhi, the obliteration of normal consciousness by the DNA-mind: the highest peak of human awareness. One, speaking in the second chapter, is Hadit, the serpent, kundalini, the trance of unity, or *dhyana*, midway between normal consciousness and Samadhi.

Two, speaking (and not speaking) in the third chapter, is the Horus twins: Ra-Hoor-Khuit (the active, or yang, left lobe) and Hoor-Pa-Kraat (the silent, or yin, right lobe): normal, dualistic consciousness.

But, as the similar symbolism of Crowley's *Book of Lies* makes overt, 0 is also the vagina, 1 the penis, and 2 the testicles, and the great magick number 012 is a glyph of coitus. Only when ordinary consciousness explodes in the shock of orgasm does the normal primate, Homo Sapiens, catch a glimpse of the DNA-mind, the Holy Guardian Angel, Shiva Dancing. (The notorious "secret" of the IXth degree of the Ordo Templi Orientis was that the Invocation of the Holy Guardian Angel is most likely to be successful if performed during actual coitus.) That this is already coded into *The Book of the Law*, 1904, and that Crowley only consciously learned the secret from the O.T.O. in 1912, are just other spooky things that happen when the Silent Lobe begins to "speak."

Of course, all of this is quite traditional and ordinary – the trans-time perspectives of the Silent Lobe were well-explored in India and the Near East millennia ago, and even the sex-magick techniques which made Crowley so controversial in his own time are merely a revival of ancient lore, as can be seen in Payne-Knight's *History of the Worship of Priapus* and Thomas Wright's *Worship of the Generative Organs,* two anthropological classics which Crowley always recommended to his students.

What is new, and alarming, about *The Book of the Law*, and most central to Crowley's commentaries, is the Law of Thelema – Do what thou wilt." "[T]hou hast no right but to do thy will." "There is no law beyond Do what thou wilt." Even this is hardly astonishing; it is the way most aristocracies and ruling elites have always acted, while preaching humility and submission to the masses. What is new and what is stressed in the title Dr. Regardie set upon these commentaries is the universalization of this *Herrenmoral. "The Law is for all,"* not just the elite. That is the shocker.

What the book seems to advocate goes beyond Nietzsche's intellectualized Social Darwinism, beyond the philosophical egotism of Max Stirner and Ayn Rand, beyond even the wildest flights of de Sade. It is not necessarily advocating the Hobbesian "war of all against all" (see below) but it is definitely a total, complete, unmitigated renunciation of all morality.

Now, I for one have never found this particularly frightening. It is an open secret, carefully hidden from the young but easily discoverable if one peeks into postgraduate texts on social science, that there is no rational basis for preferring any tribe's morality to any other tribe's morality. All are equally arbitrary, capricious and, at least partially, absurd. The morality of Roman Catholics or Fijians or communists or academic humanists or vegetarians is precisely as sensible, and as silly, as the morality of Confucians or snake-worshippers or Samoans or fascists. People will accept any one of these moralities if they have been conditioned to accept it since childhood, and can immediately see how absurd each taboo-system is if they have not been conditioned to it. To be truly educated, in the twentieth century, is to understand this central fact of anthropology, however one chooses to cope with it.

Of course, few have fully adapted to this shocking revelation (just as few have adapted yet to the 100-year-old Darwinian discovery that we are all mammals.) It is particularly amusing that Marxists and liberal humanists – whose philosophies of dialectical materialism and scientific relativism leave no room at all for absolute morality in the old sense – are still quite indignant whenever their own value-system is violated. Most intellectuals, indeed, recoil from the facts of cultural relativism as vehemently as any hard-shell Baptist; they cling to some traditional morality, usually the one in which they were raised by their parents, as if to say, "If reason leads us to amorality, to hell with reason!" In view of Buchenwald and Hiroshima, Vietnam and Watergate, there is certainly something to be said for that position.

Nonetheless, we can certainly not be very intelligent, and possibly we cannot even be sane, if we refuse to accept what we know is the truth. However fearful we may be, it might be wise to try facing up to a post-relativistic universe and seeing what we can do about living with the facts. This, evidently, is what *The Book of the Law* urges and what Crowley bravely attempted to do in the various commentaries collected in *The Law Is for All*.

In the first place, if there is no absolute morality, mankind yet needs some kind of code to regulate its interactions. (Without rules of the game, we cannot play together, as Alan Watts so charmingly said.) *The Book of the Law* gives us a possible standard for negotiation, a new basis for judgment: the individual will. "[T]hou hast no right but to do thy will. Do this, and no other shall say nay. For pure will, unassuaged of purpose, delivered from the lust of result, is every way perfect."

As Crowley comments, "In practice it is found that those who are willing to fight for their rights are respected, and let alone. The slave-spirit invites oppression." This is a hard doctrine, certainly, but history seems to bear it out. As Robert Heinlein once pointed out, when men fought duels at the slightest affront, there was a much higher standard of courtesy than at present. This is not to invite an elite of alleged supermen to exploit all and sundry, as Nietzsche's system does (or is alleged to do). *"The Law is for all."* If *The Book of the Law* does not check A's mammalian tendency to exploit or abuse B by frightening A with a bogey called Morality, it must certainly check A by encouraging B to defend his turf, "by any means necessary," as Chairman Mao used to say.

And does this mean that all conflicts of interest (or opinion) are to be settled by force, by the mightiest "war-engine"? Here we enter the center of the Crowleyan dialectic and confront the paradox of Thelema. I propose that general acceptance of the Thelemic standard would lead to much less violence, not to more.

Is it possible? Or am I just engaging in complicated sophistry? Let us see.

Outside of Machiavelli and the Klingons on *Star Trek*, one is hard put to name any predators who justified themselves on the blunt grounds, "It is my Will to conquer and exploit you." On the contrary, the most vicious and murderous behavior is virtually always "justified" by some form of tribal morality – spreading the True Religion, or maintaining Racial Purity, or defending National Security, or some such pompous rationalization. *This hypocrisy may be more necessary than we generally realize.* It may be impossible to organize even so small a crime as a lynching without some such moralistic balderdash. Certainly, it is hard to see how you could get a million men into an army, and march them off to a place where they will attempt to kill another million, who will meanwhile be trying to kill them, on the grounds that "It is my will to have a war next Tuesday." It always seems necessary to tell them "That gang over there needs to be punished for its sins" – for being Moslems, or Communists, or something foreign.

Certainly, if everybody who was starting a great enterprise, whether a war or something else, were to announce, "It is my will to start such-and-such a project; come along now, you guys," the natural tendency would be to ask, "Is it my will to go along with this – or would I rather stay where I am and carry out my own will?" Run your eye back over the worst wars, crusades and inquisitions of history, and ask if they could have been organized and carried out among people who accepted the Law of Thelema. It does seem that most of them required a population brainwashed into believing they had a "duty" to obey certain "moral" demands laid upon them by leaders allegedly inspired by God or by history or by some resonant abstraction of that sort.

It is even hard to see how the Law of Thelema,

universally applied, would lead to more homicides on an individual basis than we have at present. It can never be A's true will to see B dead; only false ethical teachings and hypocrisy can make it seem that way to A. If A is a true Thelemite, he will know, long before any homicidal thought can enter his head, that he wants B to cease certain behaviors that oppress or annoy him. If A is a true Thelemite, B will not have to guess that A is harboring such thoughts; B will know in no uncertain terms. As in the days of duello, this can only lead to a higher general standard of courtesy and more consideration all around. People only abuse one another as they do nowadays because they think they can get away with it.

Of course, it still remains that it might be A's will to steal B's car. What of it? As de Sade pointed out in his remorselessly logical way, general acceptance of this philosophy may be the best way to ensure an equitable distribution of property. Some of us – as Max Stirner argued – would certainly find this preferable to the tyranny and bureaucracy of a socialist state.

In terms of personal mental hygiene, Thelemic thinking is undoubtedly healthier than all traditional morality. If you recognize that your latest problem is totally without "moral" significance – for instance, you have a disease which you can't, by the wildest stretch of the imagination, *blame* on anybody – then it's just a question of coping with the situation as best you can. When you finally realize that people are on the same natural evolutionary continuum with bacteria and wild animals, then you can begin to deal with hostile humans the same way you deal with infections or four-legged predators – rationally, without claiming you're "right" or they're "wrong." This discourages cruel fanaticism, and encourages sane horse-trading. It is then that one fully appreciates the great liberation implicit in Crowley's "Do

What Thou Wilt" and becomes free, really free, instead of being an unwilling actor in a soap opera written by the superstitious barbarians who created morality 30,000 years ago. You are also free of anger, hatred and resentment – which are great burdens to drop. They live happiest who have understood and forgiven all.

It is in the sexual area, of course, that Crowley's teachings are most beneficial. Almost all the sexual misery and impotence on this backward planet results from sexual *morality* – except for the small fraction caused by war wounds (and even war may be the result of sexual frustration caused by stupid morality, as Wilhelm Reich argued.) Surely, the aeon-old exploitation of women would have been impossible without morality, as Crowley argues in some of the bitterest and funniest passages in these commentaries. Just as surely, every idiocy that has grafted itself onto the Women's Liberation movement is another form of morality.

It is in the sexual area that we can most clearly see that the main effect of morality has been to make people more cruel and stupid. Read up on the persecution of any sexual minority – the homosexuals, the fetishists or whoever – and you will find it hard to attribute sanity to the human race any longer. Crowley, who sees this with a deadly accuracy, also sees that any minority, if armed with morality and a sense of its own "righteousness," can become as vicious as any majority.

Crowley interprets the Law of Thelema literally, logically, consistently. The gay have the right to be gay; the straight, to be straight; the promiscuous, to be promiscuous; the monogamous, to be monogamous; the virgin, to be virgin. "Do what thou wilt shall be the whole of the Law." It is hard to find another sexual revolutionary who isn't pushing one preferred mode at the expense of the others, and thus bringing in the cruel "old morality" again in a new guise.

But all this is the sociological, surface aspect of *The Book of the Law*. More crucial, as we approach the apotheosis of the eighties, is the growing manifestation of the forces that Crowley either transmitted or created. Just to make a list of Aleister Crowley's major teachings or obsessions, all of them linked to the prophecies in the Book, is to describe the major cultural and intellectual revolutions of our time.

He sought to revive Paganism, as the native Western mystical tradition equivalent to yoga; and the new Paganism is everywhere. He opposed Christianity in general and Christian sexual morality in particular; and Christianity, especially its sexual morality, is everywhere in contemptible decline. He rediscovered the use of psychedelic drugs for consciousness expansion; and these drugs played the major, acknowledged role in the artistic innovations of the sixties and are now playing a major, but unacknowledged, role in the scientific breakthroughs of the seventies. He favored the Tarot and *I Ching* as divinatory methods, and these are the most popular divinations around these days, although the Tarot was practically forgotten in his day and the *I Ching* nearly unknown in the West. He brilliantly anticipated the liberation of women (despite his own ambiguous attitudes on the subject, the result of negative female imprints from his Fundamentalist mother); and the liberation of women is now re-making everything from the sciences to business. He predicted that contact with nonhuman intelligences would soon revolutionize all our thinking; and several sober scientists are now claiming communication with dolphins, with plants, with extraterrestrials and with a variety of "entities" impossible to categorize in our traditional terms.

Crowley also foreshadowed the revolution in epistemology – the decline of Aristotelian logic, the coming of quantum theory, Cantor's transfinite numbers, Godel's proof, relativity, Heisenberg's uncertainty principle, Bohr's complementarity, even Bell's theorem. He predicted repeatedly that the fear of death would cease by the end of the twentieth century, and geneticists are now talking about biological immortality, parapsychologists of survival beyond the body.

All of this is implicit in the symbolism of Crowley's Equinox of the Gods – the change-over from the Aeon of Osiris, the dying God, to the Aeon of Horus, the Lord of Force and Fire who dies not. Remember the explanation of those mysterious hawks associated with Uri Geller (and Dr. Pujarich, although he never mentions Crowley's prophecies, appropriately called the hawk that visited him in Israel "Horus.") The powers that Crowley transmitted and aided are quite clearly more powerful on this planet today than they were when Crowley himself died, in poverty and obscurity, in 1947.

Nobody who wants to understand the mutation occurring among the domesticated primates of Terra can afford to ignore the prophecies and visions, the wit and logic, of *The Law Is for All.*

The Lord Of Force And Fire:
A Review of *The Law is For All*
Gnostica Vol. 5, No. 4 (#40), 1976

Afterword:
Enduring Magical
Biography

By Gregory Arnott

To man I come, the number of
A man my number, Lion of Light;
I am The Beast whose Law is Love.
Love under will, his royal right—
Behold within, and not above,
One star in sight!

> – Sir Aleister Crowley, "One Star In Sight"

A miracle occurred in Upper Egypt in 1945, near
Nag Hammadi, when a couple of farmers discovered an
earthenware vessel of obvious venerability while digging for
fertilizer. Though they feared that the sealed jar might have
contained a djinn, they also suspected it might contain gold,
so they broke the seal. Instead of gold or Robin Williams
as a gaseous vertebrate, they found papyrus manuscripts, a

treasure trove much more akin to a djinn and worth far more than shiny bits of metal. The farmers might have debated the last assertion, but for many centuries before their strike to the seal, scholars and would-be believers had only been able to piece together the tenets of Gnosticism through the parts of their texts preserved by Orthodox Christian writers. This was a flawed methodology, as those writers more often than not assaulted the beliefs of the Gnostics, and their writings were often replete with slanderous lies and misapprehensions. The discovery of this surprisingly well-preserved collection of papyri – now known as the Nag Hammadi Library – would make the long-lost philosophy of Gnosticism, at once sublime and degraded, available to the world and untainted by the scourge of orthodoxy.

Around the same time as the discovery of these manuscripts, across the Mediterranean, Europe and the English Channel, a physically withered old man who had experienced another miracle in Lower Egypt forty-one years earlier was spending his last years in Hastings, England, taking heroin to assuage his asthma/ennui and praying to the sun. His life, like Gnosticism, could be described as simultaneously sublime as well as degraded, and he had spent much of his life as a scourge against orthodoxy. I don't know if he was ever aware of the discovery near Nag Hammadi. He certainly wouldn't have been around to read the translations of the manuscripts, but I am sure he was not aware of another miracle that pertained more specifically to him, emerging across the Atlantic. A thirteen-year-old boy in Brooklyn was, perhaps unknowingly, gearing up for a life of miraculous writing, speculation and anti-orthodoxy. His speculations resulted in a corpus of magical writings that I believe are as valuable as the find at Nag Hammadi. Similar to the effect of the desert happening on the understanding of Gnosticism, this young man would free the commentary on Crowley from the flawed methodology of previous writers whose works were often filled with slanderous lies and misapprehensions, a trend that continues until today.

I don't believe that Robert Anton Wilson, our thirteen-year-old protagonist, was aware of Crowley while they shared physical existence on this planet. However, I imagine that in retrospect, Wilson found it odd that his life overlapped with Crowley's – one emerging as a shoot while the other waned – for while Crowley was physically extant, Wilson was ignorant of this figure who would change his world completely. Indeed, Wilson wouldn't discover Crowley for another twenty-five years, as he approached his fortieth birthday and had already commenced his remarkable career. After this glorious meeting, it was Crowley's influence that imbued some of his most impactful writings with magic and added to his already clearly developed mischievous sense of humor. I hope, for the sake of Wilson, that it is possible to make first contact across time as well as space – both he and Crowley deserve it. What you now hold in your hands is a testament to that possible contact, another Nag Hammadi that didn't languish as long in chthonic obscurity, but is just as valuable.

Crowley has always reminded me of the philosopher de Selby, author of the dense and occasionally gnomic *Golden Hours,* the inscrutable *Country Album* and the sweeping *Codex*, amongst other works. If we read the foremost authority on de Selby, O'Nolan, we quickly learn that de Selby is perhaps best understood under the refractory lenses of his many commentators: reliable, acerbic Le Fournier; Hatchjaw; Bassett; Du Garbandier who might have been the shadowy Kraus; Le Clerque. This collection of minds swirling and sniping in an attempt to probe the infamous opponent of sleep and darkness helps us to better understand the man himself, as we might better understand our appearance when we look into, instead of a single mirror, many different mirrors placed at different angles. So it is with Crowley, who managed to get talked about a lot during his lifetime and achieved the not-insubstantial feat of being talked about long after his Greater Feast. (Of course, de Selby holds that death itself is another of mankind's rank hallucinations.)

Much of the above could indeed be said of any thinker. And yet I think de Selby and Crowley, with their sinister reputations and their surprising earnestness, compare quite nicely, not to mention their ability to glaringly and incisively reveal truths about those who speak of them in their attempts to reconcile the men with their ideas. Wilson found both men fascinating, but, perhaps tellingly, he only handled de Selby in a few of his works, while commenting upon Crowley's ideas, beliefs and practices consistently throughout most of his writing career. For this, we should be grateful; when there are many guides to a subject, some are going to be more knowledgeable than others. This isn't to say that some are more *right* than others, as we all know we should probably avoid that word while dealing with the Commentator at hand, but the best see things that the others do not. Perhaps it is that some commentators are simply more right for a particular reader, or their angle reveals aspects of the person studied that the reader has not considered up until this point. I personally have gathered more from the Hatchjaw-Bassett school of de Selby studies than from the conservative frustration of Le Fournier. I have also gained more from the sometimes credulous, sometimes purposefully misleading, commentary of Wilson upon Crowley than from that of any of The Great Beast's other commentators.

The Poet dubbed Odysseus "the man of many ways," a title that applies just as well to Crowley and Wilson; we are lucky to have one of those rare polymorphs interpret the work and ways of another. For would we love the King of Ithaca if he had been described by any other than Homer? Perhaps, but I think not. So it is with Crowley and Wilson- there have been many writers who tried to divine the essence of Crowley's life, some of whom are probably better sourced due to our linear apprehension of time, but none have ever grasped the spirit of Crowley as well as Wilson. That could be prejudice, as Wilson was and has remained my most trusted source on Crowley's life. I'd like to believe that my credulity towards Wilson's words, which he might have hated, is at least easily understood. Before reading Wilson's *Illuminatus!* and *Cosmic Trigger*, as well as Moore's *Promethea*, I had availed myself of Crowley's *777*, Waite's translations of Eliphas Levi and the writings of Austin Osman Spare – some will recognize how inauspicious of a beginning this would be for an adolescent trying to understand magic. Wilson acted as my Chapman's Homer; he was the one who brought magic and Crowley, often mistaken for a darkling figure, into the light.

This intuitive grasp of Crowley is obvious in the pieces contained in *Lion of Light*: read the relish that Wilson imbues in his writing as he introduces the many opinions of Crowley, or recites his litany of aliases as well as any crier has ever called out the titles of nobility. Wilson, across his essays and articles, reveals Crowley's tricks with the glee of a fellow traveler explaining the previously unnoticed genius of an unappreciated one whose path he has trodden with spirited, expert footsteps. Pay attention to the beginning of the pieces where Wilson adopts his best barker-for-The-Magic-Theater voice and heralds Crowley's many guises. We can also witness the temporal cross-pollination, in the way that Wilson's ambidextrous handling of the bizarrely faceted Great Beast shows us a stage in the development of model agnosticism. Wilson obviously has a deep affection for

Crowley and presents him as a prize within the curio cabinet of ideas and personalities he can introduce to you. For all that Wilson wrote and spoke about Buckminster Fuller, Korzybski, Burroughs, Reich, Lilly or a myriad of physicists and mathematicians, he loved best his totally irrational, totally reasonable Prophet of the New Aeon.

Valuably, Wilson will delight you with examples of Crowley's bawdy and ineffably witty sense of humor. At other points, Wilson astounds with his grasp of what might be deemed magical theory. For example, I believe that Wilson, in *Do What Thou Wilt*, presaged Lionel Snell's four categories of thought when he discusses Crowley's "logical-emotional-magickal-yogic" approach to discerning reality. It is also apparent that Wilson spent a lot of time considering Crowley, and that he loves Crowley for his truths almost as much as he loves him for his lies. He loved Crowley while he wielded his pen-wand to inscribe the words between these covers; it is not a rational agnostic many-personalitied observer who wrote: "The Great Beast is the end product of the evolution, the mind that knows itself to stand midway between animal and divinity ready to leap from Earth to the stars." There is a hagiographic tone in those words, although he is presenting Crowley as an idea in this instance rather than as a mere human, something beyond fascination. But Wilson is by nature inexorably many-personalitied, and elsewhere in the preceding pages he relates Crowley's flaws and contradictions. To Wilson's credit, if we are to remember the latter half of Crowley's greeting and benediction, we know that will must be carried out with love.

Aside from the volume at hand, to completely understand Wilson's relationship with Crowley and his ideas, you must walk further into the funhouse to see the reflections of Crowley that Wilson presents in his dazzling fictions.

Read, or reread; *The Sex Magicians, Illuminatus!, Masks of the Illuminati, Schrödinger's Cat* and *The Historical Illuminatus! Trilogy* to grasp the different ways that Wilson resurrects Crowley. In *The Sex Magicians,* the reader may witness the workings of Crowley's still-extant Church of Scientific Illuminism as they ride the "mama wave". Plus, the novel is full of the enthusiasm that fills *Do What Thou Wilt,* as both seem to have been written during the same halcyon afterglow of first contact that would initiate the sequence of experiments recounted in *Cosmic Trigger.* Crowley's spirit is woven into *Illuminatus!* in a way that it imbues the book with a sinister glory and provides the reader with a valuable practical instruction in magic, as brilliant of a resource as Crowley's *Liber E* or *Liber O*, in "Appendix Lamed." *The Trick Top Hat,* the second volume of *Schrödinger's Cat,* contains the biography of Hugh Crane, a beloved figure to many readers, who embodies Crowley's life as it might have been later in an alternate twentieth century. *The Widow's Son*, aside from containing some of Wilson's most prominent discourse concerning de Selby, is a veritable education in magical theory and practice, one that might have been the cause or cure of Kenneth Noid's madness. (Please read Bobby Campbell's "Avoid The Noid" in *New Trajectories 2020* for more on this intriguing, and tragic, happenstance. Therein read also "Robert Anton Wilson's Quest To Turn On The World" by A Student to better fathom the Crowley-Wilson current.)

But it is in *Masks of the Illuminati* that Wilson pens his best and most manifold depiction of his never-met hero. In this novel we are presented with a brilliant magical Bildungsroman, presided over by an Aleister Crowley who may be the most accurate fictional characterization presented to the public so far. A figure who is implicitly involved with his unknowing-student, Sir John Babcock, who is traumatizingly humorous while also assiduously constructive. The fifth chapter of *Masks* is both Wilson and Crowley at their finest. Some readers will appreciate that as much as Crowley fictionalized himself behind the names "Frater Perdurabo, Frater Ou Mh, To Mega Therion, Count McGregor, Count Vladimir Svareff, Chao Khan, Mahatma Guru Sri Paramahansa Shivaji, Baphomet, and Ipsissimus" he also was fictionalized by others under the names Oliver Haddo, Dr. Trelawny, Karswell, Hjalmar Poelzig, Apuleius Charlton, Mocata, Castevet/Marcato as well as under his what-we-certainly-can't-call-Christian name. And Wilson's depiction emerges as the most captivating and dynamic. There is such a grace in simply being believed to believe what you say, even if you don't live up to it; this is what Wilson gives to Crowley in *Masks*, along with the works herein. Wilson writes in "The Great Beast:" "grok in its fullness this fact: he really did it. You or I might conceive such a jest, but he carried it out" while writing about Crowley's desecration/reconsecration of Oscar Wilde's tomb. Like Crowley in that episode, Wilson is making his chisel mark on the sepulchre of a venerated predecessor.

In *The Widow's Son*, the ancestor of *Masks'* protagonist, another Sir John, stands nervously in the Masonic Hall, nervously wondering if any actual chisel blow will be struck to his breast. Sir John the Elder is of course not struck through the heart but instead realizes that he has been submitted to a psychodrama intended to make a metaphorical mark of enlightenment and determination upon his metaphorical heart. So it is with Wilson, who strikes his graffiti signature upon Crowley's legacy and continues it by striking a mark on the reader. In the finest tradition of what, regrettably and inaccurately, is dubbed the Great White Brotherhood, Wilson continues the process of initiation, bringing as many into the light as possible. There is a dual lesson here; that initiation is a multi-generational process that continues long after our apparent deaths, and that the intersection of fiction and reality is the happening hunting ground of magic.

In *The Encyclopedia of Fantasy* (edited by John Clute and John Grant), Crowley is referred to as "the most flamboyant proponent of Lifestyle Fantasy." I think Wilson, judging from the tone of the essays in *Lion of Light*, would have wryly conceded that the Johns might have a point. I suspect that he would have also believed their assertion might have been more profound than they could have realized. Wilson seems to appreciate Crowley's self-fictionalization and approves of Aleister's sometimes, oftentimes, baffling insistence on living his crooked life on his own crooked terms. Crowley was a rare sort whose brilliance almost oozed out of him at times, taking strange and confusing forms and sometimes shining in the spectrums invisible to the naked eye, easily mistaken for the silhouettes of shadow-boxing; is it mere luck that he had Wilson to bear witness to that scintillating strobe of existence? If we are to believe in magic, or suspect that there might be some sort of pervasive force with an occasionally perverse sense of humor alive in the world, is the word "miracle" too much of a reach?

It would be apropos in the light of Wilson's own philosophy to ask the reader to decide for themselves. Personally, I hope "miracle" isn't too far off the mark; Wilson and Crowley both deserve to be aware that the testament of Contact in this book, penned long after one had left this plane and published a relatively substantial length of time after the passage of the other, has been preserved. As *Wilson's Do What Thou Wilt* is a biographical piece written in preparation of an unrealized longer piece, it does seem appropriate that Martin Wagner's discovery of the manuscript may have been precipitated by a query of Prop Anon's as he was preparing the first full biography of Wilson. Magic seems to be prone to tautological happenstance; recursive thought, the Ouroboros wyrm under another name, is mentioned in Wilson's essays, after all. As a final note on fiction, I would be amiss if I didn't mention that de Selby is a bit of finely crafted fiction. He was an invention of Brian O'Nolan (Ó Nualláin), who is better known as Flann O'Brien – de Selby's best material wasn't even available until after O'Nolan/Ó Nualláin/O'Brien had shuffled off his mortal-coil. For that matter, Aleister Crowley was a fictional creation of Edward Alexander Crowley, a rather peculiar result of his time and space who chose to persist in his folly, with egregious self-reference, until the end.

It should also be noted that at the time an improbable find happened in the Egyptian desert and Crowley was shuffling around Netherwood, Robert Anton Wilson was Robert Edward Wilson. Magic might have been afoot then, and there are still so many stars in sight.

23 RIFFS ON ROBERT ANTON WILSON, ALEISTER CROWLEY, PSYCHEDELICS, INTUITION, AND EVERYDAY METAPHYSICS

By R. Michael Johnson

Intended as a – hopefully amusing – disquisition on Wilson's 50 year-old "lost" manuscript *Do What Thou Wilt*, and on Wilson's reading of Crowley in general:

1.) Mind Stuff: Considered within Robert Anton Wilson's long history of self-experimentation and the attempt to see what his mind could do if pushed far enough (chronicled most famously in *Cosmic Trigger vol. 1: The Final Secret of the Illuminati*), he tells us in the follow-up experiment in autobiography, *Cosmic Trigger vol. 2: Down To Earth*, in a short essay, "Choose Your Hallucinations," (pp.195-198 Hilaritas Press ed.) about his path from "Strict Materialist" and "compulsive Rationalist" to someone who had developed all four aspects of Carl Jung's "self". Jung saw the complete "self" as being the quadrumvirate of Thinking, Sensing, Emotions, and Intuition.

Wilson's early education in mathematics and logic, physics, and other physical sciences, plus an enormous amount of reading in virtually every field of human thought ("I was a monster of erudition", he told early interviewers, and he told another that his early reading was "omnidirectional"), possibly culminating with his discovery of Korzybski's *Science and Sanity* at age 18 in 1950 and work in Engineering, all helped solidify one of Jung's aspects of the "self": "Thinking."

As for the other three aspects, for Jung, of the "functional self" – "sensation", "feeling", and "intuition" – Wilson describes how cannabis helped develop his "sensory-sensual manifold" (Sensation), and how undergoing Reichian therapy helped alleviate the muscular armoring we all have from living in Authoritarian societies and that he "learned to scream and weep again, as I had as a child." (Emotion) He ends the brief essay – some of his best writing about cannabis – with these lines: "I still didn't know what to do to develop Jung's fourth faculty . . . Intuition. That had to wait until I discovered Acid and Aleister Crowley."

2.) As for: what the hell "is" intuition, anyway? When Einstein told an interviewer late in his life, "I believe in intuitions and inspirations . . . I sometimes FEEL that I am right. I do not KNOW that I am right," we all nod. When Swedish filmmaker Ingmar Bergman said, "I throw a spear into the darkness. That is intuition. Then I must send an army into the darkness to find the spear. That is intellect," we *feel* like we know what he's talking about. Then we have Steve

Jobs tell us, "Your time is limited, so don't waste it living someone else's life. Don't be trapped by dogma – which is living with the results of other people's thinking. Don't let the noise of others' opinions drown out your own inner voice. And most important, have the courage to follow your heart and intuition," some of us might feel all charged-up and ready to get going doing our creative work. And yet: these quotes seem to act as *incantations*. They don't tell us what intuition is, how it works, where it resides, etc. (NB: there are some readers who saw "incantations," and remembered: those *work! They work really well!* Those readers should probably put down this book and go Do Your Thing. Best to ya!)

In Jung's 1921 *Psychological Types*, he writes a lot about intuition but even he seems to be at sea trying to tell us what it "is": His first attempt at a definition there appears to be this: "Intuition as the function of unconscious perception is wholly directed upon outer objects in the extraverted attitude." A few of us can gloss this, while some will have a rough time with it. This seems like it fits the sociologist Peter Berger's assessment of Jung. Berger saw Jung's work as part of a movement among thinkers who developed private, subjective interpretive schemes within religious thought. While putatively these are statements about human psychology, they often feel like private, subjective poetic-like statements.

Here's one that seems straightforward to me, but you be the judge: "Intuition appears either in a *subjective* or an *objective* form: the former is perception of unconscious psychic facts whose origin is essentially subjective; the latter is a perception of facts which depend upon subliminal perceptions of the objects and upon the thoughts and feelings occasioned thereby." Yea. I guess I sorta already (maybe?) assumed it was something like that. If some Readers have studied Korzybski's General Semantics, they may see that, when looking for the "referent" with some of these abstractions, it quickly becomes unwieldy, then much of it seems to suddenly vaporize and disappear with an audible POP. Later in his life Jung got together with quantum physicist Wolgang Pauli and tried to pin down intuition and meaning in their acausal connective principle, AKA: synchronicity. For Jung, neuroimaging machines were a long way off.

Let's keep hacking and try another from Jung. Intuition is "by no means a mere perception, or awareness, but an active, creative process that builds into the object just as much as it takes out." Hmmm. Some of us have not cracked the Jung Code just yet. Maybe. He really *does* seem to "know" what this mysterious faculty "Intuition" is, though. Probably the virtuoso Reader of Difficult Texts, Robert Anton Wilson, had a better purchase on Jung's private vocabulary. This seems quite probable, simply due, for example, to RAW's demonstrations, 1970-2007, of readings in mathematics and quantum mechanics, but also deciphering the densities of the private language-codes of such figures as James Joyce (e.g., *Finnegans Wake*), Ezra Pound (e.g., the *Cantos*), and Crowley (e.g., *The Book of Lies*), and numerous other texts that present notorious difficulties for even highly educated readers.

Brain-waves? Inklings? Premonitions? Hunches? Sneaking suspicions? Satori? Educated guesses?

Is intuition really just another word for creativity? Imagination? Insight? Foresight? Instinct? The "A-Ha" experience, or the "lightbulb going off"? Maybe a "gut feeling"? (Since RAW's death researchers have found human gut microbiome-to-brain influences that would have blown his mind, though since the early 1950s he thought of the body as a unity and not in Cartesian "mind-body" ways.

Maybe intuition really does have something to do with a "gut feeling," literally? Similarly, RAW would've been interested in the new "polyvagal theory" of Stephen Porges, methinks. Also: all the latest on the profound significance for human well-being of the endocannabinoid system! The gut microbiome-brain nexus, the polyvagal theory and the endocannabinoid system are all two-way streets from the brain to other parts of the body and back to the brain, and all three systems were virtually unknown in 1973-74, when RAW's *Do What Thou Wilt* was composed.)

What can we actually SAY about intuition that's meaningful, besides, "I knows it when I feels it" or "I grok in its fullness"? Does it matter, does it suffice if we all *seem* to "know" what we're getting at when we talk of our "intuition" regarding a certain space/time event? What might have LSD and Crowley done to help Robert Anton Wilson develop his intuition? What sort of effect does the writer produce in the reader's nervous system when he asks questions that don't seem to have easy answers? Let us see. We'll walk metaphorically around the chiaroscuro periphery of this question, from darkness toward light, hoping to gain some insight.

3.) Getting into Crowley: In *Cosmic Trigger Vol 1*, RAW – as he will be known henceforth – tells us that he had lunch with Alan Watts and his wife in 1970, and Watts told RAW about "the best book I've read in years," a biography of Aleister Crowley by Crowley's ex-secretary, Israel Regardie, titled *Eye In The Triangle*. Because Watts had never given RAW a bum steer, RAW avidly read the book, and then "I'd soon plowed my way through all of Crowley's books still in print and began a correspondence with Dr. Regardie." (*CT1*, pp.65-66 Hilaritas ed.) No mean feat!

Now: if it took LSD and Crowley to help RAW develop his Intuition, we can only guess that the addition of these aspects to his life was a resounding success, because soon after 1970, from 1972-74 he published his first books, at or approaching age 40: a book on forbidden words; one on sex, drugs and magick; a comic novel based on tantric sex magick; and a book on female breasts in history. Then, finally, in 1975, Dell published the counterculture classic trilogy of *Illuminatus!* novels, which had mostly been written between 1968-1971. RAW then published another 30-odd more books until his death in 2007. He'd gotten a mountain of articles in print in various periodicals since 1959, but 1970-71 seems to be something of a watershed moment in his life. Maybe LSD and Crowleyan magick and RAW's onslaught in book-publishing merely coincided, but maybe it had to do with the development of Intuition.

In *Do What Thou Wilt*, his 1974 book on Crowley (herein), RAW is discussing the history of Hippocrates's four humors, Rosicrucians, Sufis and the history of Alchemy – all of which coalesce and become synergetic in Crowley's overall work – and RAW sees the balancing of four-ness in the history of magick as bringing on an "equilibrium", a vital balance which is a theme that runs throughout much of RAW's work. One of the most essential aspects of developing and attaining equilibrium is the "transcendence of the conventional ego": "Crowley has further extended this formula . . . by including in the forces to be balanced, those faculties of the psyche known as intuition, feeling, reason and sensation, and their corresponding methodologies: magick, yoga, logic, and experimental science." Whatever Jung meant by those four faculties of the self/ego, RAW extends Jung via Crowley by denoting a corresponding *method* for personal development. Here Jung's "thinking" would seem to be addressed by logic and experimental science, "feeling" and possibly "sensation" by yoga, while magick would seem to address "intuition," but careful readings of RAW on magick and Crowley – and psychedelics – appear to spill over into development of all four of Jung's aspects of the self, and would largely make up Crowley's "Great Work" of developing all of the faculties to the *nth* degree. But how?

Mutt: Hey man, they just do.

Jute: Not good enough!

4.) In his earlier intensive study of Korzybski's magnum opus, *Science and Sanity* – which he once read in an entire weekend, and, through the years, read many times while stoned on cannabis – RAW would've encountered this passage, early in the book: "Creative scientists know very well from observation of themselves, that all creative work starts as a 'feeling', 'inclination', 'suspicion', 'intuition', 'hunch', or some other un-speakable affective state, which only at a later date, after a sort of nursing, takes the shape of a verbal expression, worked out later in a rationalized, coherent, linguistic scheme called a theory." (p.22, 4th ed.) What Korzybski seems to be getting at here is the origin of creative ideas, the origin of knowledge. *Not* trivial.

Jung, by way of Spinoza, seems to add to this: "Intuitive cognition, therefore, possesses an intrinsic character of certainty and conviction which enabled Spinoza to uphold the '*scientia intuitiva*' as the highest form of cognition." Clearly RAW assumes all creative work is like this: before you've thought about how you're going to approach writing an essay, or solving a problem in physics, *something* comes to you. However, RAW thought intuition could be wrong sometimes and needs to be checked with logic or experimentation. Anyway, let us call all this "intuition" for now, until we enter something more material, perhaps something that weighs around three pounds, has neurons and a colloidal substrate.

In US culture, post-1945, it seems a common assumption that the Arts and Humanities are fueled by intuition or creativity while Sciences are "logical" and use strict methodology. But as Spinoza and Korzybski pointed out, creative/intuitive work is essential in Physics, Chemistry and Biology too. Indeed, Thomas Kuhn thought all sciences developed initially in a pre-paradigm phase in which various thinkers about some unknown phenomena posit likely guesses as to what the hell is going on. At some point there is no consensus on any particular theory. Then, folks start inventing experiments, and gradually, a consensus develops about What The Hell Is Going On, called a paradigm. It's soon taken to be the correct interpretation, and most scientists are merely working to solve a series of puzzles within the paradigm, but as time passes, unsolvable issues begin to pile up, then a younger crew of scientists come up with a better approach that encompasses the old paradigm, accounts for most of the unsolvables, and overthrows the old order, which had become dogmatic and stodgy anyway.

But Kuhn largely misses what someone like Nietzsche thought about early science: "Do you really believe that the sciences would have ever originated and grown if the way had not been prepared by magicians, alchemists, astrologers, and witches whose promises and pretensions first had to create a thirst, a hunger, a taste for hidden and forbidden powers?" (*The Gay Science*, Book 4, aphorism #300) Though this historical link of magic and science is usually hidden in mainstream historical discourse on the sciences, RAW was steeped in these ideas, not only from Nietzsche, but such texts as Frances Yates's *Giordano Bruno and the Hermetic Tradition*, Andrew Dickson White's *The History of the Warfare of Science With Theology in Christendom*, Joseph Needham's multi-volume *Science and Civilisation in Ancient China*, and Lynn Thorndike's *A History of Magic and Experimental Science* (8 vols, 1923-1958). Additionally, around six months after he finished his book on Crowley,

RAW published an article in the neo-pagan magazine *Green Egg* (June 1974), on "The Origins of Magick," and he opens by quoting Will Durant, from *Our Oriental Heritage*, "Magick begins in superstition, and ends in science." To which RAW appends, "*Per contra*, Mr. Durant: magick begins in science, and sometimes degenerates into superstition." RAW was keepin' it 100.

Still, aye: "a taste for hidden and forbidden powers!" If you don't currently have this taste, you might be readin' the wrong book.

As we shall see, both Crowley and RAW find much of vital interest in this intuitive/creative aspect of science and think the tenets of good scientific experimentation ought to be generalized to anyone who has the taste for hidden and forbidden powers. (Or maybe not: Crowley was more aristocratic and elitist: see #7, below.) Or more simply: everyone who seeks to develop themselves to their fullest potencies.

Whatever this faculty of intuition is, it seems of paramount importance. We all want to develop our own intuition, whether we know it or not.

But we still don't know how it works.

5.) Consciousness and instruments: RAW and Leary, taking a page from Alchemy and/or Buddhism, thought scientists using their instruments (microscopes, telescopes, etc.) too often overlooked the most fundamental instrument: the human perceptual systems. And, just as technical apparatuses need to be cleaned and polished, so should scientists "polish their instruments", and RAW and Leary meant: doing yoga, cannabis, and even psychedelics or any other gimmick that at least temporarily erodes that old albatross, the Ego. It seems probable that Crowley was the first to compare human perception enhancement to scientific instruments, at least as far back as 1907, in his writings about hashish. RAW quotes Crowley on "empirical mysticism" and the use of cannabis in relation to scientific knowledge:

"Hashish at least gives proof of a new order of consciousness, and (it seems to me) it is this *prima facie* case that mystics have always needed to make out, and never have made out.

But to-day I claim the hashish phenomena of the first importance; and I demand investigation.

And I assert – more of less *ex cathedra* – that meditation will revolutionize our conception of the universe, just as the microscope has done.

"Then my friend the physiologist remarks: 'But if you disturb the observing faculty with drugs and a special mental training, your results will be invalid.'"

"And I reply: 'But if you disturb the observing faculty with lenses and a special mental training, your results will be invalid.'"

"And he smiles gently: 'Patient experiment will prove to you that the microscope is reliable.'"

"And I smile gently: 'Patient experiment will prove to you that meditation is reliable.'" (See *Sex, Drugs and Magick*, RAW, Hilaritas ed, pp.156-158: RAW points out that the rhetoric of perceptual enhancement with drugs and scientific instruments used by subsequent writers such as Aldous Huxley, John Lilly, and Alan Watts, was prefigured decades earlier by Crowley. As for Crowley demanding "investigation", we now have a number of books on how cannabis can enhance our human potential, and I heartily recommend *Elevated: Cannabis As A Tool For Mind Enhancement*, by Sebastián Marincolo, Hilaritas Press, and *Healing With Cannabis* by Cheryl Pellerin, Skyhorse.)

On polishing the instrument: Because no matter how "objective" the scientist's work, they were still operating from within a critical set of assumptions about their projects.

And some of those assumptions were occluded from their perceptions. From the 1970s to the 2020s, if scientists are doing non-"scientific" things in order to polish/purify/refine their instruments hardly any of them are admitting it. And this, ironically, is due to a set of larger societal assumptions about what is "rational" and "responsible." Nevertheless, if we read widely in the physical sciences, we will find many anecdotes about great scientists polishing their instruments. Nobel physicist Richard Feynman smoked cannabis and spent time in isolation tanks. Neuroscientist Christof Koch talked openly about the profound effect a flotation tank had on him. Co-discoverer of the structure of DNA, Francis Crick, according to Matt Ridley's *Francis Crick: Discoverer of the Genetic Code*, smoked cannabis and did LSD (although it seems dubious, he had LSD in 1953 to help him discern the structure of DNA). The neurologist Oliver Sacks tried and enjoyed many mind-expanding drugs. Nobelist Kary Mullis, who discovered a major improvement in the technique of obtaining the polymerase chain reaction, credited LSD for the initial insight. Etc. (Probably many other lesser-known scientists are staying mum about their altered states, because of a lingering general taboo.) The philosopher and neuroscientist Susan Blackmore agrees with Leary and RAW and sees the purification of the main instrument as an idea taken from Alchemy, and she echoes Aldous Huxley's metaphor of consciousness as a "reducing valve", an idea Huxley probably got from Henri Bergson. (*Cannabis: Philosophy For Everyone*, ed. Jacquette, p.39)

RAW has his character Albert Einstein thinking to himself in the novel *Masks of the Illuminati*: "But the nervous system, *meine Gott*, is the instrument which reads all other instruments." (p.100, Dell, 1981)

One of the key ideas from Aleister Crowley is found in his *Eight Lectures on Yoga*:

We place no reliance
On Virgin or Pigeon;
Our method is science,
Our aim is religion.

Crowley adds to this: "Our common sense, guided by experience, based on observation, will be sufficient."

Or, as RAW writes in *Do What Thou Wilt*, "Aleister Crowley's life work was to create a new system of judgment – a four-part methodology which follows science in combining logic and empiricism, but transcends science by including magick and yoga, It was his claim, and it is our claim here, that this logical-empirical-magick-yoga method will be the normal mode of knowledge in the future."

Crowley's overall practice of magick was founded on a basic scientific method in a kind of large-scale pragmatic, libertarian, DIY set of physiological experiments to find out what the human nervous system is capable of ("religion"), which, in using "religion" as the stated goal, was a cosmically hilarious (and true enough!) rhetorical ploy, and might have been meant to piss off orthodox religious people more than anyone else. Why, then, are his methods – even the mention of his name – considered taboo, *déclassé* or "out of bounds"' among the credentialed Scientific class? Why the Iron Curtain between Science and, basically, Everything Else? Does it have to do with that word, "Religion"? We're getting to it. We're beginning to close in. Let's see.

6.) Knowledge: RAW was one of the great Generalist intellectuals of the 20th century. He was seemingly interested in everything. A significant appeal, to the present writer, of RAW's oeuvre was his exceedingly expansive scope with regard to knowledge, and, of all intellectual discourse on topics like this, the sociology of knowledge seems the most interesting. RAW himself thought the Neapolitan philosopher

Giambattista Vico (1668-1744) originated this branch of meta-knowledge (writing and thinking knowledgeably about knowledge: how ideas arise, attain valence, and how they're propagated over space/time, etc.), and some "experts" in the sociology of knowledge cite Vico as the "Father," but more often: Marx, Nietzsche, Durkheim, Weber, Scheler, or Mannheim. Suffice: the topic had long been about the social substrates in which thinkers operate: who and where you are and which groups you're affiliated with greatly influences your ideas, mentalities, ideologies and beliefs. It seems likely, based on his writings about the sociology of knowledge, that RAW read Werner Stark's 1958 book on the topic, although this is speculation, as I can't recall RAW citing Stark. His wife Arlen may have influenced him here, as she had a degree in Sociology. Clearly, RAW had an abiding interest in the subject and addresses the topic of the abuse of the sociology of knowledge explicitly in his Shavian preface to *Wilhelm Reich In Hell* (see "Strange Loops and the Sociology of Knowledge", Hilaritas Press ed, pp.31-35).

RAW was particularly taken by Berger and Luckmann's 1966 *The Social Construction of Reality: A Treatise In The Sociology of Knowledge*, because both sociologists were students of Alfred Schutz, who was himself a student of Edmund Husserl, the Grand Poo-Bah of Phenomenology. Peter Berger and Thomas Luckmann, in importing Phenomenology to Sociology, assert early in their treatise that, hitherto, the sociology of knowledge had been too often confined to what the history of ideas were, or what intellectuals thought, and they sought to define "knowledge" as "everything that passes for knowledge in a society" (p.14-15, "Introduction", ibid.).

What had already been a discipline concerned with relativism and "relations" became even more heavily concerned with this provisional quality of knowledge, and in another of his books, Berger gave a quick definition of what the topic was when he wrote, "The sociology of knowledge, more clearly than any other branch of sociology, makes clear what is meant by saying that the sociologist is the guy who keeps asking, 'Says who?'." (*Invitation To Sociology*, Berger, pp.110-111).

In a very wide number of writings by RAW, he lauds the idea of areas of knowledge keeping up with profound breakthroughs in the sciences, and if we look at his Introduction to Regardie's bio of Crowley, *The Eye in The Triangle*, he points out that Regardie's book is like the first works that introduced the public to Einstein's relativity, Joyce's *Finnegans Wake*, or Picasso's cubism . . . the latter two of which seem to extend the new theory of relativity in physics to the novel and painting. RAW further extends this notion of relativity to Ezra Pound's experiments in poetry, Frank Lloyd Wright's architecture, and Freud and Jung's discovery of psychological relativism. "Korzybski and the General Semanticists, Garfinkel and the Ethnomethodologists, and all psychologists working in perception theory, have made this variety of relativism even more obvious than it was to Freud and Jung." He goes on to assert that "Aleister Crowley was, in my opinion, one of the most original and important thinkers of this era – right up there with such titans as Einstein and Joyce." Crowley's work yields yet another perspective on Relativity Writ Large.

Rarely were the great Generalist intellectuals of the 20th century so expansive in scope as to include magick or the occult, along with Einstein and Joyce. Because this was so rare, RAW's inclusion of Crowley among the relativizers of knowledge – as "everything that passes for knowledge in a society" – begs a concomitant thought that then must be: *why* has this area of thought been so marginalized? Practice of magick like Crowley's system(s) seems to be thought of as anathema to modern, enlightened "rationality," and thus – maybe? – too much linked to the oppressive, irrational forces of the Organized Church ("Our aim is religion") that kept scientific inquiry repressed until the 17th century.

But when we read Crowley, he's a most formidable foe of established Christianity. And, as we've seen, a proponent of scientific doubt and method. Clearly, a major reason he valued doubt and experiment was his reaction to his upbringing in a fundamentalist Christian sect, the Plymouth Brethren. Then what could be the reasons for the marginalization of magickal and occult practices and Crowley himself, in the supposed "rational" 20th-21st centuries?

7.) Illumination immanent: As we read through the 50 years-lost and now found text of RAW's *Do What Thou Wilt: An Introduction to Aleister Crowley* it's striking how RAW seems, in late 1973/early 1974, so sure that a new practice for obtaining knowledge will catch on and revolutionize all the sciences. While scientific experimentation and logic and doubt have, together, proven fantastically revolutionary, RAW thinks in 1973 it can get even better. One thinker – among many – that Crowley insisted magicians read was David Hume, The Master of Those Who Don't Know, and one of the greatest exponents of doubt and empiricism.

But still: How can all of us be much smarter? As RAW writes in *Do What Thou Wilt*, "We all act as if our nervous systems were delivering us the Absolute Truth, while in fact, we are receiving abstractions which may or may not be the truth. The only way we can approximate to truth is by finding some method (or methods) of calibrating and testing our nervous system's reports." And thus, like Crowley, we can all use Science, which RAW places in an historical context: a synthesis of craft methods from medieval guilds (empiricism), and logical thought. But also: "Magick and yoga are two other methods widely believed effective throughout history . . . "

[Above I made it sound as if Crowley was a democratizer of occult magickal knowledge. RAW was, but Crowley wasn't. Regardie writes about Crowley, "To seduce the aspirant by the assumption that any idiot could attain was altogether beneath him. He preached an aristocracy of spirit, a brotherhood of illuminati . . ." (*Eye in The Triangle*, p.435) RAW writes in *Do What Thou Wilt*, "It may be said that Crowley's goal in life was to deliver the arts of mysticism from dogmatists, fanatics, theologians, and fools, making them available to persons of logical and scientific mind." A more specific aristocracy, but aristocracy nonetheless. In an interview RAW did in 2001 with a guy only identified as "Joe", a Jack Parsons enthusiast, RAW told him, "My work as I see it consists of a series of attempts to translate the experimental element of mysticism into a set of models that grown-up men and women can understand and use, amputating the archaic vocabulary that doesn't make sense anymore." So, RAW was much more egalitarian politically than our Uncle Al.]

This idea of adding yoga and magick to logic and experimentation would still, 50-odd years later, qualify as an idealized method of attaining or creating knowledge. And RAW often discussed these ideas. In his 1980 book, *The Illuminati Papers* he writes about ideas as the source of all wealth, and there are four basic modes of attaining knowledge: *mechanical association*: you touch a hot stove and learn to never do that again, in a sort of Pavlovian response. This method is quick, easy and probably led to survival. *Logic* "can consider whether a system of ideas is self-coherent." *Experimental method* helps us to discover whether ideas are always true, always false, or sometimes true, sometimes false. The fourth mode is *Intuition*: "Intuition ALONE can generate new ideas and associations, new technology, new wealth." Note his idea of intuition as the source of new ideas, like his beloved Korzybski in #4, above. RAW then discusses how all these systems can react together and adds that "Intuition can be totally wrong if not checked by logic or experiment." (see "Dissociation of Ideas," ibid, And/Or Press, p.117) Let's not forget that our "Intuition" was what told us the world was flat. Again: we all know what "intuition" is, but let's press on.

8.) Now, one of the most striking things to me about reading RAW's *Do What Thou Wilt* was his consideration of Crowley as mentally ill, and his sort of "so what?" stance, based on so many other geniuses who were clearly either mentally ill also, or merely Weird As Fuck, as the young people might say today. The chapter that covers this, "A First Effort At Understanding", begins thus: "It is undeniable that Aleister Crowley was 'psychotic' (by normal standards) part of the time and 'neurotic' most of the time. Such an admission does not close the discussion about the value of his life's work, however, but merely opens it."

RAW then cites a number of artists and religious visionaries who would be seen similarly in the Crowley boat. Attending to my admiration for RAW's sociology of knowledge would be this unflinching openness toward discussing favorite poetic and artistic figures and their illnesses and uglinesses. How refreshing to just admit some of your favorite artists – and here, we must consider, I postulate, Crowley as some sort of species of Religious Virtuoso – were "sick." RAW was fantastic at separating the person's Work from their illnesses or fuck-ups. Other examples come easily to mind: Ezra Pound's antisemitism and support for Mussolini; Wilhelm Reich's extreme paranoia; Picasso's politics; Jung's unsavory assumptions about "race"; DW Griffith's racism, etc. If RAW were alive today, he would have some exceedingly interesting things to say about "cancel culture," I hazard. No matter how screwed up some artist or thinker was, the Work remains. Let us take pleasure in the Work; all else is secondary. I humbly ask the Reader to ponder the merits of RAW's position here.

RAW had a long, evolving history and understanding of fairly severe mental illnesses like schizophrenia, from seeing through the lenses of thinkers like Jung (who, along with his patients, displayed a level of precognition and statements that were later seen as prophetic), to R.D. Laing in the 1960s and early 1970s (it's society that makes people mentally ill; the schizophrenics are just adapting to it, and their illness gives them insight we "normals" don't have), to the consensus interpretation of the early 21st century (schizophrenia is a biochemical imbalance in the nervous system, caused by we know not what; so far: genes on multiple chromosomes expressing too much of what was once good?).

Finally: some of us might find it of interest that his two detectives in *Masks of the Illuminati*, James Joyce and Albert Einstein, both geniuses of the highest order, had offspring who were diagnosed with schizophrenia. A third figure in the novel – who steals the show – is Aleister Crowley, prankster extraordinaire. RAW doesn't address Crowley's mental illness there, though; that novel was written after *Do What Thou Wilt*.

9.) Visual tests were the first thing. (NB: I am assuming right-handed people below; for left-handers, reverse the two terms, although you all may know this is an oversimplification. Sorry!) After a series of corpus callosotomies – brain surgeries that sever the superhighway of neurons that bridge the two lobes of the brain in order to stop intractable epileptic seizures – Roger Sperry, Michael Gazzaniga and crew found that images projected to the right visual field, i.e., to the left hemisphere of the brain: patients had the language to describe what they saw. But show them the same image to the left visual field – which, because the brain does "crossing over" – the image was sent to be processed by the right hemisphere: people couldn't say what they saw. They'd grope for the word, feeling they know the answer, but it wasn't coming to them. Similar experiments on "split-brain" patients that sought to find out about touch, smell, and sound revealed similar results. I suspect most readers of this book know the basic story behind these experiments conducted by Sperry in the late 1950s into the 1970s, for which he won a Nobel in 1981. He and his colleagues showed that when the corpus callosum was cut it revealed that, basically, those patients had two separate "minds", each mind functioning differently but both minds being totally human.

Here's the thing: the best science seems to place intuition as primarily a right-hemisphere/lobe thing. Play! Tell silly jokes. Paint even if you don't know how. Listen with all your attention to your music. Read poetry and novels. Have better and better conversations, 'cuz it really is an "art" too. There are a lot of things you *think* you want in order to finally start being happy, but they probably aren't necessary.

Caveat: always remember the two lobes are *complementary*; we're at our best when they're both contributing to the situation. It's just that the left lobe seems to have taken over as captain around 1650 or so and the right has been relegated to swabbing the deck. (For Iain McGilchrist, the left lobe is the Emissary; the right the Master, but the Emissary has taken over.) And thus, we race toward disaster.

To vastly oversimplify, the left hemisphere "does"

speech and abstract, logical, if-this-then-that thinking. When you make a list and systematically check off each "item" as it is accomplished, such as an essay in which you riff about 23 aspects of some idea, that's a fairly left-brained thing. When we do non-verbal communication, that's the right hemisphere, primarily. Although we non-split-brained people are *always using both hemispheres*, each hemisphere goes about doing its thing in different ways. The crux seems to be this: the right hemisphere is how we see the world before we fall back on our prior conceptualizations about it. Those concepts are worked by the left brain. And the right hemisphere listens to what the left is doing, but the left is sort of "autistic" and doesn't listen to the right hemisphere; the left sees itself as the The Big Cheese, but it's locked into a series of "ideas" about the world "out there"; the right hemisphere is us living as part of the world, but it doesn't express this in language. If we are to realize Crowley's goal of Knowledge and Conversation with our Holy Guardian Angel, we need to learn to "be" in our right hemisphere. There we find clear signals about what's good to know, but the brain doesn't read this as language. It's a metaphor when it gets "languaged." The right hemisphere concocts this metaphor, and sends it to the left hemisphere, which promptly forgets where it came from, assumes IT made the metaphor, and then it forgets how metaphors work. It can't remember that "Time is money" is literally gibberish.

Jerome Bruner, at the forefront early on in thinking of hemispheric lateralization:

"One thing has become increasingly clear in pursuing the nature of knowing. It is that the conventional apparatus of the psychologist – both his instruments of investigation and the conceptual tools he uses in the interpretation of his data – leaves one approach unexplored. It is an approach whose medium of exchange seems to be the metaphor paid out by the left hand. It is a way that grows happy hunches and 'lucky' guesses, that is stirred into connective activity by the poet and the necromancer looking sidewise rather than directly. Their hunches and intuitions generate a grammar of their own – searching out connections, suggesting similarities, weaving ideas loosely in a trial web . . ." (*On Knowing: Essays for The Left Hand*, pp.2-5, 1962)

About the role of "searching out connections" in the age of Q-Anon? 'Nuff said? If only some people had the self-knowledge of their own nervous system, where their *ingenium* was and how it worked, and a philosophy of doubt under their belts. If only.

The science of hemispheric lateralization heavily implies that what is "implicit" is working in the right hemisphere. This includes understanding what others mean, which we tend to think is a straightforward left-brain-language thing, but it's not. Expression, tone, nuance, and body language is largely mediated by the right lobe. So much depends on the context of what is conveyed. The right hemisphere is really good at metaphor, and understanding seems more than a clear, straightforward "totally correct" interpretation of communication: "understanding" seems more like a sort of "tuning" toward what was conveyed. And "tuning" here is, clearly, a metaphor.

The Age of Reason ushered in an acceleration of a culture that hasn't stopped. It was/is an age of rapid development of science: empiricism and logic. A great deal of human suffering has been alleviated by left-brain approaches to solving problems. And good ideas that promoted overall human happiness, such as separation of Church and State, toleration, fraternity, and constitutional government, seem very "rational" and left-brained. The ever-finer details and codifications of these ideas involved rationality, and largely, the left hemisphere of the brain. But, like the physical sciences, these ideas were initially dreamed-up, imagined, created. By intuition. By the right hemisphere, which "thinks" in large jumps and sees the whole scenario in an all-at-once-ness. The details, the grunt work, was hammered home by the left hemisphere. And, to cut to the chase: the left hemisphere has become ascendent for the last 300 years. The acceleration of culture: largely left-lobe stellar achievements. The right lobe ("Master") has some language, some syntax, but not much. While the great ideas were dreamed up by it, it stands quietly in the corner now, watching the left brain ("Emissary") run the Show. And while "rationality" does fantastic things, it tends to dominate to the point where it doesn't see the whole picture. Therefore, in a mere 300-odd years, we've noted a number of nuclear near-misses that could have ended human life on the planet, we've overpopulated, are at the brink of climate catastrophe as I write, everyone has microplastic in their body, and fascism has again threatened to take hold in the richest countries. The petri-dish conditions we've created may have ushered in the Age of Pandemics, which have so far seen a large chunk of humans at their nadir, tribally politicizing science and global health as a massive conspiracy against their "liberty." Nationalism seems to be the most fervent irrational "religion" of our time. There are bank failures and massive inequalities, the eight billion humans are at risk of running out of usable water, global deforestation marches on. AI has some of us worried because of its hyper-rapid acceleration of power, everything in economics is still about constant "growth", even though that's largely what got us here, and is the same ideology as the cancer cell: monomanias, money-grubbing, power trips, and State violence seem as given as a way to "solve" very human problems. Perhaps even structurally deeper, a majority of humans are identifying themselves with their own socially-derived Ego, which Crowley and RAW would say is a huge mistake. Etc., etc., etc.

In *Do What Thou Wilt*'s "Potency and Impotence" chapter, RAW seems to link political authoritarianism to two instances of "trained impotence," which in Crowleyan terms is "conscious will . . . at odds with . . . the True Will": females losing the natural ability to orgasm during sex, and the loss of ESP powers, especially telepathy "during those decades in which 'all responsible scientists' claimed there was no such thing." The first claim reminds us of RAW's deep engagement with the psychology and sociology of Wilhelm Reich, through the 1950s and into the mid-1970s; the second seems reminiscent of one of his great adversaries: the overly conservative and stodgy "Citadel" scientific establishment, who all-too-often dogmatically claim to know what's possible, and what's not even worth investigating. The *locus classicus* for his ideas about this are found in *The New Inquisition: Irrational Rationalism and the Citadel of Science*.

In the "Aeon Of Horus" chapter of *Do What Thou Wilt*, RAW writes – in 1973 – that "the dualistic consciousness of Ra-Hoor-Khuit and Hoor-Par-Kraat, the mentality of the Man of Earth, signifies the normal ego imprinted on the first four neurological circuits of forward vs. back, dominate vs. submit, dexterous reason vs. passive intuition, sexually restricted vs. sexually free [. . .] will continue to rule, for a short while yet, leading humanity and possibly all earth's biosphere to ruin and destruction."

("For a while yet.")

The above passage from 1973 has RAW drawing from Leary's then Seven Circuit Model, which would soon become the Eight Circuit Model. (See, e.g, *Quantum Psychology* by RAW or *Info-Psychology* by Timothy Leary.) The salient point for us, here, is the message about the Four Terrestrial Circuits, 1-through-4, of which every human takes mammalian imprints and which are then taken to be "just facts" about the world. *But we can transcend* these largely accidentally-derived circuits. With techniques and substances like magick and psychedelics.

Clearly, we (the ultra Royal "we") are not in equilibrium. The science heavily implies that intuition is primarily a right-brained thing. A common, serviceable definition for intuition is "the ability to understand immediately without conscious reasoning." (This reminds me of Stephen Colbert's term "truthiness": asserting something is true because it *feels* true, even though there's no evidence it is true: RAW emphasized that scientific experimentation and logic follow thinking about intuitive knowledge.) And it's heavily linked to the way the right lobe works. Humanity *seems* to need a resurgence of holistic thinking in order to survive into the 22nd century.

Soon after the CalTech split brain research was published, it was largely seen as weird and wonderful stuff. Many researchers wrote about how strange it is that we could have two brains, two consciousnesses, two "minds" in our one three-pound glob of water, neurons, salt, sugar, and blood. And so it was in 1972, when UC San Francisco and Stanford psychologist Robert E. Ornstein published his *The Psychology of Consciousness*, which did enormous work in gnostically popularizing not only the neurobiological findings that came out of split-brain research, but in suggesting that "Eastern" modes of being: yoga, meditation, koans from Zen, Buddhist and Hindu ideas about the "self" and the world, might provide a move toward more of an equilibrium in the West. Ornstein reserved a particular affinity for Sufis: Islamic mystics and their humor and practices. Ornstein was friends with Idries Shah. There are a number of interesting books from the late 1960s/early 1970s on brain hemisphericalization in mammals in evolution, and in humans especially, but

Ornstein's was my favorite. No doubt RAW read it.

Very soon after, the pop-psych dumbed-down ideas of people being a "type" of either left-brained ("logical") or "right-brained" ("artistic") took hold in popular culture. Ornstein's interest in the topic waned, and he studied many other aspects of the brain around health and evolution. He came back to the topic 25 years later and, assuming that research would show the two lobes really are much more alike than the pop-psy books thought, he discovered the research found the "division of the mind is profound, and it begins earlier than we had thought, not in early human society, not in our remote humanoid ancestors, not in monkeys, but before primates." (*The Right Mind*, 1999, p. 4)

Trying further to boil down the research on the hemispheres, the right/holistic/"silent" lobe doesn't work on algorithms or exact definitions of words or orders of items unchanging, but it works with patterns, sympathies, correspondences, analogies, relationships . . . intuition.

Not only high-falutin' imaging machines have given us scientific understanding into the right hemisphere and intuition, but those unfortunates who had strokes or garish automobile accidents have aided us as well. The most outstanding example this writer can give at the moment is Jill Bolte Taylor's book *My Stroke Of Insight*. She was a Harvard neuroanatomist who had a massive stroke in her left hemisphere, and it made her into a neuroanatomist-artist of considerable rhetoric.

One of RAW's favorite models for what happened to him when he began to receive signals from the Sirius star system was that he's pushed his nervous system so far with psychedelics, kabbalah, yoga, cannabis, reading *Finnegans Wake* and writing feverishly to stave off poverty that his right hemisphere invaded his left. In *Prometheus Rising* he locates the post-terrestrial Neurogenetic circuit in the right neocortex, while the 5th circuit of enlightened hedonistic pleasure was obviously mostly a right lobe thing. In the Spring issue of his magazine, *Trajectories*, 1979, he says that the best futurist thinking comes from the right hemisphere. Indeed, the rise of neuroscience was for RAW the beginning of post-primate Psychology (1987: *Dark Nerve* magazine). He also, over his 48 years of writing, entertained Paul MacLean's "triune" model, popularized in Carl Sagan's *Dragons of Eden*. (Sagan: another cannabis freak whose signal difference with RAW, besides Sagan pretending to protect real science from hooey, was perhaps: he never "came out" as a cannabis enthusiast while alive. For more on Sagan and cannabis and the right hemisphere, see "Carl Sagan, Cannabis, and the Right Brain Hemisphere," by Sebastián Marincolo, in *What Hashish Did to Walter Benjamin*, pp. 156-166.) RAW returned to the triune brain model in an answer given in an interview with a Bulgarian magazine late in his life:

Q: What's mankind's problem right now?

RAW: Too much midbrain activity (mammalian conditioning) and not enough forebrain activity (human creativity.) (see *TSOG*, Hilaritas Press, p. 208)

RAW's novel within his *Schrodinger's Cat* trilogy, *The Trick Top Hat,* has the title being a metaphor for the human brain, answering his colleague William S. Burroughs's metaphoric appellation for the brain: "The Soft Machine". RAW more than once noted how the human brain delights in reading about how wonderfully complex it is, taking a page from Nietzsche's riff on how the human intellect's "knowledge" was a form of self-flattery. RAW for a while, alienated by the pop-psych reductionism of the Right/Left findings, also entertained Karl Pribram's holographic brain model. Over his entire career, he was fascinated by what he'd gotten about semantics and the nervous system from Korzybski, and the 8-Circuit Model that he collaborated with Leary in building, becoming the Model's most articulate and comprehensive advocate.

He was also stimulated in thinking about cybernetics and information theory and the brain (with the information theory lick he may have presaged the most cutting-edge theory of how psychedelics work, as we shall see), and his generalist's intellectual bent towards playful ideas, like the left hemisphere being a "digital computer" while the right lobe was analog. Or the left was Aristotelian and linear while the right was synergistic and non-linear. (see *The Starseed Signals*, Hilaritas, p. 341) Or the left hemisphere was Pavlov's Dog while the right hemisphere was Schrodinger's Cat (Erik Davis noted that Leary's use of "techno-biological mystical materialism" language appealed to and influenced RAW, and they both used metaphors from that realm to write about the brain, among others). RAW was also hugely influenced by Nietzsche, and had riffed that the left lobe was Apollonian/rational while the right was Dionysian/ecstatic.

RAW repeated that the brain/nervous system was *the* source of all ideas and real wealth and it makes all "realities." Because it's so profoundly central to . . . seemingly everything, every moment of our lives, it's cosmically "personal" when we realize this. (You're using it now! . . . and when you're asleep. At every nanosecond, only to end – probably? – at your death.) Riffs like this one, attributed to physicist Emerson M. Pugh: "If the brain were so simple, we could understand it, we would be so simple we couldn't," appeal to this sense of unfathomable incommensurability of the brain. Metaphors for the brain seem to only make it funnier: by the age of the computer, the ways the brain manifests itself (e.g., language) was "hardware", while the brain itself was "wetware." RAW had to run with it: the surrealism about how, with its folds, the human brain looks like a plate of lasagna (See the antic *Reality Is What You Can Get Away With*). To stay alive and thinking, keep your plate of lasagna flying, literally: picture a gigantic lasagna hovering over suburban homes in New Jersey, like an alien spaceship in a 1950s film and you get the picture. Jokes like his friend George Carlin's: "They say only 10 percent of the brain's function is known. Apparently, the function of the remaining 90 percent is to keep us from discovering its function" seem entirely appropriate. An ironic distance was required when we realized the utterly profound, seemingly absurd nature of the brain . . . because it's the Thing that's discussing itself *now*. Who's in control? Or *what* is in control?

At one point and similar to Ornstein, Wilson perceived that popular psychology's dilution of the right-left brain model had become a turn-off for Neuroscientists, and he assumed that the whole thing had gone the wrong way down a one-way street, intellectually. In a 1985 interview with V. Vale, RAW thinks maybe the right/left model had possibly been oversold, but he still thought it a legit model, adding the "back brain" as more primitive and that the frontal cortex probably contained Leary's higher "circuits." (See *Robert Anton Wilson: Beyond Conspiracy Theory*, V. Vale; Re/Search, pp. 25-26.) By the time he wrote his 1993 introduction to *The Selected Letters of Philip K. Dick*, 1977-1979, RAW thought the dual hemispheric model was outdated. (page 9, ibid.) Both he and his friend PKD had used this model in the 1970s and 80s to try to explain the extremely bizarre things that had happened to them. (See RAW, *Beyond Chaos and Beyond*, p.372; and Erik Davis's scholarly yet readable and wonderful *High Weirdness: Drugs, Esoterica and Visionary Experience in the Seventies*, pp. 259-260; 323-324; 478 note #72.)

The right-left model was most decidedly *not* dead.

Crowley, long before the 1960s explosion of knowledge about our two minds, urged his students to write with both hands. He seemed to have intuitively found out that this exercise activates both lobes, because the left hemisphere controls the right side of the body, and vice-versa. Oh, he was "on" to something, alright. RAW: Rituals of magick are "physiological experiments." Moreover: "The magician induces highly unusual experiences in his own nervous system" which "enlarge our understanding of the Mind and its relationship to the Cosmos."

Wilson's most extensive writing and speculations about the human nervous system/brain are probably found in *Prometheus Rising*. At any rate, you can't go wrong starting there on this overall topic.

To carry on in this left/right lobe research, have a look at Iain McGilchrist's 2009 *The Master and His Emissary*, a landmark on the topic to contend and grapple with. RAW would've loved this one. Shorter but also in the same vein and wonderful is Leonard Shlain's *The Alphabet Versus the Goddess: The Conflict Between Word and Image*. RAW was alive to read this, and loved it.

10.) On saving the world: you can only do what thou wilt. But that's a lot. My gawd, it could be everything. If you don't understand what your "will" is and you assume it means behaving like an asshole, please read RAW's *Do What Thou Wilt* (contained herein) closely, as if your life depends on it. Some are fucking in the forests. Some are consuming less. Many are engaged in some aspect of Crowley's grand project, studying cabala, yoga, astral travel, the tarot deck, or meditation, or any number of anthropotechnics. Including Science and Art. Many are, shall we say, "politically active."

If you're a Generalist like RAW and not a Specialist, you

know you're on the outs with mainstream intellectual culture. As Gary Lachman writes, the Western occult tradition and the right hemisphere always attracted Generalists over Specialists and the Western esoteric tradition has been "subject to the kind of left-brain aggression that, McGilchrist argues, the right brain has been enduring for some time now." (*Lost Knowledge of the Imagination*, see pp. 27-28.)

Disobedience will probably figure strongly. You might use sex, cannabis, magick, pranks, and psychedelics. Or all of those. Or not. If you limn the outlines of your own new religion, you're probably doing something right. If you attain telepathic communication with the Plant Kingdom, it seems a good guess you're onto something good. RAW liked to remind us that *ecstasy* was Greek for "outside of oneself" or even "out of the body." This seems like the least – and most – we can strive for. That ecstatic "Self" will seem a helluva lot more than you ever thought. To the point where it spills over into a whole new order, rendering the previous "self" as miniscule, even trivial. See for yourself! Inform yourself and act without fear. The mystic Helen Keller said, "Life is either a daring adventure or nothing (*Let Us Have Faith*). Science may have found a cure for most evils, but it has found no remedy for the worst of them all – the apathy of human beings (*My Religion*). Security is mostly a superstition. It does not exist in nature, nor do the children of men as a whole experience it" (*The Open Door*). I pancaked all three of her quotes into one, assuming she wouldn't have objected.

There's a funny problem with Keller's "faith". Crowley once pitted Faith and Doubt against each other and what he found was this: "I slept with faith and found a corpse in my arms on awakening; I drank and danced all night with doubt and found her a virgin in the morning." (*The Book Of Lies*, 45, "Chinese Music.") Maybe *you* can make Faith come out on top, but I Doubt it. And no, I'm not tryna pick a fight with

Helen Keller, fer crissakes.

11.) Knowledge of spiritual mysteries: gnosis. Intuition, though we've located it in the right hemisphere, still eludes those of us who seek to obtain it easily upon mere invocation. Clearly, aside from waiting for it to visit us as a random accident, we, like RAW based on his reading of Jung, want to "have" Intuition at our beck and call. Can we? Clearly, we have to work to activate it from our silent right hemisphere. What takes us "out of ourselves"? Whatever it is, it seems a royal road to Intuition. I notice I obtain random creative thoughts "from out of the blue" when taking a hot shower. I don't ask for Intuition going in; it just comes, fairly reliably. I step into the shower thinking of nothing, like the latest government jobs report or the spell of hot weather moving in. Suddenly: I get an Idea, from "out of nowhere." Afterwards, with a towel on, I make notes.

Other times, ideas come, seemingly, from out of a dream. Asked whether I wanted to contribute to a book on RAW and Crowley I said yes, not having any idea about what to write. I made a list of five or six topics, then went to bed. In the middle of the night, I got up to pee and as I'm standing there, I received a message that reminded me of what RAW had written about Jung, Intuition, and how "That had to wait until I discovered Acid and Aleister Crowley", as noted in #1, above. I thought I'd forgotten that. Fighting off sleep, I turned on the light and made a note about this, seeming to remember it was in *Cosmic Trigger Vol 2*, then went to sleep. I checked the next day: it was there. And hence this weirdo's long essay. Where was this memory, and how did it arrive here, then? Plato thought we all knew everything, we just needed to engage in dialectical talk with others to recover this knowledge. That has always seemed dreamy and fanciful and even sorta arrogant to me. And yet . . .

Rhythmic action like walking and bicycle riding
are other reliable exercises to call this elusive Force into
consciousness. (It could be that our endogenous cannabinoids
are kicking in, if ya wanna get scientific about it.) I see
such seemingly mundane actions as underrated magickal
operations. Hey, your mileage may vary.

By the way, Ezra Pound scholar Peter Makin once wrote
an essay on Pound's use of 9th century Irish philosopher
Scotus Erigena, who once told us, "All that is, is light."
(Ponder *that!*) Makin noted that Erigena thought – in the 800s
CE! – that personal intuition and awareness of proportion
in nature served as a constant corrective for the "intellect."
Just a thought. The Neoplatonists (like Erigena) kept the
magic/intuition/gnosis strain alive from at least the 4th
century BCE, and this notion of equilibrium keeps showing
up, doesn't it? Erigena here seems to have been excessively
ahead of his time.

12.) Ecstasy would seem to be amenable to
neuroscientific studies. Examples of science studying yoga
are fairly solid. (Quoting Ring Lardner, "You could look it
up.") Studies about the scientific basis of Crowleyan magick
look pretty sparse to me, but the situation's better than it was
in 1973. The magickal procedure of astral travel that RAW
describes in *Do What Thou Wilt* involves "seeing" a second
physical body of "you" across from "you." Since RAW
wrote this, much has been learned about the neuroscience
of, say, proprioception – the embodied feeling of yourself in
a space, which is located in the right hemisphere. We know
which areas of the brain light up in fMRI images when we
are asked to imagine our bodies in space. And in *Kabbalah:
A Neurocognitive Approach to Mystical Experiences* by
Moshe Idel and Shahar Arzy, they showed that what 13th
century kabbalist Abraham Abulafia did to get out of his

body: chant Hebrew letters while paying close attention to his head movements and breathing patterns, imagining himself without a body and with one, while mentally rotating the Hebrew letters, producing a dissociative state and a "doppelganger": this is now amenable to scientific study. It works, and now we know why, because we've stimulated key brain regions that lead to similar effects.

It would seem that more studies are forthcoming, finally. However, many practitioners of magick will shrug and say, "Of course! You needed an fMRI machine to show 'proof'?" Crowley emphasized in *Book VI: Liber O*: "In this book it is spoken of the Sephiroth and the Paths; of Spirits and Conjurations; of Gods, Spheres, Planes, and many other things which may or may not exist. It is immaterial whether they exist or not. By doing certain things certain results will follow; students are most earnestly warned against attributing objective reality or philosophical validity to any of them . . . There is little danger that any student, however idle or stupid, will fail to get some result; but there is great danger that he will be led astray, obsessed and overwhelmed by his results . . ." What is already subjective and "obvious" to the magician will be increasingly shown to be "objective" science. And for the Epoch we grew up in, only the latter is a "fact." We can ignore it or embrace it. Or shrug and say "Told ya so."

In a 1981 article in *High Times*, "Cabala: Tasting the Forbidden Fruit of the Tree of Life," RAW writes, "Cabala, like dope, is a deliberate attempt to overthrow the linear left brain and allow the contents of the holistic right brain to flood the field of consciousness. When you are walking down the street and every license plate seems part of one conscious message – one endless narrative – you are thinking like a very advanced theoretical Cabalist. (Or else you're stoned out of your gourd.)"

Regarding the overthrow of the linear left brain: recall the feelings you had while reading Lewis Carroll, or some book on the nature of infinity, or an article on famous logical paradoxes. Or when you first had a good long look at Escher's stuff, or watched a David Lynch film. In Gregory Bateson's cybernetic ideas about wisdom, any opening to the experience of the irrational makes us more whole. And that was RAW's goal in reading Jung on the quadrumvirate "self." And Jung's "Intuition" seems "irrational" enough to us. Amid a long review of books by Philip K. Dick, Terence McKenna and Fred Alan Wolf in *Chaos and Beyond: The Best of Trajectories,* RAW grapples with the tremendously weird experiences related in all three books, and finds a common denominator in the very serious role of nonsense that shows up in the space/time events of these authors. He related it to his readings of Mary Baker Eddy: "I once spent a lot of time brooding over why Mrs. Eddy makes so much sense on one page and then seemingly degenerates into total gibberish on the next page. I got my first clue about this mystery when reading Aleister Crowley, who does the same thing but with tons more of literary flair, humor and panache than Mrs. Eddy. 'Nonsense frees us from conditioned thinking,' I decided, 'but only if we're not quite sure it's nonsense.'" (op. cit: p.234.)

RAW then links this to the nonsense of Zen masters, Sufis, shamans, and the cognitive "reframing" of psychologists, who use it to get us out of our conditioned reality-tunnels and allow more information to flood our brains, information which would presumably be instantiated as energy in the nervous system. A switch to "nonsense" knocks us out of our hardened categories, at least temporarily. With Eddy's Christian Science, it may account for its seemingly magickal "mind healing." We should take nonsense more seriously, perhaps. Certainly, Crowley did.

The three books that comprise *777* are so filled with data and links between data, correspondence tables and what they "mean" that the reader's alternation between "important" and "nonsense!" probably alters consciousness by dimming down the left lobe and letting the right lobe take the spotlight, but we will not dogmatize about such speculation; the Reader must see for herself.

During his terrific essay on "Sexual Alchemy" (collected in *Email To The Universe*, Hilaritas, pp. 212-222), RAW navigates the abstruse coded language of 17th century tantric/sex magick writings, and suddenly shifts into the scientific mode: "The processes involved can be defined very materialistically, in terms of exercising to move the center of Consciousness from usual domination by the left brain hemisphere and the sympathetic (active) nervous system to balance between both hemispheres and a growing ability to relax into the parasympathetic (passive, receptive) nervous system. The old mystic terminology lingers on chiefly because it is poetically precise and psychologically highly suggestive."

Jung had tried to explain sex magick as the psyche's attempt to integrate sexual passion with religion, while Freud seemed to see it as evil. Chalk one up for Jung over Freud here.

But remember: RAW actually *did* tantric sex-magick. He didn't just read or theorize about it.

13.) On self-experimentation in general: By doing certain things certain results will follow. This seems the essence of the scientific method writ large: set up a regimen, follow it to the letter, then write down your results and observations. Keep notes. The regimen was already a creative act: build on it. Results will turn out to be both objective and subjective, and should be productive of further experimentation. These procedures seem limitless. Can I control my breathing in a certain way for X amount of time? Can I memorize this very long poem and what are some tricks to make it easier? What are some gimmicks to improve my musicianship? You are the designer, subject, and analyzer of your own experience. This has often been called Personal Science or "N-of-1" science. You can do pragmatic self-analysis. You can be some sort of Mad Scientist. And just about anything can be investigated. Increasingly, in the age of Internet and "mind hacks", you can share your results with others who are working in similar areas.

RAW decided, around 1962, to see what his nervous system was capable of when he pushed it with meditation, breathing, yoga, psychedelics, cannabis, writing, and immersion in dense and difficult texts, etc.: 14 years (or so) of it was chronicled in *Cosmic Trigger Vol 1*. His discovery of Crowley via Watts would have occurred in the eighth or ninth year of his self-experimentation. After 14 years, among other things, he had a variety of ESP experiences, including an uncanny "contact" with alien intelligences, which was one of the ultimate challenges to his interpretive schemes, his ontology and epistemology. Lest seriously adverse outcomes occur, he has cautioned the inexperienced in Magick and Psychedelics to first get grounded in the history of Philosophy, including doubt. Read about the psychedelic first, have a guide, be able to describe what "set and setting" mean so someone who knows nothing about it could understand. The student should also have studied Logic, and undergone at least one form of psychotherapy. RAW earned a degree in the psychology of perception and had a deep understanding of Adelbert Ames's transactional psychology, and phenomenology: it would be a good idea to know at least the basics in this, first. All of this *at minimum!*

The Gnostics, the mystics, a number of fine scientists and artists, have all *wanted to know*. They either consciously sought extraordinary experience or it was thrust upon them, due to their prior studies, "accidents" and/or predispositions. RAW says Crowley – one of the greatest self-experimenters of all time – was "psychotic" some of the time and "neurotic" most of the time. He never met Crowley, so it was an interpretation based on everything he read by and about him, and conversations with people like Grady McMurtry. I don't think you have to be "weird" to do extensive self-experimentation, regardless. It seems probable that ignorance is so endemic that the self-experimenter will be seen as a weirdo simply for the experimenting bit. Citizens of the U.S. can see their experiments as good ol' fashioned Pragmatism, our single contribution to Western Philosophy.

The reader of RAW will notice almost all of his favorite artists and "religious" figures were self-experimenters. Leary, Lilly, Pound, Joyce, his Berkeley physicist friends that MIT professor David Kaiser called "the hippie physicists" . . . and, of course, Crowley. RAW was totally enamored with experimenters, innovators, trailblazers, and doers. The history of self-experimentation in the sciences is rich, and of course Albert Hofmann accidentally ingested a huge dose of LSD, but then continued to experiment on himself with it. Ballsy! Alexander "Sasha" Shulgin, who RAW knew, concocted hundreds of psychedelic compounds and either tried them all himself, or had an elite crew of psychonauts report back to him their findings: dosage, effects, duration, etc. To me, one of the most thrilling examples of self-experimentation in medicine was an account I read about in my early 20s: stomach ulcers were thought to be mostly a product of psychological stress. Barry Marshall thought, against all medical orthodoxy, that this was wrong. He thought it was caused by a bacterium. To prove it he drank a petri dish of cultivated *Heliobacter pylori* bacteria and quickly felt an acidic stomach, nausea, gastritis, and very bad breath. He took an antibiotic and his symptoms went away. He won a Nobel Prize for this. The late Seth Roberts influenced many in his philosophy of self-experimentation, and we miss him. The Professor Tyler Cowan called Roberts's overarching theme of self-experimentation "the highest stage of science." Best-selling writer Timothy Ferriss is largely known as a gonzo self-experimenter. We may see all of this as a legacy of the Gnostics, and then the first 15th century experimental scientists. But as RAW pointed out, the earliest "makers": guild craftspeople, led to experimental science.

RAW: "I don't believe anything, but I have suspicions." Does suspicion seem close enough to intuition here?

Gnosticism: aye. But you say, "Hey man . . . Crowley said to *doubt* your results, no matter how weird and wild they are, and Wilson's thing was model *ag*nosticism: never believe any of your models of 'reality' but be informed about all your models and be ready for changes . . ." Precisely! If Crowley and Wilson are the royal road to any gnosis, if they are to be teaching us anything, it's how to *not be a dumbass*. Always be ready to have a laugh at yourself for being wrong. Scientists are wrong all the time, because they're constantly trying out things to see if they better describe the phenomena than some other small piece of information. Anyone can be right about who the 33rd President was, or what time the Yankees game starts tonight. That crap is trivial. Think big, and prepare to be wrong, and you're probably one of the more intelligent ones around. Being wrong is a huge part of being very intelligent. What are the actual rewards for being "right" all the time? (Trick Q: *no one* is right all the time. *No one*.) What did Crowley mean by "Soldiers and Hunchbacks"?

!?!?!?!?!?!?!?!?!?!?!?!?

14.) For examples from Crowley and RAW giving us things to experiment with, simply open any of their books. (NB the chapter "A Crowleyan Curriculum" in *Do What Thou Wilt*.) RAW explicitly labeled as "exercizes" things *to do* to more deeply learn what had previously been discussed in the chapter, and was adamant about the reader not just reading about the exercises, but *doing* them. (See esp. *Prometheus Rising* and *Quantum Psychology*.) But RAW has maybe two or three times as many exercises within the body of his texts, including his fiction. He's often not explicitly saying, "Hey Reader: try this!", but the careful reader will note that prompts to try something often show up in his work. See the five different one-pager "Dissociation of Ideas" in *The Illuminati Papers*. See the pop quizzes that show up in *Illuminati Papers*, *The New Inquisition*, *Right Where You Are Sitting Now* and other places. RAW explains how magick works in one of the Appendices of *Illuminatus!* (Magick: "Invoke often. Repeat": we see this in advertising and other places, possibly right where you are sitting now.)

In his *Historical Illuminatus Chronicles*, set in the late 18th century, Sigismundo Malatesta, the young hero, was studying under a magician: "He had been working on a new exercise Abraham had given him: to look, each day, for ten beautiful things in Napoli he had never noticed before. 'It reminds you that the things you worry about do not comprise all existence,' Abraham said." (*The Earth Will Shake*, p. 240, Hilaritas ed.) Try this one for anxiety?

In *Masks of the Illuminati*, Sir John, mentored by George Cecil Jones, who was "simultaneously devouring tons of mystical literature from all nations and all ages, dumped on him ten volumes at a time by Jones," is clearly being made to go through the Golden Dawn exercises that Crowley later published in *The Equinox* and which showed up later as the goldmine *777 And Other Qabalistic Writings of Aleister*

Crowley, a boot camp/magickal encyclopedia of gematria, mythology, comparative religion, other esotericism, and the vast numbers of correspondences within these elements. Even though he protests that he is a Christian, Jones insists Sir John read a text on Buddhism: "The refrain, 'everyone you meet is a Buddha,' began to drive him to despair; it was so nonsensical; it was repeated so often, in so many different ways; it was obvious that he would have to understand it before he began to comprehend what Buddhism was all about. He, therefore, at Jones' suggestion, tried to *see* the Buddha in everyone he met – and then he understood quickly." (*Masks of the Illuminati*, p. 64, op.cit: I contend that RAW is asking the Reader to go along with this exercise, along with Sir John. For a narrative and experience of the rigors of being initiated into the Golden Dawn, read pp. 60-80 of that novel, and study Crowley's *777* at the same time.) A companion to the description of the astral travel section of *Do What Thou Wilt* is in *Masks*, pp. 112-115. See for yourself.

RAW writes about Crowley's exercise of developing two antagonistic personalities, keyed to two pieces of jewelry. This exercise blew my mind when I did it. If you're an actor and you haven't heard about this, you need to check it out. (RAW describes this Crowley exercise in his introduction for *Eye in The Triangle*)

My all-time favorite exercise to boost the imagination that RAW links to Crowley is this: you're sitting there, reading this book. Why? What led you to this book? What led you to the room you're in? Keep going back, from, "I'm reading this book because . . ." Go back further than how your parents met. At some point you don't know "facts", so speculate. If you get good enough you end up with atoms, subatomic particles, the Big Bang, or before it.

RAW has done fantastic work popularizing Korzybski's

"extensionalizing" exercises with language, including writing entire books in E-Prime: English without the forms of "be", and any one of us might learn a lot about ourselves simply by re-stating what we mean anytime we say "X "is" Y, because whatever it "is", it's surely more than that. We subconsciously think "X equals Y" when we say it "is." Try it. He also talked about trying to say "I" less, to get out of the derived social Ego.

An entire book could be written on RAW, self-experimentation and his endless "exercizes." Suffice: find one exercize and work with that. Don't lust after results. Be earnest but in no rush. Be careful and deliberate and have fun with it. Go to the completion you set up in the first place and don't cut corners; you might find a *blue sapphire* in one of those corners one day. By doing certain things, certain things result. Take notes. Stop and move to the next exercize/operation when the last one got boring or wasn't working for you. Be creative with choosing exercizes. Alter and combine them. Simplify them. Do the Work. RAW spent seven or eight pages writing about the people who didn't do the exercizes in *Prometheus Rising* or in Crowley's books. He chalked the non-doers to "magical thinking" (hilarious irony!) and the hatred of work. (see *Undoing Yourself With Energized Meditation*, by Christopher Hyatt, introduction by RAW.)

Indeed on "work," Both Crowley and RAW were in love with that sort of hard work that suited them. And they want *you* to exert yourself towards those same ends. Actually, if you're the sort they want: they demand it. You know who you are.

15.) The eminent Richard Kaczynski, in his definitive bio of Crowley, *Perdurabo*, tells us Crowley's psychedelic of choice (LSD hadn't been discovered yet) was *Anhalonium lewinii*, which is basically peyote. Kaczynski gives us a funny anecdote about a party in 1913 in which Katherine Mansfield might have ingested Crowley's psychedelic. Or maybe it was merely hashish.

RAW's first psychedelic was also peyote, on December 28th, 1962, in an old slave cabin in the woods near Yellow Springs, Ohio. (See *Cosmic Trigger vol. 1*, Part One for experiences on 40 peyote trips.)

Remember RAW wrote about Jung's 4th aspect of the realized "self", Intuition: "That had to wait until I discovered Acid and Aleister Crowley." RAW met and became friends with Leary in 1964; in *Cosmic Trigger vol 2*, he admits, "Between 1969 and 1973 I was doing a lot more acid than I admitted in the first *Cosmic Trigger*." (*CT2*, p.51, Hilaritas ed.) Without telling us the exact date when he first did LSD – as he does with peyote – RAW saw, in *CT1*, another American Hysteria coming down in real time, and waxes warmly about the metaprogramming wonder of cannabis and yoga. RAW had obtained an easy familiarity with the psychedelic peyote buttons by late 1963.

The naif may ask, "Why did these guys do that old world Native American psychedelic?" Quick answer: RAW in 1962 was at the beginning of his self-experimentation and was intellectually neophilic. He'd read ultra-conservative Russell Kirk's glowing review of Huxley's *The Doors of Perception*, Kirk's piece in *National Review*, which is cosmically hilarious in and of itself. A jazz musician gave RAW the peyote. Huxley's drug for that 1954 book was mescaline; Huxley was much-admired as a fellow Generalist by RAW.

But again, why use peyote/mescaline?

But maybe that's like saying, Why do you need to know?

"We can no longer be told what to do; we must learn by our own scientific experiments in consciousness expansion what we really are, beyond the superficial personality imprinted by social reward-punishment conditioning if there is no Sun-King at the apex of a hierarchy, guiding and leading us all, if 'every man and every woman is a star,' we have not only the right, but the duty to expand our consciousness and our powers to the utmost. This is the final meaning of the Great Work, and of Crowley's slogan of 'Scientific Illuminism.'" – *Do What Thou Wilt*, chapter "Aeon of Horus."

This "superficial personality" AKA "ego" seems an albatross around our necks. We want to do certain things and see what certain results we obtain. If these psychedelics encourage ecstasy – that is, if they allow us to get "outside ourselves", all the better. They do that. Magick and cannabis and psychedelic drugs and sex-magick (and extreme sports!) limit the limiting Ego and allow an expanded view of phenomenal reality, before the body clears those molecules from action in the brain/blood.

There seems much to be said, but for now, let this suffice.

16.) Explanation for how psychedelics work: Okay, okay, the current favorite of mine – and apparently, the leading scientific interpretation – is that a group of brain modules consisting of the medial prefrontal cortex, the inferior parietal lobule, the posterior cingulate cortex, the lateral temporal cortex, the dorsal medial prefrontal cortex and the hippocampus formation . . . working together called the Default Mode Network (DMN), all work in concert to link the more evolutionarily recent "cortex" brain with older and "deeper" structures involved in emotion and memory. When you're doing basically nothing, these structures are lit up in the imaging machine. Doing "nothing" would mean daydreaming, reflecting on ourselves, worrying. We're not playing chess, working on an article about Crowley, or planning a getaway vacation, step by step. When we are engaged in the outside world, the attentional areas take over, and Michael Pollan describes it like a see-saw relationship with the DMN, which exerts a top-down influence on other parts of the brain. This Default Mode Network *seems to be the neural correlate of the "self."* The Ego.

Cut to the chase: psychedelic drugs and *very* accomplished meditators, as studied in fMRI machines (which measure blood flow and energy in different parts of the brain) dim the DMN greatly, and the "ego" seems to vanish. Robin Carhart-Harris thinks psychedelics and advanced meditation allows for more information to flood the brain. More chaos. Let Eris in to do Her Thang, and you get – literally – fantastic results. When you successfully get outside yourself – *ek-stasis* you lose your ego and experience more of the booming, buzzing confusion that is "Reality." This model crosses the tees and dots the eyes of Huxley's hypothesis of "reducing valve." Indeed, this psychedelic dampening of the Default Mode Network is likened to the consciousness of babies, and Michael Pollan interviewed a UC Berkeley scholar of baby consciousness with regard to psychedelic use by adults, Alison Gopnik. The idea is that infants haven't wired up their DMN yet, and when you, an adult, do psychedelics, what you experience is similar to what babies are experiencing, except you really have been sued, gotten a degree, have a mortgage, felt romantic heartbreak, etc. But still: Babies be trippin, yo! (See *How To Change Your Mind*, Michael Pollan, pp. 300-329. This book made it into the *New York Times* best-seller list, which many of us take as a Good Sign.)

Carhart-Harris is preceded in this notion of non-equilibrium flows in the brain by neuroscientist Marcus Raichle, and probably, before Raichle, by Erwin Schrödinger in his *What Is Life?*. In *Do What Thou Wilt*, RAW writes of the desire for "equilibrium," and we should see the apparent paradox as more a case of complementarity: if we achieve non-equilibrium flows in the nervous system via magick or psychedelics, the overall thrust would be that the more people who reach non-ordinary states via non-equilibrium flows, the more Western society would begin to go back towards an equilibrium between the hemispheres. This term "equilibrium" in the area of Thermodynamics is a synonym for "death"; life thrives on non-equilibrium in a way that's a Goldilocks situation: just the right amount of non-balance between chaos and stasis. Total stasis, total equilibrium, is, at least thermodynamically, equivalent to death. The Belgian chemist Ilya Prigogine (Nobel: 1977) thought societies work the same way, as "dissipative structures": non-equilibrium states in society at the very least indicate that determinism is no longer viable, and that change requires chaos. We probably need a tad more chaos, overall. At minimum, psychedelics would seem to give us a longer moment in new phenomenal realities before a return to stasis.

(*More* chaos? Isn't the threat of global warming under fascist leaders in a pandemic quite enough as it is? Again: we probably got to this point largely due to too much of the wrong non-equilibrium: the "rational" left-hemisphere-dom-inated kind. There are signs it's starting to swing back: all Philosophy really does begin in right-brain wonder, and over the past 40 years or so, many if not most philosophers have returned to right-brain philosophical thinking after the years of Logical Positivism, according to McGilchrist. There will always be hardworking, tinkering rational-logical thinkers who enjoy that, but now is the time for the intrepid mystical types to explore the dissolution of Ego and see what's there, via magickal operations, psychedelic use and other creative gimmicks that monkey-wrench the left brain for a while, then allow it back to see if all the right brain items dredged are actually viable. A living philosopher whose work I've always found wonderfully provoking is Justin E.H. Smith, who very recently came out as a psychedelic user. Some of us read a particular author and wonder at some point, "She seems like she's done acid. I wonder . . . ?" I thought that about Smith years ago, and only now does he confirm it. I seem to be implying that one psychedelic person can metaphysically "sniff out" another through their voice or work, and I'm not sure if I am saying that. Maybe I am. But I think it's a weak sense. Let us call it . . . intuitive?)

In Late Modernism we see a move away from looking to authority figures to looking inward; the Neoliberal mind's assumption that "free markets" will solve everything has not gone away but has withered. Incessant talk of "the self" remains, but there's more public discourse and rethinking about values in a world of insanely abundant wealth that yet has hunger, homelessness, lack of health care, bad schools, primitive racism, and other inequalities. Since the pandemic, notions of work seem to have shifted. Those born after 1960 have largely abandoned organized religion. Prof. Christopher Partridge, part of the "occulture" strain in academic thinking about religion, writes, "Influenced far more by popular culture and subcultural peer pressure, there has, again, been a shift away from the authoritarian aspects of religion and toward the creation of personal spiritual paths. As Helen Berger and Douglas Ezzy comment of contemporary Wicca in their study of teenage witchcraft, 'the emphasis in ritual and all self-transformation techniques is individual discovery and self-development. There is no clear list of behaviors, such as those that exist in Islam, Judaism, or Christianity, that adherents are expected to change or adopt.'" (Partridge, "Occulture Is Ordinary", in *Contemporary Esotericism*, ed. Asprem and Granholm, Routledge, pp. 115-116.)

The Romanian scholar of magic and esotericism,

Ioan Culianu, was invited to a national science fiction conference a few weeks before he was murdered in 1991, a crime which still hasn't been solved. One panel he sat on had as a discussion topic, "Is all magic bad magic?" Culianu defended magic: "Magic is not about disorder. On the contrary, it establishes a peaceful coexistence with the unconscious when this coexistence is under attack." (See, *Eros, Magic, and the Murder of Professor Culianu*, by Ted Anton, p.12, Northwestern U. Press.) Culianu was invited to that conference by the writer John *Crowley,* and *nota bene* the name of the author of the book. Probably only a coincidence . . .

And the State suppression of research into cannabis and psychedelics is rapidly thawing as I write this. RAW intuited this and told Philip Farber in a 1991 *High Times* interview, "I'm beginning to think that there's a real chance that research will be legalized again. There are more and more people in the psychotherapeutic professions who are speaking out, and it has been relegalized for research purposes in several countries in Europe: in Switzerland, Germany and Holland, among others. There is definitely a movement toward, at least, legalizing research again. It does seem, with the passing of time, that more and more people can see how stupid it is to forbid scientific research in an area where the research that was done thirty years ago was so promising."

My point: there seems to be some very good news amid all the bad, and who knows where culture and human existence is heading? I don't. Neither does Ray Kurzweil.

Around 1990, academic scholars began taking Crowley seriously. Who would've seen that coming in 1973? There seems no good reason to believe academia won't try to catch up with unaffiliated intellectuals and scholars in writing on the topic of Robert Anton Wilson.

RAW guessed right in that "information theory" lick in

#9, above. Uncertainty is baked into "reality" but in order to survive we developed what's now called "predictive coding," an isomorphism to Leary and RAW's "reality tunnel": quick guesses/storified structures as to what's going on. The brain's predictive code makes up stories for us to explain what's going on. And after a while, we think "our" story is "the" story. Depressed people stay in Default Mode and their own "story" too often; it's as if they ruminate and practice depressed thoughts, and then those thoughts become "reality" for them. They're suppressing entropy: they're suppressing information flow. Not on purpose! Doing a psychedelic dims the DMN, and that's one explanation for how these substances seem to provide drastically quick relief for some people who were depressed. They receive enormous – chaotic, entropic – information-flows in their nervous system.

To add to that, early in late 2022 – early 2023, researchers at UC Davis have found that the psychedelics (LSD, DMT, psilocybin), all of which look, molecularly, like serotonin – which is why those drugs work: they dock in serotonin receptors – the classic psychedelics, unlike serotonin, are "greasy" in that they can do something serotonin can't: they infiltrate the neuron itself, and there are receptors in there, too. And when they greasily slide into your neurons and dock in intracellular serotonin receptors, they cause growth in the dendritic spines, tree-like branches that are part of the neuron. Depressed, traumatized people have withered dendritic spines. Psychedelics appear to cause neural growth. November of 2022: a *single dose* of synthetic psilocybin in a randomized double-blind study, "the largest of its kind," "improved depression in people with a treatment-resistant form of the disease." Serotonin is apparently not greasy enough to make effects inside the neuron like a slippery-slidey psilocybin molecule can. As of this writing, we're waiting for these studies about psychedelics getting *inside* the neuron to be replicated. What do psychedelics do for non-depressed, non-traumatized, non-PTSD people? It's complicated, but it hardly seems "bad." Not at all. Far from it!

Lest we equate the DMN with stupidity or the Ego, it's of course not that simple. "Working at a remove from the sensory processing of the outside world, the default mode network is most active when engaged in higher-level 'metacognitive' processes such as self-reflection, mental time travel, mental constructions (such as the self or ego), moral reasoning, and 'theory of mind' – the ability to attribute mental states to others, as when we try to imagine 'what it is like' to be someone else." (*How To Change Your Mind,* Pollan, Penguin, p. 302.) RAW thought the Ego was important historically, so we could get to the advanced technological age where we could seek to alleviate ourselves of it, or squelch it at will.

Does this DMN action work with cannabis? Descriptions of the enhanced cannabis state makes it seem likely, but we're not sure. Cannabis – the "trippy" THC aspect – works not by docking in serotonin receptors, but in CB1/ anandamide ones. Still: a sufficient amount of THC seems to dampen the Ego. Furthermore, Iain McGilchrist's copious descriptions (In *The Master and His Emissary*) of how the right hemisphere works often makes it sound like a cannabis effect. We need *much* more open scientific research on this. What is the relationship between the DMN going offline and the right hemisphere (parts of it?) going online? We'd love to *know*.

Furthermore: the idea that psychedelics work by explanation from information theory, and allowing more entropy/chaos makes intuitive sense. RAW would describe Joyce's *Finnegans Wake* as maximally info-dense. Actually, every writer I've read regarding that book resorts to similar claims, which are obviously true if you've looked at that book. But if the more information increases in a text means the more it resembles chaos in the overwhelmed reader's brain leading to psychedelic effects: this seems like an interesting model for RAW and his expressed love of not only *Finnegans Wake*, but all the "inexhaustible" texts he loved, because they contained not puzzles to be solved, but "puzzles to be worked on," which, together with "inexhaustibility" were his criteria for a great book, as he told the present writer in an interview in 2003. Further, readers of RAW will note he often talked about "psychedelic" texts, which would be a metaphor. Books are not psychedelic drugs, but he seems to have intuitively linked the two to information so dense it acts like chaos in the nervous system. Leary linked books to psychedelics before he left Harvard, sick of the academic "game." The library had proven, historically, more dangerous to society than mind-altering drugs, Leary asserted. If and only if we define "dangerous" as a threat to authoritarian-pa-triarchal established order . . .

In a discussion of Crowley's *The Book of Lies* (1912), Richard Kaczynski notes that so much of the book's meaning "lies not in its literal interpretation, but in the highly codified meaning of its words that one is tempted to call it a stylistic forebear of James Joyce's *Finnegans Wake* (1939) – although Joyce never met or read AC." (*Perdurabo*, p. 562.) RAW of course noted similarities in Crowley and Joyce. In 1923 Crowley published an article "The Genius of Mr. James Joyce," based on his readings of *Portrait of the Artist as a Young Man*, and *Ulysses*.

It would seem that if there are psychedelic effects in reading and deciphering books like *Finnegans Wake* and *The Book of Lies*, the chaos is more controllable than that of an Ego-flattening "heroic dose" (taking a page from another *Wake* reader and psychedelic virtuoso, Terence McKenna) of, say, psilocybin. Further, according to Claude Shannon's earth-shattering 1948 paper *The Mathematical Theory of Communication*, which all this information/chaos/entropy/ theory of how psychedelics work in the brain stems from, the quality of information is in the sort of "yoga" (from Sanskrit: "union" or "yoke") of the text and the particular nervous system of the reader. Certain readers are far more prepared to encounter a book like *Finnegans Wake* and "make sense" of it, while quite a lot of people – judging by a lifetime of talking to people about that work and sometimes showing them the first page, by way of illustrating how dense and weird it "is" – are not prepared at all, at all. Shannon's theory of information has to do with our nervous system's ability to predict what's coming next, based on what we're encountering "now." The degree of unpredictability correlates mathematically with the amount of information "in" a text. Clearly, a reader who approaches a given "dense" text – in this case, the *Wake* – is far more equipped to ride the dense chaotic waves if they're well-read in, say: Vico, Irish history, Joyce's life and previous books, and etymology, than someone who's a committed reader of the *New York Times* best-seller list.

This would seem amenable to scientific study: to what extent does the DMN dim down when the accomplished reader engages in *Finnegans Wake*? As I wrote, a dense text would seem to present a more controlled chaos (sorry about the oxymoron!) than a full-blown psychedelic trip. Can certain books be lumped in with Crowleyan magick and psychedelic drugs? And how does all this circle back to the topic of Intuition?

17.) Nor has the constant critique of "the self" slowed down. A most powerful criticism of its salience or even reality probably came first with Buddhism. In our times, a multi-pronged attack on it was mounted by the French post-structuralists, and it's spilled over into the sciences since the 1970s. The Jamaican-British Marxist Foucauldian social theorist Stuart Hall once asked why we talk about literary characters when human beings are social fictions themselves? The humanist scholar Norman O. Brown, on a hike with Dale Pendell, said, "I am what is mine. Personality is the original personal property." Jung was asked what the "self" was and he said he thought it was an expression of the unity of the personality. RAW's friend David Jay Brown takes the psychedelicized stance that we are "an everlasting field of consciousness in physical form." The poet Stanley Kunitz intuited that "At the core of one's existence is a pool of energy that has nothing to do with personal identity, but that falls away from self, blends into the natural universe. Man has only a bit part to play in the whole marvelous show of creation."

Here's RAW's mentor Alan Watts: "I regard the actual self as an entire cosmos [or whatever is], operating in that particular way, time and place that we call the individual organism. The organism's sense of ego is an additional operation of this totality – a kind of resonance or echoing [like singing in the bathtub], which enhances experience. I also connect the ego with the organism's capacity for conscious attention, i.e, for a type of awareness similar to a spotlight, that can focus upon those areas of experience that we call things and events, simultaneously ignoring everything outside those areas. All these ego functions seem to be real and effective. But they are functions of the larger self, and I cannot feel the ego as something apart from that self, and certainly not as the real and final ground of my being." (1964 letter to Gordon Ragle, *Collected Letters of Alan Watts*, p. 457)

In an interview with *The Sun* in 1987, RAW said,

"The ego is important, culturally and historically, but when it becomes convinced it's the only game, it becomes compulsive." He adds that eventually the Ego will be "flooded with trans-ego levels of consciousness, the ego mutates and becomes something else and can have a very important function in the future. Especially if it lives long enough. The evolutionary potentials of the human race haven't been discovered yet. We've been at a very primitive level, fighting for our survival for most of our existence. And fighting one another for survival." (collected in *Natural Law*, Hilaritas pp. 156-158.)

An avalanche of 21st century social research suggests our selves are shaped far more by our friends than most people think. Even to the point of weight gain or loss: if your friends are fatter than you, you'll gain weight. If your friends are thinner, you'll probably lose pounds. We don't know if there's some subtle swapping of bacteria that influences this or not. We now know – another fantastic and fairly recent cascade of research that RAW missed out on – that our DNA is being *constantly* modified in its expression by our thoughts and environment: the field of epigenetics. (In RAW's thinking during the period 1973-74, DNA is "ageless, trans-egoistic and immortal," which still seems true enough.)

Whatever we "are" we have more bacteria, viruses, fungi phages, and other archaea than we have human cells that "belong" in humans. But this is misleading, as we've been like that for a very, very long time. Many of these bacteria and viruses interact intimately with our DNA and epigenome to help keep us safe. It's complex. To put it mildly. The air we breathe contains microorganisms. We breathe them out, they're taken up by other humans, animals, plants, etc.

It seems culture and nature flow through us, that we're semi-permeable membranes, that we influence our environment and other living things by proximity. Even when you're fresh out of the shower, the "clean" unitary "self" is probably a vast fiction . . . that almost everyone believes in.

As for the moronic "War On Drugs" – yeah, it's a "war" on people who use the sorts of drugs that feel threatening to politicians and other authoritarians, advertisers, and pharmacy companies, but it seems even stupider than that, as Tao Lin puts it in his book *Trip: Psychedelics, Alienation and Change*: "One similarity between psychedelics and drugs is that we are always experiencing both, are always on fluctuating amounts of serotonin, DMT, GABA, adenosine, oxytocin, dopamine, opioids, cannabinoids, and hundreds of other compounds for which we've evolved receptors. The amounts we are on, and their ratios, determine, or at least strongly influence, our realities. 'Life itself is a drug experience,' said Dennis McKenna, who earned a PhD in botanical science in 1984 and has published around forty papers on psychedelics, in an interview in 1994." (*Trip*, p. 65.) Tao Lin also writes about the invention of pesticides in 20th century warfare, now worldwide and affecting everyone's microbiome. Switching to Third Person: "Tens of trillions of bacteria, fungi, archaea, and protists, representing probably one to five hundred species, lived in his eyes, mouth, esophagus, stomach, intestines, genitals, skin, and lungs. Each microbe was a cell made up of tens of millions of giant molecules called proteins. Each microbe affected Tao's consciousness at all times by, among other means, creating neurotransmitters and other compounds for him to absorb, including ones he needed but couldn't make, like vitamins C, K2, B1, B2, B5, B6, B7, B9 and B12." (op. cit, pp. 257-262.)

Indeed, we're swaddled and barraged by particulates, microbes, and chemicals. Increasingly this order is called the "exposome."

We're now getting brain implants and other cybernetic augmentations. At what point are we bona fide cyborgs?

An ancient retrovirus has been linked to addiction behavior. Whatever the "self" is, it seems it can be hijacked, and we might not even know it. You thought you were this way 'cuz ya "made bad choices" but actually, you couldn't help it. It was you plus your parasite; you plus a virus added, you in addition to a genetic expression gone awry. "Normal"? Some philosophers and psychologists think our innate ideas prevent us from seeing certain things about ourselves. There are microorganisms like *toxoplasmosis gondii* that you don't even know you have, but it acts like a parasite in the brain and you find yourself *blasé* toward oncoming traffic, guns wielded in your environment, etc. It's more common than you probably think and is contracted via eating insufficiently cooked meat. Or contact with cat feces. There is no cure. Probably most who have it don't know they do. Although hormonal expression affects us in profound ways, even most educated people have little self-knowledge of these effects on our "selves." Are you still "you" when you're hangry? Drunk? Have the flu? How has Internet changed your "self"? *Is* there a "self"?

Any one of us could add to this list, easily. The Eight Circuit Model of Leary and RAW posits at minimum four different "selves" in every living human. That's 32 billion selves in the world, roughly. But then some of us (no doubt: you, 'cuz you're reading this) have activated higher "selves". So: more than 32 billion. Way more. RAW once entertained the idea that there are an uncountably high-may-as-well-be-infinite number of each of us, if the "Many Worlds" interpretation of quantum mechanics is true . . . but you only really care about the self that's reading this book right now. Presumably, in a universe next door, there's a copy of yourself sitting in the same room, but reading *Gravity's Rainbow* instead of this book. There's also a you in the same room in a parallel universe, but wearing different colored underwear and reading *The Story of O* or *Introduction to Business*, 17th edition. But we care about our "self," now. I know that's how I "am."

We hope that, whatever we "are," that IT is at least *awake*.

In RAW's Foreword to Scott Michaelson's book on Crowley, *Portable Darkness,* he addresses Uncle Al and this slipperiness of the fictive "self", viz: "A single ego is an absurdly narrow vantage point from which to view the world, he explained. Who has ears, let him hear."

Quick!: How many different egos have you had in the past three days?

Further, in *Do What Thou Wilt*, the gnostic aspects of our selves are addressed: "We do not know our true will or our true mind in authoritarian society because we are trained from infancy to repress both. The resultant of all these repressions *acting convexly from outside* is *experienced concavely from inside* as the defined self; it has been defined by others. 'The ego is a conspiracy by society for which you take the blame,' said Modecai the Foul, high priest of a Crowlyean magick society in California; in other words, the 'I' which is seeking to escape the social trap *is* that trap." (Many years later, this idea that invented ego getting the blame was written in Sigismundo's diary in the woods in southern Ohio, *Nature's God*: "Ego is a social fiction for which one person at a time gets all the blame." – p. 121, Hilaritas ed. "Mordecai the Foul" was one of RAW's Discordian aliases.)

Buddha was on to something: this Ego really has got to go. Like having relatives over for more than three days. But that Ego seems intransigent. It keeps coming back like a case of herpes simplex.

Okay, so the "self" we all take so seriously is a conspiracy by authoritarian society and fake, defined by others so we take the blame, a social trap, a symphony of inherited viscera, of non-originally human microorganisms gumming up and influencing and hijacking our "natural" pristine human bods; the ego is a socially-derived aspect of dubious validity, extremely dynamic, and it's heavily informed by non-conscious factors.

Still: we must pretend it's "real." Or: realize our True Self, via magick and/or psychedelics. And furthermore, we believe that we do have free will. Even those philosophers who deny free will admit they go about their days acting as if they had it. They have to, or they'd go bonkers. Exercize: Go an entire week believing that everything that you do is predetermined. Write down your results . . .

So, when we or Crowley or RAW do magick and psychedelics and these things allow us to experience ecstasy – standing outside our "selves"– what significance does this "self" have? Who "are" we when we're in a state of ecstasy? What does our intuition tell us? Is that ecstatic state our lost birthright? Is it our True Self?

Suddenly, this fictional world seems *more than real*. Doesn't it? And so we act within that world. Here's how I take it: All this just means we grew up with a lot of wrong knowledge, but our teachers probably meant well. Carry on!

18.) Recent (post-1945) cognitive science has a lot to say about . . . not just the "unconscious" but the "cognitive unconscious." The findings in that field show it's vast, that our conscious "self" is but a small part of who we "are," and that we cannot have "direct conscious awareness" of most of what goes on in our minds. *Unconscious* thought is at least 95% of what goes on. The struggle to gain control of ourselves involves interacting with largely unconscious processes and conceptual schemes we can't really articulate for ourselves, yet these things guide us, and as we struggle, we posit a "higher" (better) aspect of us going at it tooth and claw with a "lower" (amoral, irrational, "bad") aspect. All this is sobering, ain't it? Maybe it depends on how you look at it. For one, we're all in the same sorts of fictive boats.

If we're guided by hopelessly unconscious metaphors, what good is trying to realize our "True Self?" George Lakoff, cognitive neuro linguist, and philosopher Mark Johnson, who are on the same page, write: "When you try to find your 'true self' you are using another, usually unconscious metaphorical conceptualization . . . When we consciously reason about how to gain mastery over ourselves, or how to protect our vulnerable 'inner self' or how to find our 'true self,' it is the hidden hand of the unconscious conceptual system that makes such reasoning 'common sense.'"

Johnson and Lakoff say we're all trying to realize our true self, or to "take a good look at ourselves," or gain control over ourselves. "Though we are only occasionally aware of it, we are all metaphysicians – not in some ivory-tower sense – but as part of our everyday capacity to make sense of our experience. It is through conceptual systems that we are able to make sense of everyday life, and our everyday metaphysics is embodied in those conceptual systems."

For cognitive psychologists (which has only been a thing since around 1956, but remember how Jumping Jesus* works), any structure or mental operation that can be studied is "cognitive." It's hardly about "conscious thinking." (This business of adding "cognitive" before a word like "unconsciousness" feels a lot like RAW and Leary adding "neuro-" to everything, to remind us that it's a human thing to be doing mathematics, only it should properly be called "neuro-mathematics," because who knows how the highly advanced silicon-based aliens do their Number Game?) All the unconscious processes embodied are "cognitive."

And this realm is *vast*! Motor operations, mental imagery, and emotions: cognitive. They've found that what you did the other day – when you sat around, watched a movie, ate lunch, wrote some email and then went for a walk – is almost unfathomably complex. It's almost miraculous. I like the metaphor of angels participating in our cognitive unconscious. You may prefer Other Things.

~•~

* The Jumping Jesus Phenomenon was RAW's amusing description of the rapidly accelerating logarithmic accumulation of knowledge over time.

~•~

I'm writing about this because it's *trippy*; it's psychedelic (to me, at least). It seems to present what "Intuition" might be from another angle, and our intellectual culture still hasn't caught up. A final quote from Lakoff and Johnson:

"When we understand all that constitutes the cognitive unconscious, our understanding of the nature of consciousness is vastly enlarged. Consciousness goes way beyond mere awareness of something, beyond the mere experience of qualia (the qualitative senses of say, pain or color), beyond the awareness that you are aware, and beyond the multiple takes on immediate experience provided by various centers of the brain. Consciousness certainly involves all of the above plus the immeasurably vaster constitutive framework provided by the cognitive unconscious, which must be operating for us to be aware of anything at all." (See *Philosophy In The Flesh*, Lakoff and Johnson, pp. 9-13.)

When I began this piece, my favorite model for Intuition was that it somehow "bubbled up" from this vast realm of the cognitive unconscious. Suddenly, we got an idea. Maybe it's in the cognitive unconscious, and then it makes its way to the right hemisphere? Maybe intuition's link to the cognitive unconscious is tenuous? If so, why? If the sudden flash of knowledge originates in this unconscious processing realm, can magick and/or psychedelics summon it to the right hemisphere and waking consciousness?

To think this sorta stuff comes out in the Age of Horus! In *our* Aeon!

Now: you may reject all or part of this. I think it's basically correct, but I'm no academic cognitive scientist or PhD philosopher. My question to you: what if they're right? Here's how I'd answer:

Do what thou wilt.

19.) Everything I'm writing about here is all made up. I mean: it's in books. It's from my reading and reflections. But it's still *made up*. You have to understand this, and by understand, I mean a sort of "tuning-toward." I hate to be "serious." I like to have fun sometimes. I do like to yank a chain now and again and have my own chain yanked, but here I'm pretty serious. All this is made up. Someone dreamed it up, someone processed it through experiment and wrote it down. Does it make any difference?

20.) Pisces: Recently a book came out called *Why Fish Don't Exist*. I read it and enjoyed it. It's mostly about a woman finding herself and her sexuality and her young-person's admiration for a Biologist named David Starr Jordan, who was one of the early heavies on the faculty of Stanford. I won't ruin it for you. Anyway, Jordan was an Ichthyologist, and one of the greats. He was resilient, bouncing back from his life-work being wiped out by accident not once but twice. As the book moved into modern times, we find out there were – starting in the 1960s – renegade groups of Taxonomists who had a huge problem with the entire history of classification and categorization of animals and plants. They saw that we can now do genetic sequencing and find the last common ancestor (*clade*; the technique and field is called *Cladistics*) of each species, which would be a far more cutting-edge way to do Taxonomy. More accurate. Also: it would totally revolutionize Taxonomy. One of their findings was that, of all the "fish" in the ocean, the diversity of their evolutionary backgrounds was strikingly extensive. They all *look like* fish, from the outside; their evolutionary path was quite something different. To simplify, it was found that the category "fish" doesn't exist in Cladistics. We made up all our categories, then reified (made them "real"), and then *forgot* we made these categories up! The hardcore Cladists are kinda frustrated that everyone still seems to want to think with the Old Categories. While I feel for the Cladists, I do find all this cosmically poignant.

How much thinking are we doing in categories that are already outmoded and inferior, only we don't know it yet? My intuition tells me the number is much larger than one. (Food? Sex? Sleep? Work? Health? Entertainment? How haunting the category of: We Don't Know What We Don't Know!)

For example, with regards to Biological Sex, as I write there's a Moral Panic in the US because a huge swath of the American public seems to work with the category: "Gender means you're either born a Man or a Woman." What seems profoundly ignorant to me, is that these people ignore the evidence that this isn't a black/white issue. Clearly, there have always been people who are gender fluid. Furthermore, a small amount of education would've shown these Moral Crusaders the common phenomena of intersexuality, not to mention chromosomal and gonadal sex differences, and the urge to transition to the gender they feel they always were. Why be cruel to people who have always felt they had the wrong genitalia? They want to harmonize their own sexual self-identity with their genitalia. How does that harm anyone else? Why is it your business? My point: it seems glaringly obvious that you'd have to be not only an idiot, but a Blithering Idiot, to think these transgender people want to "recruit" children or somehow "infect" you with their gender fluidity, or, most idiotically, "They're doing this just to piss me off!". But apart from calling people "idiots". I should rather think, "They're working with faulty categories."

Back to Cladistics: Here was yet another "new" intellectual field that blew my mind. I love reading about how everything I thought I knew was wrong, and that things are actually far, far weirder and of a magnitude and scope I hadn't realized. I had a month-long anxiety attack when I read my first books on quantum mechanics. But it was a "good" anxiety, like an acid trip that is a bit too much, but suddenly you're also laughing so hard you get a side ache and feel great. Then: anxiety, etc.

I later had most of my models spaghettified when I read Robert Anton Wilson. And Lakoff and Johnson's 1979 *Metaphors We Live By* – mentioned above – acted like a long-lasting mild psychedelic for me. More than a microdose, though. They put on a lot of flesh, some bones, and even eyebrows to Norman O. Brown's "All that is, is metaphor." RAW cited Brown's quote often. My gawd, is it true! (Or, according to my epistemology: provisionally true, as of this date.)

RAW got me to read Korzybski, Joyce's *Finnegans Wake*, Vico's *The New Science*, Pound's *Cantos*, and his everything-taken-as-knowledge stance influenced me to read Berger and Luckmann's *The Social Construction of Reality*. All of these are magick books to me; they're all psychedelic. They changed me, utterly. I'm sorta high much more of the time due to all they wrote, meant and implied. I continually re-read them. RAW got me into Crowley, by gawd. It was the sex magick, I admit it: entry drug. RAW's *Sex, Drugs*

and Magick interacts, comments upon, and elaborates on
Do What Thou Wilt, the two books written within 18 months
of each other: sold me on what scholar George Feuerstein
calls "California Tantra" and Crowleyan sex magick. (orig.
1973, Playboy Press as only *Sex and Drugs*, because Hefner
thought only gays were into "magic"; best edition available:
Hilaritas Press, because 'twas updated by RAW before he
died and with lots of extra commentary by others.)

All these Immortal Holy Works pointed me, in different
directions, toward vastnesses I didn't even know existed,
but I began to inhabit parts of that seemingly fathomless
cognitive terrain. I don't know if it was the books, the yoga,
the cannabis, my experiences with psychedelics, or all of
these combined synergistically and contributed in their own
ways, but I suspect it was some exertion, some striving, some
yoga that brought me into inexhaustible wonder, and RAW
once said that's all the religion anyone needs. I know *it's all I
need*. Reading about Science led me to Religion, but not like
any religion you see on teevee.

21.) Epistemologies get us high. Or should. Ontologies,
for me, come out of epistemologies. It may work differently
for you. I hope you have an even better conceptual scheme,
or set of 'em, than I do.

But magick can really change the world. Sounds trite,
but lemme try'n give a few examples. Someone was telling
me about Boswell and Dr. Johnson, in the 1770s, going
from London to check out parts of Scotland. When Johnson
wrote about it, the forms of land they had to move through
to get to Edinburgh were a real pain in the ass, and Johnson
detailed that. In 1798, Wordsworth and Coleridge published
their *Lyrical Ballads*, (mostly by Wordsworth) and they
were both so mystically taken by the landscapes of the Lake
District and Wales ("Tintern Abbey") that these poems not

only kicked off the Romantic movement, but they, in a sense, "created Nature": the power of the poems showed how mystically magically marvelous the beauty of the natural world is; Wordsworth and Coleridge may have invented tourism, which affects entire economies today. There was a time where the only "beauty" was to be found in artworks, architecture, and The City. Let us consider this poetry as a magickal operation that utterly changed the world.

Closer to our time, Jack Parsons, a dedicated Thelemite and head of Crowley's OTO lodge in Los Angeles, post-WWII, was a rocket scientist who advocated for space exploration and human spaceflight, and made significant contributions to those fields, particularly using his knowledge of chemistry to concoct better rocket fuels with his proto-Jet Propulsion Laboratory colleagues Malina and Forman. Smoking cannabis and drinking while tinkering and testing possible superior methods of rocketry, they were key in getting humans on the moon. Like RAW discovering LSD and Crowley and developing his Intuition and publishing all those books, it's difficult to know to what degree Parsons's deep involvement with Crowley and the OTO contributed to human space-walks, but it had to influence that knowledge at least a bit. Maybe a lot.

Stewart Brand, founder of the *Whole Earth Catalog,* did some LSD one day on the roof of his North Beach, San Francisco apartment and realized he'd never seen a picture of Earth from space. He thought humans seeing a picture of their planet could change their consciousness. So Brand, with the help of such friends as Buckminster Fuller, convinced NASA to take this photo. It appeared on the cover of the *Whole Earth Catalog* in 1969.

Douglas Englebart, who earned a PhD in Electrical Engineering with a specialty in computers from Berkeley in 1955 was a hiking (not quite at the level of Crowley's mountaineering) and LSD enthusiast. Aided by Steward Brand, Englebart put on the "mother of all demos" in San Francisco in 1968. This 90 minute presentation demonstrated for the first time the computer mouse, hypertext, windows, graphics, video conferencing, word processing (thanks, Doug!), and collaborationist real-time editing of texts, etc. Not bad!

Robert Anton Wilson, with a number of Discordian, magick and psychedelic aficionado friends, starting in the late 1960s and going full force by around 1975, conducted a series of pranks and social experiments they called Operation Mindfuck. In the wake of the JFK hit, Watergate, and the torrent of revelations about FBI and CIA operations, RAW and friends, with virtually zero funding, sought to undermine all authority, everywhere by monkeywrenching ideas that fed into consensus "reality." The quotes around that word would be an atomic aspect of the entire OM. They couldn't let people continue to sleepwalk through the carnage of Vietnam while becoming consumerist robots in suburbs. As Douglas Rushkoff wrote about OM:

"Operation Mindfuck sought to suggest that anything anyone in the counterculture was doing at any time might just be part of an elaborate prank. This put outsiders in a difficult position: The only safe assumption was that anything a hippie was doing was part of Operation Mindfuck — some sort of trick or game. But because this could only lead to paranoia, one had to assume that whatever they were doing was probably harmless. They were, after all, just pranks. For their part, the counterculture agitators hoped the assumption that they were just jesters would keep them safe from any real persecution." (Bing/Google: Rushkoff's "Operation Mindfuck 2.0")

With the rise of Q-Anon and Trump, Rushkoff and a number of other commentators think maybe this prankish social experiment/magickal working conducted by a small group of psychedelicized "hippies" . . . perhaps worked a little "too well." Their ideas became mainstream, then repurposed by the fascist Right. In a 2014 book, Prof. of Communications Studies at the U. of Iowa, Kembrew McLeod, analyzed the "blowback" that this all-too-successful magickal operation had. In making fun of right wing paranoia and conspiracy theories about mind control, social science, secret societies, collectivism, and Wicca, "This condition of suspicion was duly satirized by a group of mind-bending pranksters known as the Discordians. Their irreverent actions, combined with those of other sixties troublemakers, helped fuel a conservative backlash that fundamentally altered America's social and political landscape." (See *Pranksters: Making Mischief In The Modern World*, pp. 150-164, NYU Press.). The number of books post-Trump's election are seemingly growing by the week. See especially *Kill All Normies* by Angela Nagel and *Operation Mindfuck: Q-Anon and the Cult of Donald Trump*, by Robert Guffey. Jesse Walker's chapter, "Operation Mindfuck", pp. 219-259 of *The United States of Paranoia: A Conspiracy Theory* is not-to-be-missed as background here. For RAW's take on all this as of 1977, see *Cosmic Trigger Vol.1*, Hilaritas Press ed, pp. 51-65. Also see *Historia Discordia: The Origins of the Discordian Society*, and *The Prankster and The Conspiracy*, both by Adam Gorightly. Actually the number of books that touch on this topic is too large for this essay. Start there?)

Sometimes, your magickal working gets out of hand, and I only have this to say on all that: RAW was an enthusiastic fan of quasi-occult, absolutely Horror writer H.P. Lovecraft, who penned the immortal line in his short story, "The Strange Case of Charles Dexter Ward": "Don't call up what you cannot put down." Sometimes you *think* you're only playing and can mostly control "it", but sometimes you can't.

To be clear about the effects of OM: social causation is complex in the extreme, and the link between cause and effect – especially with this sort of operation – would seem tenuous, and although there undoubtedly were some very real social effects by around 1975, the causation (from a series of pranks!) would seem to diminish over time. Those who claim, in 2023, that RAW's actions, even obliquely, led to the Jan 6th coup attempt, or even Trump's election in 2016, look like idiots to me. Was there some small amount of (horribly ironic) influence? I think so. But that influence was miniscule compared to, say, the Citizens United case. Or John Roberts's SCOTUS, ruling that Corporations Are People. (Puts a new, even more absurd wrinkle in our discussion of the "Self", don't it?) Or the 2008 banking collapse. Or having a black POTUS in a very racist country. Or the rise of Internet. Or, if we want to point to a popular culture influence other than Operation Mindfuck from the time of the Nixon Administration, the metaphors of "Red Pill" and "Blue Pill" from *The Matrix* movies seem to have influenced the fascist/ Right *far more* than the Discordian Society. (And no, I'm not blaming the Wachowskis for Trump!)

On the other hand, I simply don't know to what degree the 1648 Treaty of Westphalia, which ended the Thirty Years War, influenced me in having a bowl of oatmeal and some kefir today. I really don't know. Should I be worried?

There are 83,941 other stories in the naked city about how magick and psychedelics have changed the world. These have been five of them.

22.) Alien contact: Crowley's magick seemed to have led to alien contact by a trans-dimensional being named Aiwass, and the "reception" of the prophetic *The Book of the Law* on April 8-10, 1904 in Cairo, Egypt. Talk about *unheimlich*! Some corners of popular culture in the 21st century have pointed to Crowley's magical workings as opening up the era of UFOs: he did weird stuff, one of his students was Jack Parsons, whose work led to JPL and space travel, then Roswell, then Betty and Barney Hill, various ESP experiences by diverse people, etc. About this I'm dubious, but refuse to dogmatize. Suffice: Crowley and his wife Rose Kelly had an extraordinary experience in 1904, and, whether or not it was "automatic writing", it does seem to be a dictated/received text. Kinda like how the Prophet received *The Qu'ran*.

RAW's friend Philip K. Dick wrote a 944 page book (there were many more pages of notes, like thousands more) of philosophical speculation about his own contact by extraterrestrial intelligence. I'm frankly fazed, flummoxed and disoriented when I try to figure out what happened to him. It seems too easy to just point to his use of amphetamines, or a supposedly schizotypal personality. I very tentatively assume LOTS of psychedelics and unbounded reading and imagination accounts for the exceedingly weird experience – including alien contact – at La Chorrera, as told by the McKenna Brothers. Terence's *True Hallucinations* is one of the all-time Weird Travelogues, an astounding story that, to the extent it's true, is better than most fiction.

One of the Fathers of Modern Rationality, Rene Descartes, said an angel appeared to him in a dream and told him the modern conquest of nature would be done via math and measurement. Descartes, seeking to find a necessary link between his (bad) separation of Mind and Body, posited the pineal gland, an endocrine gland in the middle of your brain. This idea was very creative thought and also scientific balderdash, but we now know that one of the things the pineal gland does is secrete DMT. Curiouser, mysteriouser, siriuser . . .

And, RAW's contact with Sirius: hey, he's not the only one. In Ingrid Rowland's *Giordano Bruno: Philosopher/Heretic* she notes Bruno whimsically referred to Sirius's influence. Nobel winner for Literature, Doris Lessing, had an odd contact with Sirius. The composer Karlheinz Stockhausen claimed he came from a planet near Sirius. Other friends who had bizarre contact with otherworldly intelligence include Leary and Lilly. RAW has links to others and their contacts and affiliations with Sirius in his *Cosmic Trigger vol 1*. RAW's dear friend and collaborator Robert Shea told interviewer Neal Wilgus, apropos of RAW, that "It frequently helps an artist to imagine that the work he is creating has a separate life of its own and is being transmitted to him . . . ," and Shea cites Vladimir Nabokov, Igor Stravinsky, John Keats, and psychoanalyst Charles Rycroft as other examples. Speaking of *The Qu'ran*: 53:49: "He [Allah] it is Who is the Lord of Sirius."

A RAW speculation: LSD opens up "noise" (here, again, in the early 1970s, intuitively prefiguring the latest scientific hypothesis about how psychedelics work!) into the nervous system, and that his friend John Lilly also thought he was contacted by ETs. RAW writes (1971? 1972?) that he'd known other LSD users who had the same experience. (See *Sex, Drugs & Magick: A Journey Beyond Limits*, in chapter "Tibetan Space-Time-Warp Star-Nova Trips," pp. 276-277, Hilaritas ed. For an interesting discussion of "Entities" like these, see *Trialogues On the Edge of the West*, pp. 92-107, Bear & Co. Mathematician Ralph Abraham, Terence McKenna, and Biologist Rupert Sheldrake weigh in with intellectual jazz.)

Not all of these names are associated with psychedelics or magic. The one thing they all have in common: they are all brilliant, imaginative artists with their Intuitive faculties highly developed. Even Descartes. Other than that, I do not know. A very smart person once told us, "Whereof one cannot speak, thereof one must remain silent." I've done magick and psychedelics, I'm very weird, I'm a musician, and I haven't been contacted (Yet). I will not speculate further.

23.) The idea that writing in itself is a magical act has been around since Thoth/Hermes. Just as Jung interpreted alchemy as the alchemists doing experiments in order to change themselves, and if you happened to change a base metal into gold, cool, so many writers seek to communicate effectively with others, but might be doing it primarily to cause change in themselves. Makes sense.

If you've read this far, I have you thinking about such things as Intuition, simply 'cuz I brought it up so often. Magick works by invoking often, then repeating the invocation.

It's getting easier to be public with your psychedelic use; it seems like it's getting easier to talk about your magickal experiments. Still: we can see our "coming out" as a political act. And you have your reasons for *not* coming out. You don't wanna deal with the Idiots, who are Legion. *Tempus loquendi, tempus tacendi*: I got that from Pound's Canto XXXI: "There is a time to speak and a time to stay silent." Something like that.

I'll close here by pointing out we are all perfectly formed grapes who want and need to ripen, develop Knowledge, Love and Will. That is our raisin d'etre.

– R. Michael Johnson
Penngrove, CA, Unistat
March 25, 2023

PUBLISHER'S NOTES

Do What Thou Wilt, a Robert Anton Wilson manuscript hidden for nearly 50 years, arrives at Harvard University, and soon after, the creation of *Lion of Light* becomes a priority at Hilaritas Press. As Mike Gathers describes in his Editor's Note, Hilaritas Press learned about the manuscript, and while Rasa began the process of gaining permission to publish from Harvard, and then from other sources, a group of the usual suspects from amongst the Robert Anton Wilson Trust Advisors began to coalesce around the idea of a book of RAW's writings on Crowley. As Mike says, "A team of Chad Nelson, Oz Fritz, Michael Johnson and myself gelled together."

We thought you might like to know a little bit about that team whose gelling produced this amazing addition to RAW's canon.

Mike Gathers

Mike Gathers discovered Robert Anton Wilson through Timothy Leary and deoxy.org sometime around 1997, and immediately took to the Eight Circuit Model of Consciousness. He aspires to bring the Eight Circuit model up to date with modern neuroscience and developmental psychology and place it in a relational context in conjunction with Antero Alli's embodiment context. He hosts the Hilaritas Press Podcast and enjoys helping Hilaritas continue to publish new books such as this one. A father of two teenage boys and husband of 23+5 years, he has a background in engineering and psychotherapy. He currently works coaching men in creating a meaningful life while volunteering as a leader and administrator in the ManKind Project. He lives in Golden, Colorado. For more on Mike and his work on the Eight Circuits, see https://linktr.ee/mgathers23.

Chad Nelson

Chad Nelson lives in Providence, Rhode Island with his wife and two cats. When not engaged in RAW studies, he is a practicing attorney, yogi, and outdoor enthusiast. He edited Hilaritas Press' 2021 release, *Natural Law, Or Don't Put a Rubber On Your Willy and Other Writings From a Natural Outlaw*.

Oz Fritz works as a sound engineer and music producer. Reading *Cosmic Trigger* at age 21 introduced him to Aleister Crowley and other prominent experimental researchers of expanded awareness. This book changed his life. Oz likes to read and write in his spare time. Other interests include hiking, gardening, traveling, listening to music, watching films, and philosophy. His current project presents a lay person's approach to understanding *The Logic of Sense* by Gilles Deleuze in a 36-part video series. He maintains a blog at: oz-mix.blogspot.com containing several essays and reviews based on the writings of Robert Anton Wilson, Aleister Crowley and related subjects. He is also writing a memoir of his adventures in the music business working with artists like Bill Laswell, Tom Waits, Primus and Ornette Coleman among many others. Oz lives in the foothills of the Sierra Mountains in Northern California with his best friend and their cat.

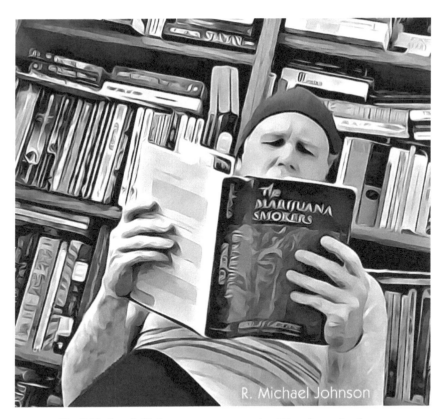

R. Michael Johnson

R. Michael Johnson grew up in Glendora, in the
eastern San Gabriel Valley sprawl of Los Angeles, lived
on the Los Angeles harbor at San Pedro, then moved to
Berkeley, California, in 2005. He's lived in rural Penngrove
in Sonoma County – California's "wine country" for
over 10 years. He's played rock guitar for over 45 years,
taking breaks now and then to sleep, shower, and watch
Turner Classic Movies. Besides Robert Anton Wilson's
entire oeuvre, his interests are cycling and yoga. He has an
omnivorous appetite for books and ideas, and has long been
drawn to marginal writers and non-mainstream topics, in
addition to his love of classic books and the sociology of
knowledge. He's just the kind of nut you'd read in a book
like this.

LION OF LIGHT:
A SEARCH FOR A COVER

Some words about the *Lion of Light* cover we
didn't use . . .

When considering a cover for *Lion of Light*, I had the thought to begin the design with the help of Artificial Intelligence. I tried producing a graphic that reflected Crowley and a "lion of light." I used six different AI graphic rendering programs, and was not too thrilled with the result. I came to realize that with these programs, while "borrowing" from millions of graphics available for bots to peruse, a successful rendering was largely dependent on the human interface – with what vocabulary did the human use to create a spectacular result when prompting the bot? I saw that many of the renderings I liked used thick paragraphs of descriptors which the AI could consume, and that complexity and, dare I say, human ingenuity, produced the best results. I figured that maybe someone else might be better at communicating with an AI.

So I went to the RAW community online and offered a Call for Art. We received about 50 pieces of AI art from about a dozen people. Some of them were spectacular, turning Crowley into a Marvel superhero, or making Crowley into a kind of lion-human hybrid. I decided to make my favorites into sample book covers, each with a text design for the title and author's name that reflected, graphically, some aspect of the AI's rendering. While all of the submissions that I liked were lush with color and interesting details, one graphic we received just made me laugh. It was a graphic Chris Mazur found of a child-like black and white cartoon figure* that I was sure was just a joke on Chris' part.

~•~

* We tried to track down the creator of the image, but without success. A woman who we think may have created it seems to have disappeared from the net in 2021!

~•~

I decided to lighten the mood here at Hilaritas Press, and I gave Chris' drawing a goofy frame and text in an appropriate font, and included the design in a group of fifteen "finalists" that I presented to the four editors working on this publication, and also to the some 23 people who we call the RAW Trust Advisors (friends of Bob, and/or experts on RAW's work). I made Chris' design #15 in the list of fifteen, and I was sure it would provide a laugh. When I started to get responses from the editors and advisors, I was a bit shocked to find that #15 got the second highest number of thumbs up! The reasoning was intriguing. Oz Fritz offered some compelling thoughts.

Oz wrote:

"After reviewing these cover ideas again, #15 remains, by far, my favorite. My second choice is #1 but would like to see the font straight on, not angled. #6 seems a good, more conservative option. The second two alternatives were chosen in consideration of marketing purposes.

"Apart from what I said regarding #15 before, its simplicity and lack of pretension, it seems like a great tabla rasa, free from bias and overt, superficial association with occult or New Age publications. Below the surface of this tabla rasa, symbolically, Horus = the Crowned and Conquering Child."

Oz later reconsidered and wrote:

"After careful consideration, trying to look at the bigger picture beyond my personal preference, I've decided to withdraw my vote for #15. Though I do like the metaphor that this presents a book for "children" (like myself) to higher consciousness – newborn babes in Spirit , if you will – I think that likely that will get lost upon anyone new to Crowley as will the symbolism of the Crowned and Conquering Child. It may get seen as childish rather than child-like and turn some people off."

Bobby Campbell (author of *RAW Art* and other great comic explorations) suggested we choose a more appropriate cover, but make a special limited run using #15 – a special collector's edition. In the end, we went with the number one choice, and it is likely that making a special limited edition may not come together. I decided instead to give readers a little insight into the process by writing this addendum, and giving Chris' design a little bit of the serious recognition I'm still not entirely sure it deserves. What do you think? Would it have been a good cover?

– Richard Rasa, *Curious Publisher*

HILARITAS
PRESS

Publishing the Books of Robert Anton Wilson
and Other Adventurous Thinkers

www.hilaritaspress.com

Made in United States
Troutdale, OR
09/26/2024

23165057R00186